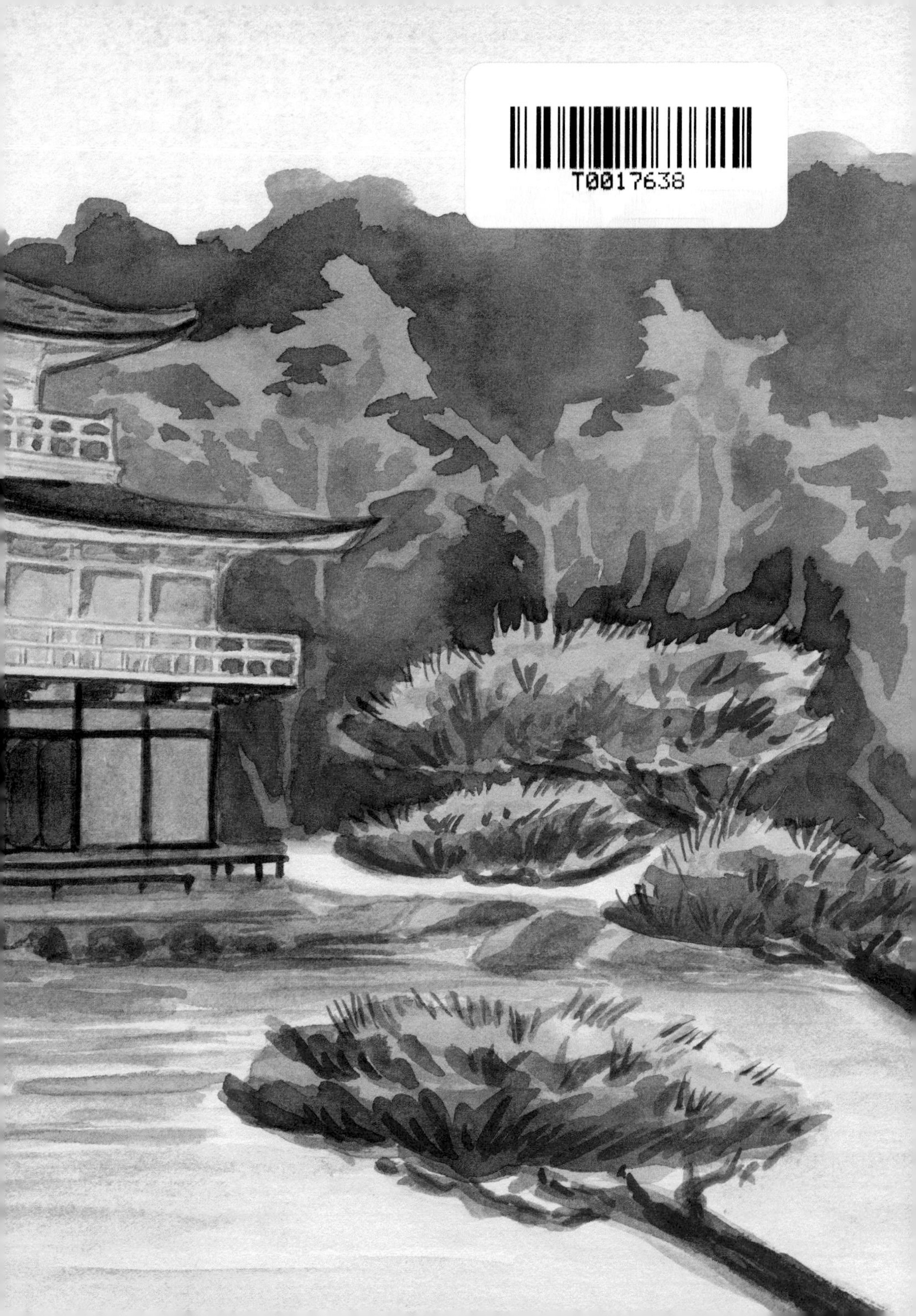

# My Travels in JAPAN

AUDRY NICKLIN

**TUTTLE** Publishing

Tokyo │ Rutland, Vermont │ Singapore

# Contents

Adventurous Beginnings **4**

Flying to Japan **8**

Meeting with Friends in Yokohama **12**

Traveling to Hiroshima **16**

Day Trip to Miyajima **28**

Himeji and Osaka **50**

Exploring Osaka **59**

Mount Koya 67

To Nara and Kyoto 75

Seeing the Sights in Kyoto 84

Kyoto Shrines and Temples 91

Arriving in Tokyo 103

All Day in Tokyo 109

Going Home 112

How to Start Your Own Travel Journal 121

# Adventurous Beginnings

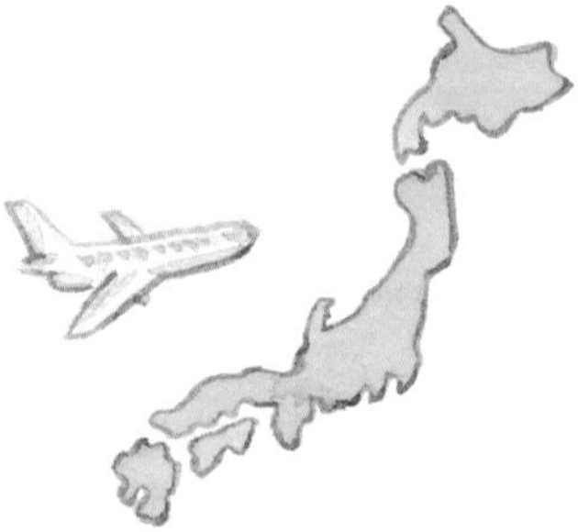

My first attempt to visit Japan was through a study-abroad program.

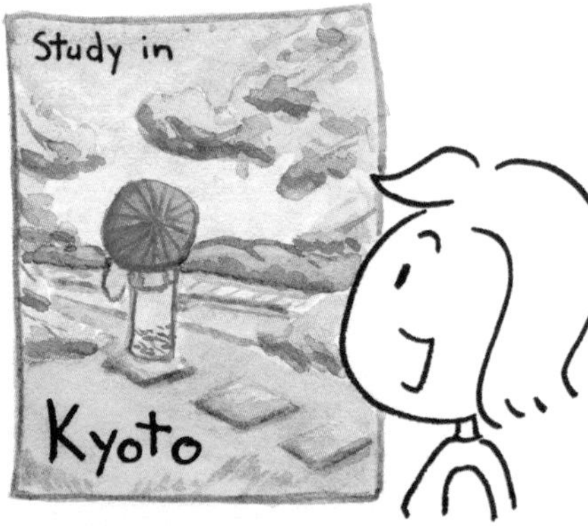
Study in
Kyoto

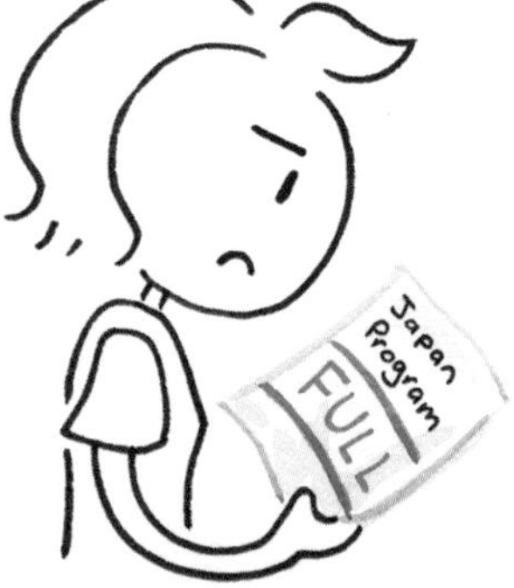
Japan Program
FULL

After going through the application process, I was rejected.

That summer I went to China instead.

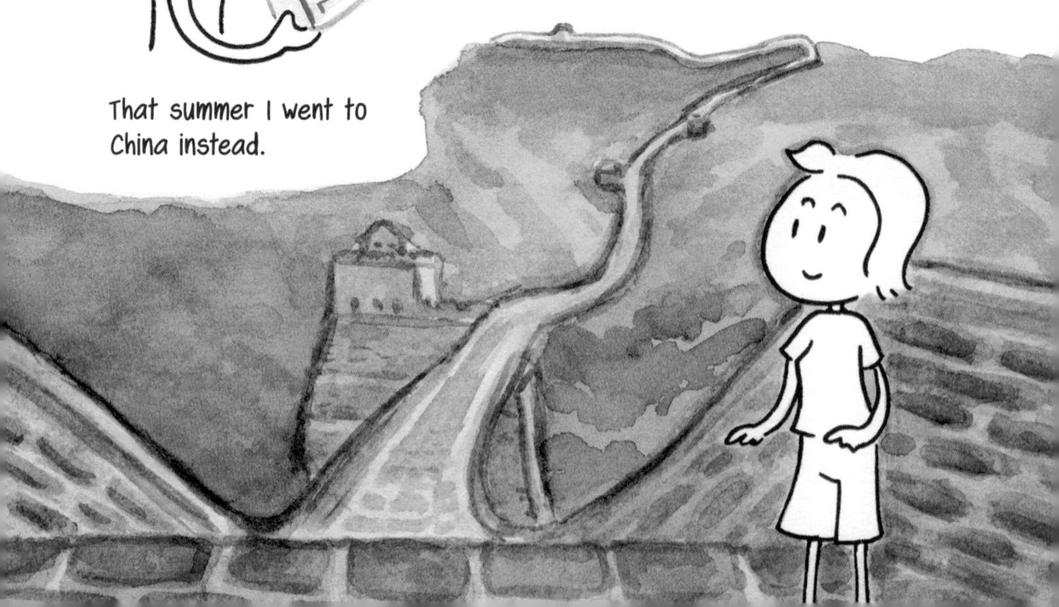

Fast forward eight years. I was now married and my husband, Connor, was asked to go to Japan on business. Unfortunately the timing was poor, so once again I was unable to go. I was extremely disappointed.

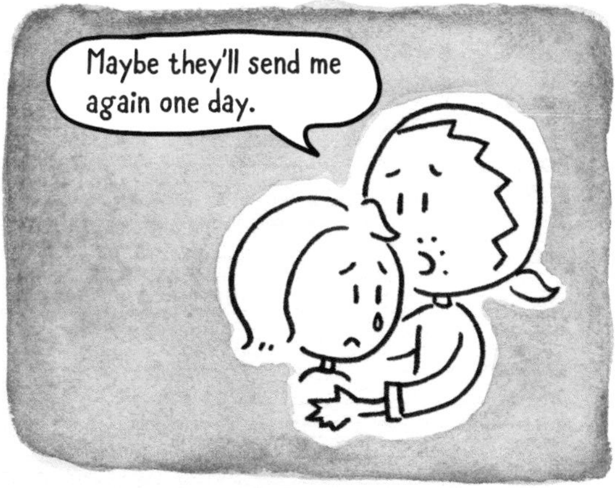
Maybe they'll send me again one day.

Two years later, Connor was asked to travel to Japan again. By this time I had returned to school.

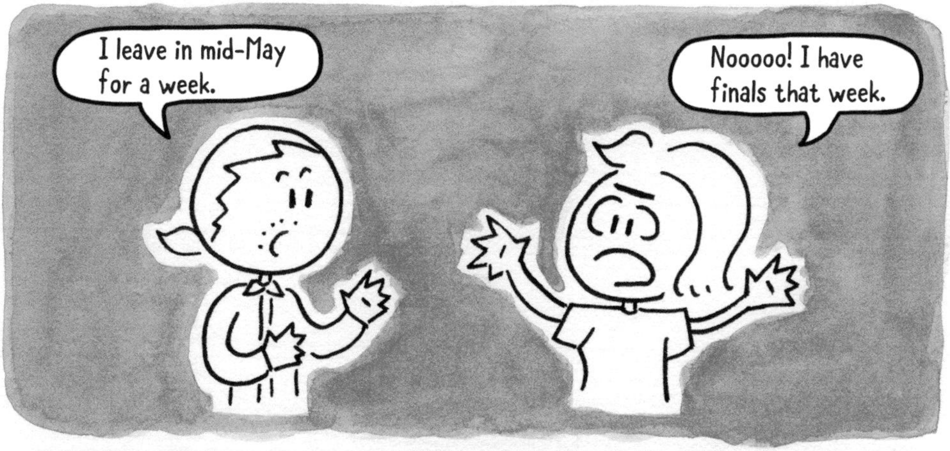
I leave in mid-May for a week.
Nooooo! I have finals that week.

Fate finally smiled on me because they delayed Connor's trip by a week and asked him to stay in Japan for longer. My finals would be done and I could finally visit!

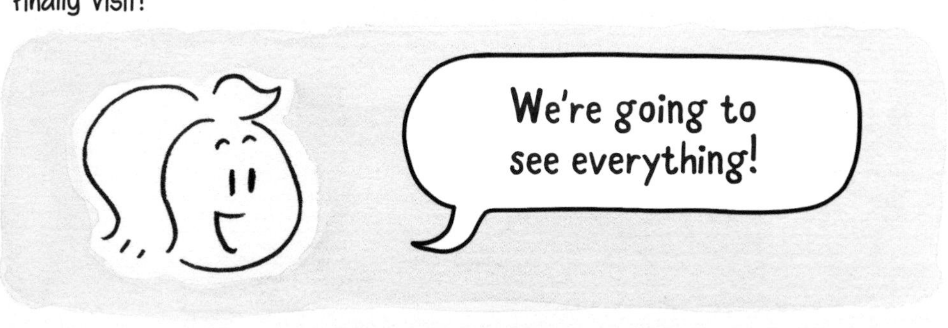
We're going to see everything!

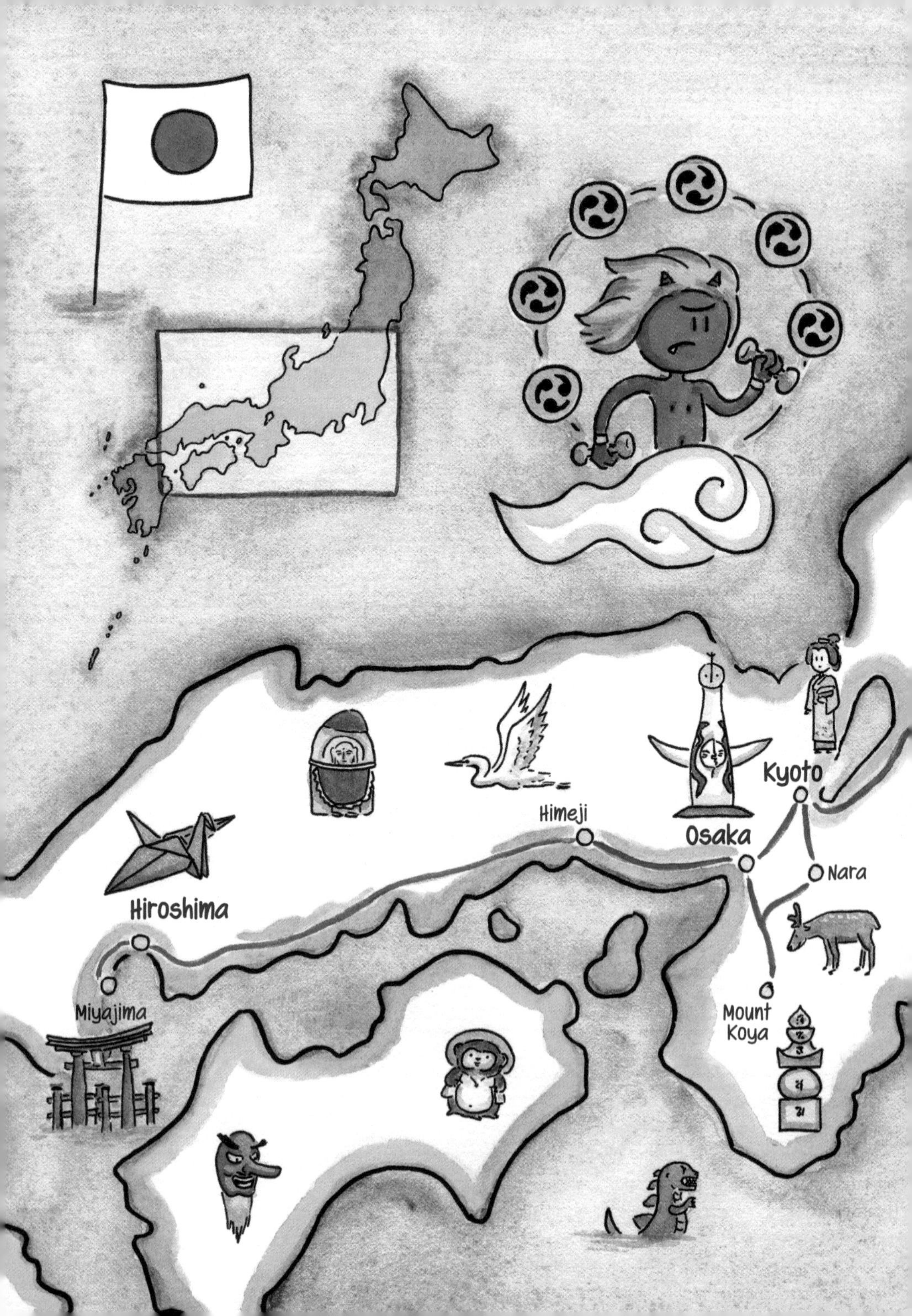
Kyoto
Himeji
Osaka
Nara
Hiroshima
Miyajima
Mount Koya

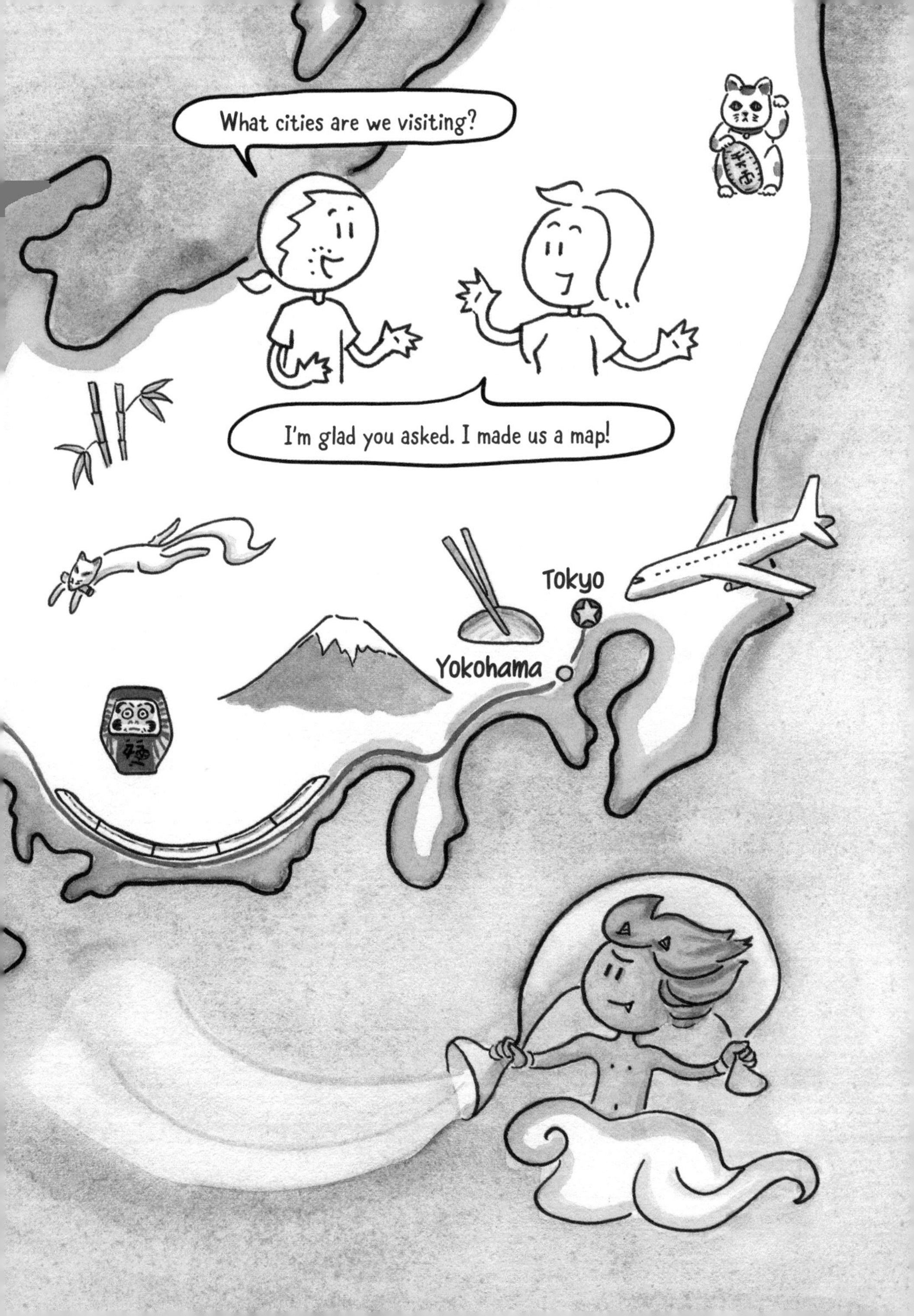
What cities are we visiting?
I'm glad you asked. I made us a map!
Tokyo
Yokohama

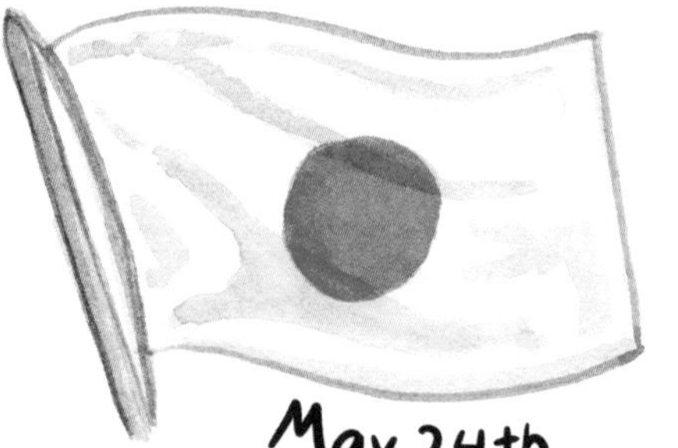

# Flying to Japan

May 24th

While waiting in the security line at Mineta San Jose International Airport . . .

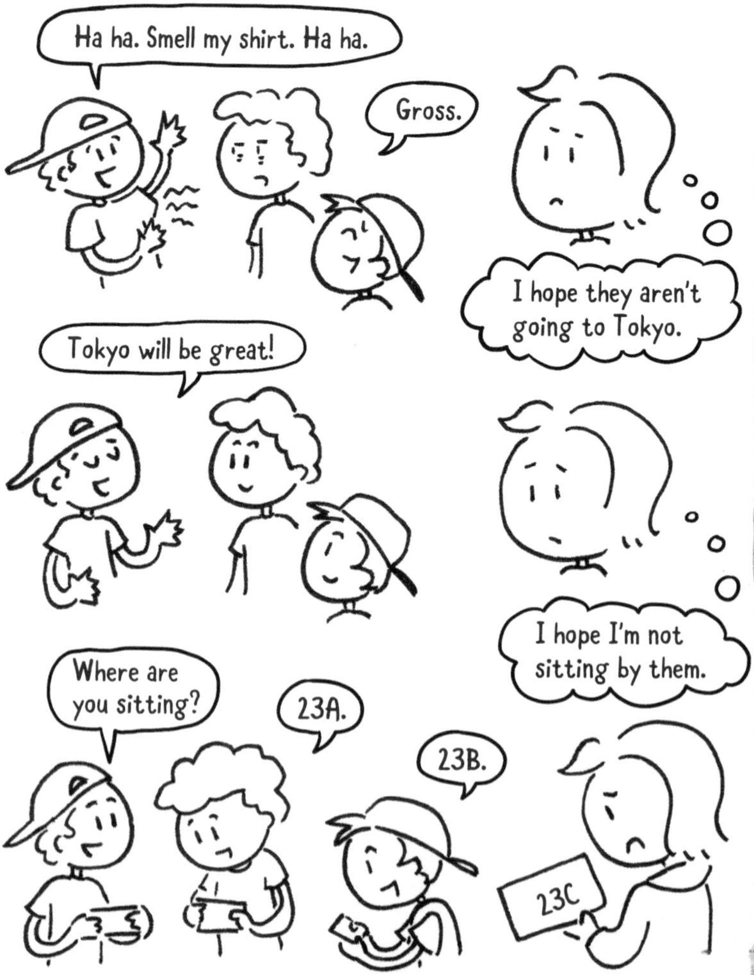
Ha ha. Smell my shirt. Ha ha.
Gross.
I hope they aren't going to Tokyo.
Tokyo will be great!
I hope I'm not sitting by them.
Where are you sitting?
23A.
23B.
23C

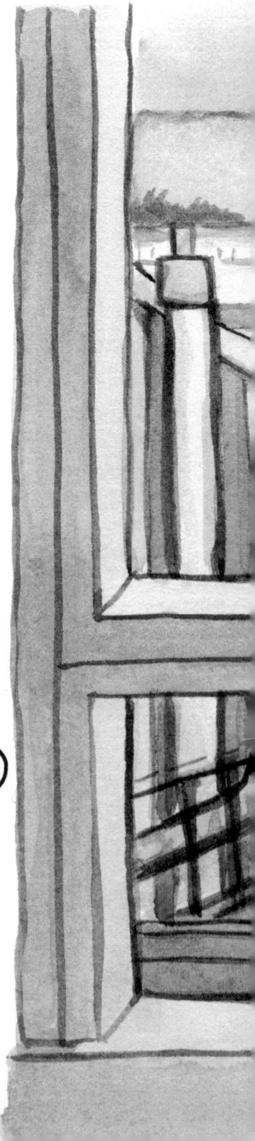

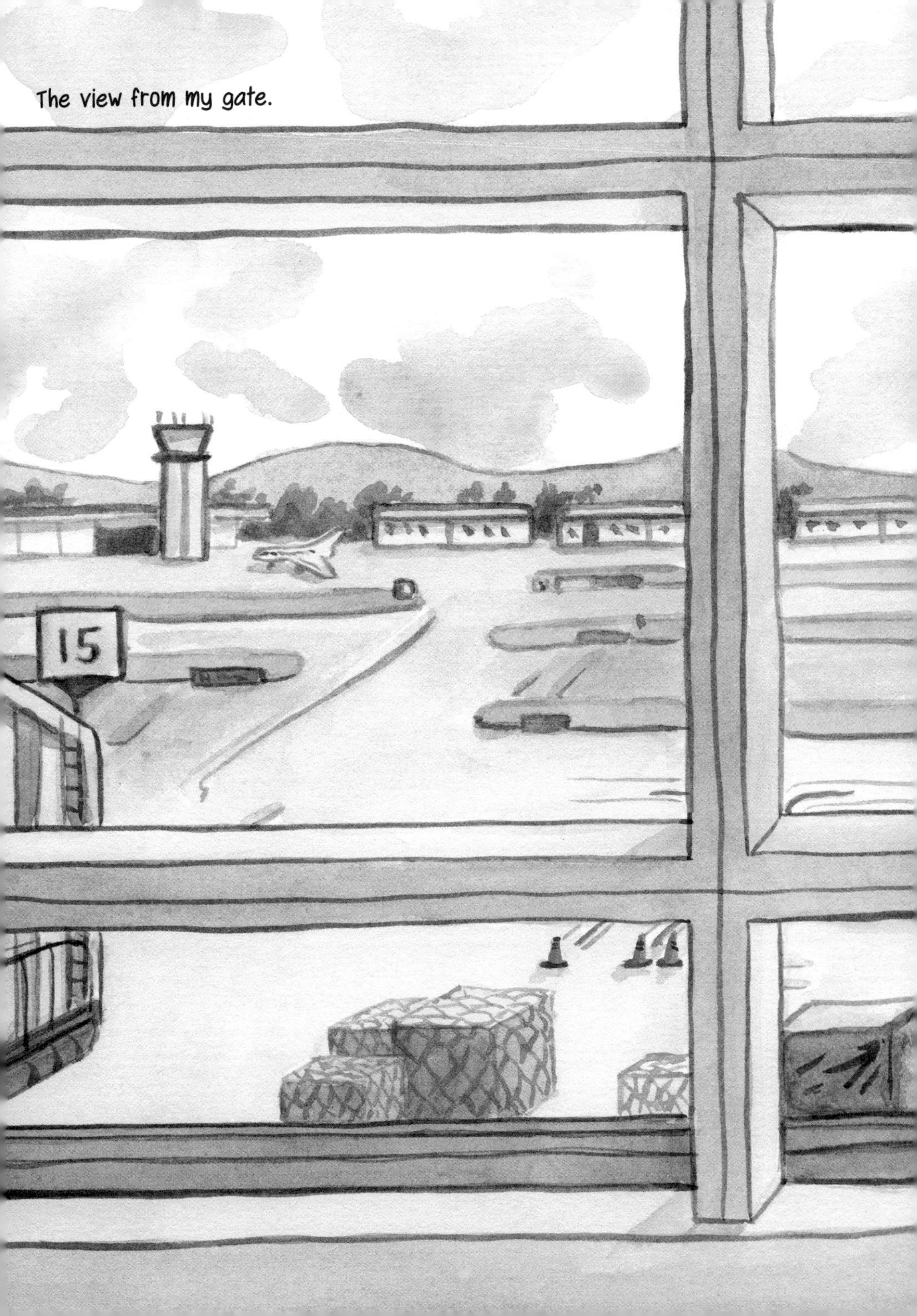
The view from my gate.
15

My seatmates ended up being awesome. We chatted for a bit and I learned that they were three brothers going on vacation to Thailand.

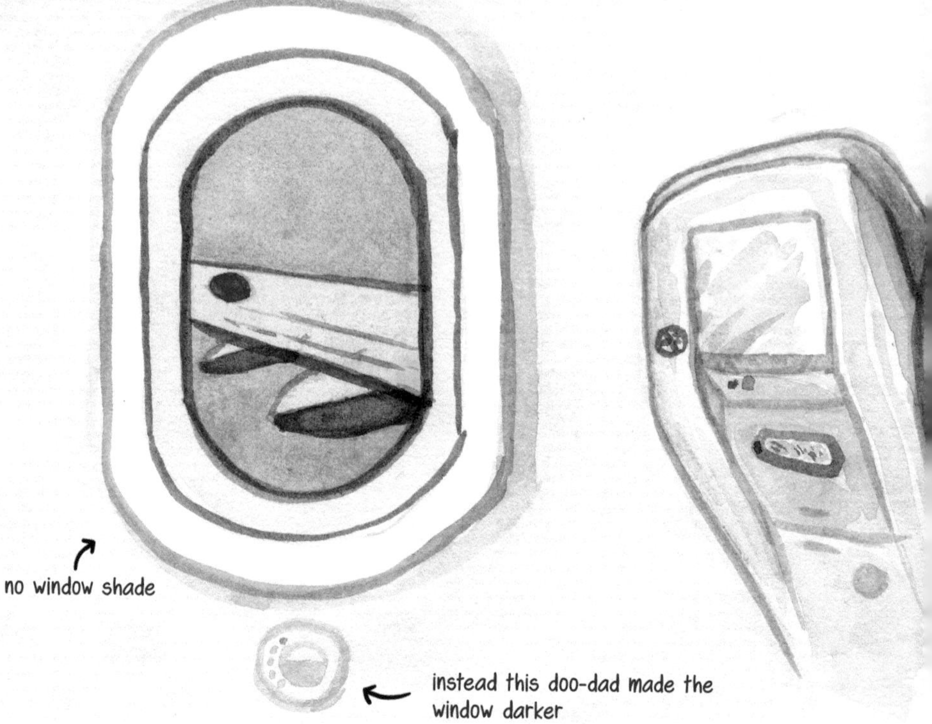
no window shade
instead this doo-dad made the window darker

During dinner we jointly tried to figure out what we were eating.

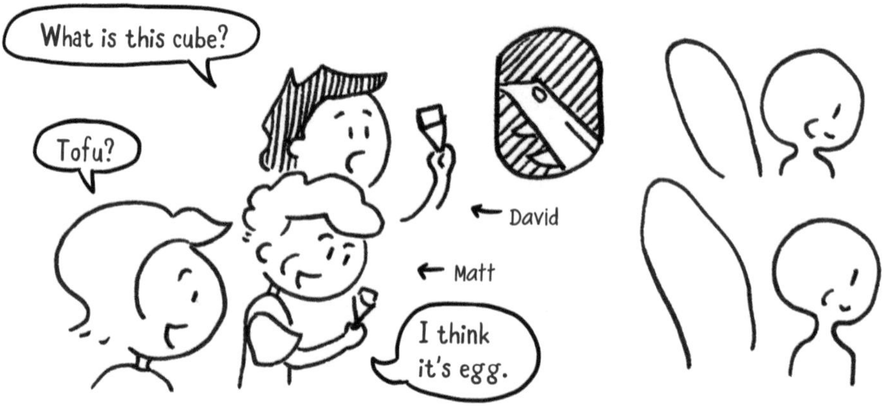
What is this cube?
Tofu?
David
Matt
I think it's egg.

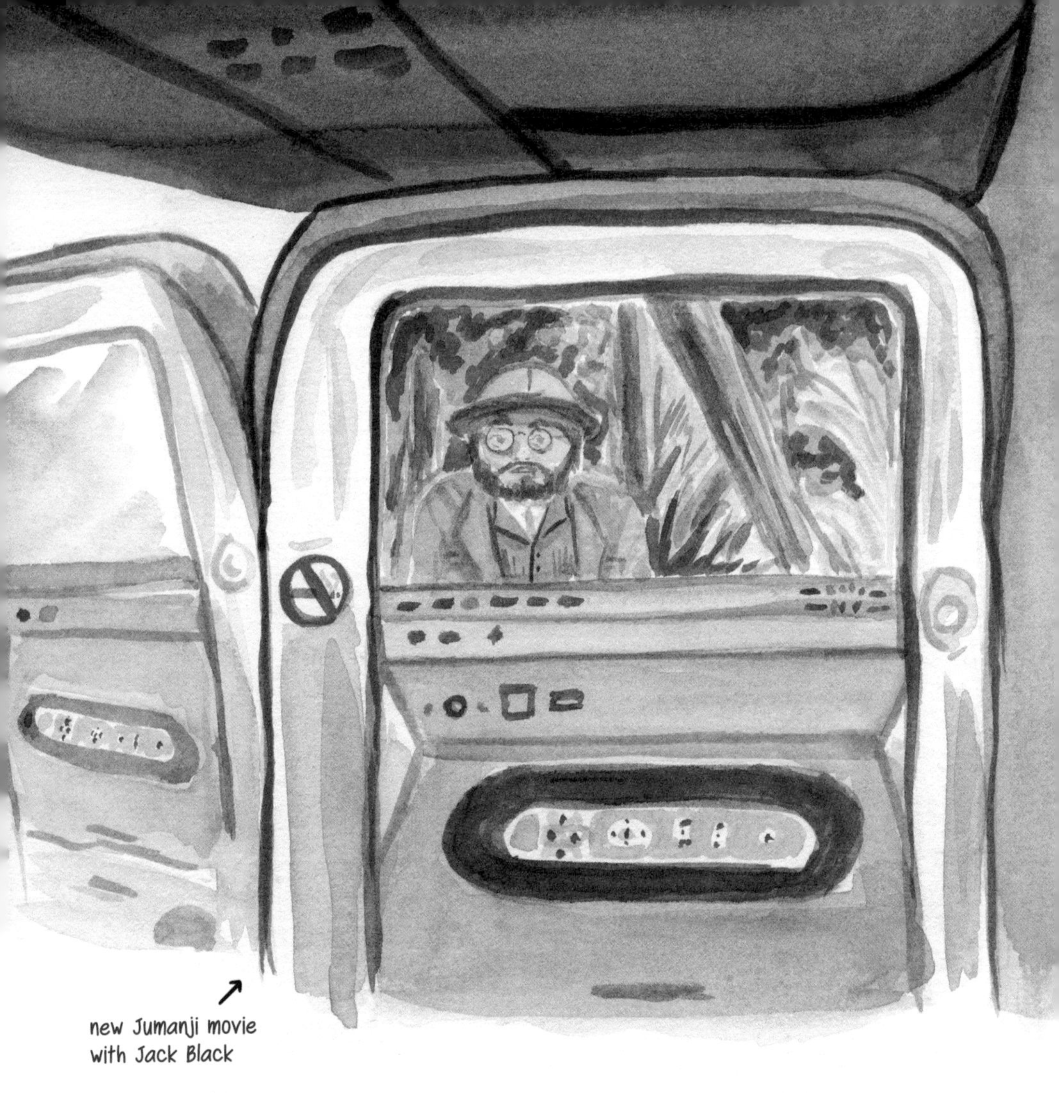
new Jumanji movie
with Jack Black

A little girl watched me while I was painting the rough draft for this page, so I gave her an impromptu demo.

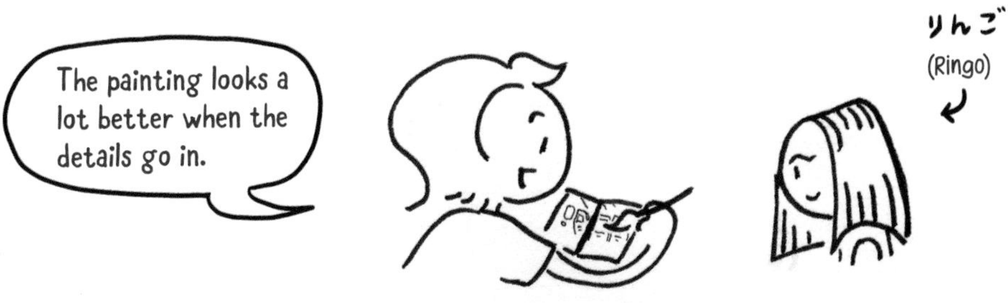
The painting looks a lot better when the details go in.
りんご
(Ringo)

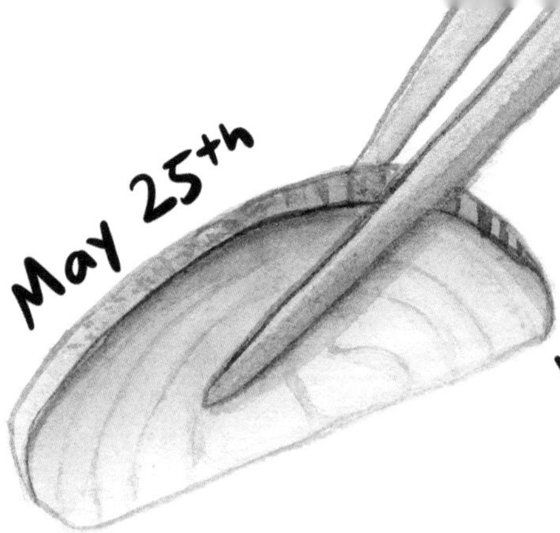

May 25th

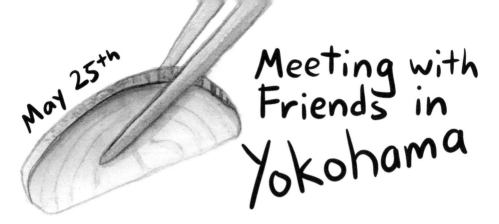

# Meeting with Friends in Yokohama

After getting through customs I went to the place where Connor said he would wait for me, but he wasn't there.

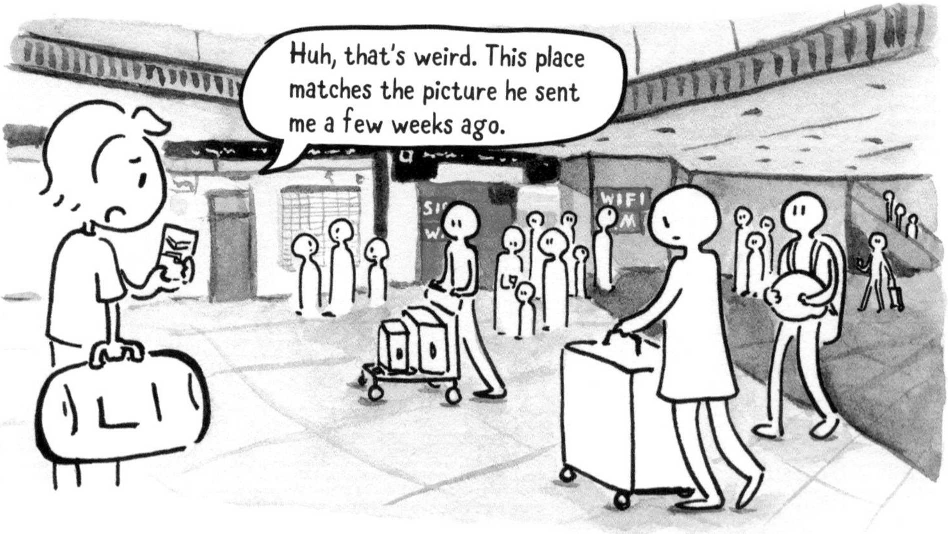
Huh, that's weird. This place matches the picture he sent me a few weeks ago.
WIFI

Connor was going to buy me a SIM card for my phone when we met. Without him, I was all alone with no money and no cell phone service. I panicked and cried for a little bit. Eventually I thought to connect to the airport wifi and learned he was going to be late.

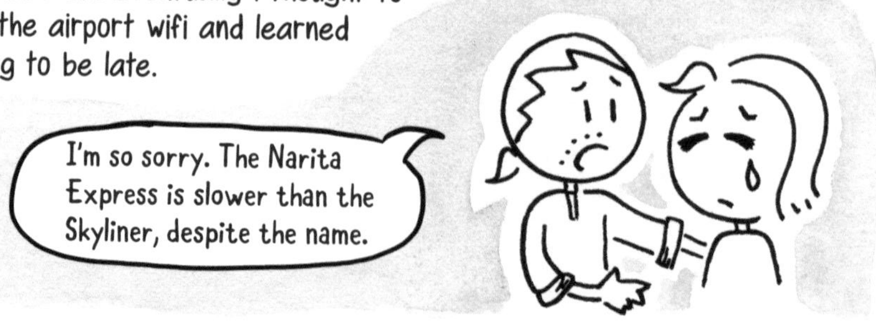
I'm so sorry. The Narita Express is slower than the Skyliner, despite the name.

We picked up our Japan Rail passes, then got onto a train to Yokohama.

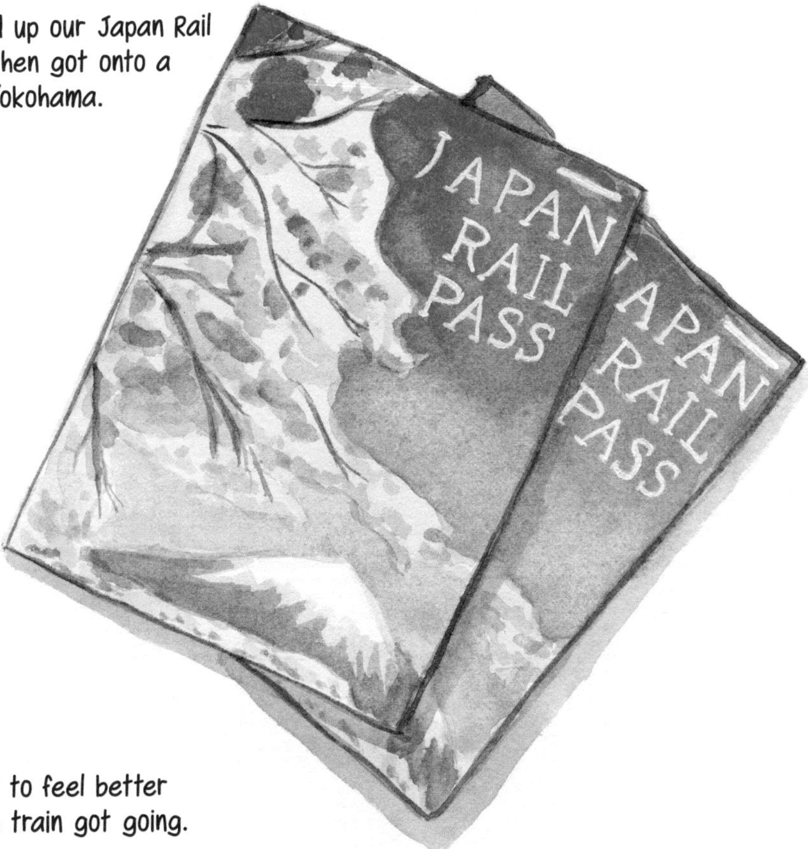
JAPAN RAIL PASS
JAPAN RAIL PASS

I started to feel better once the train got going.

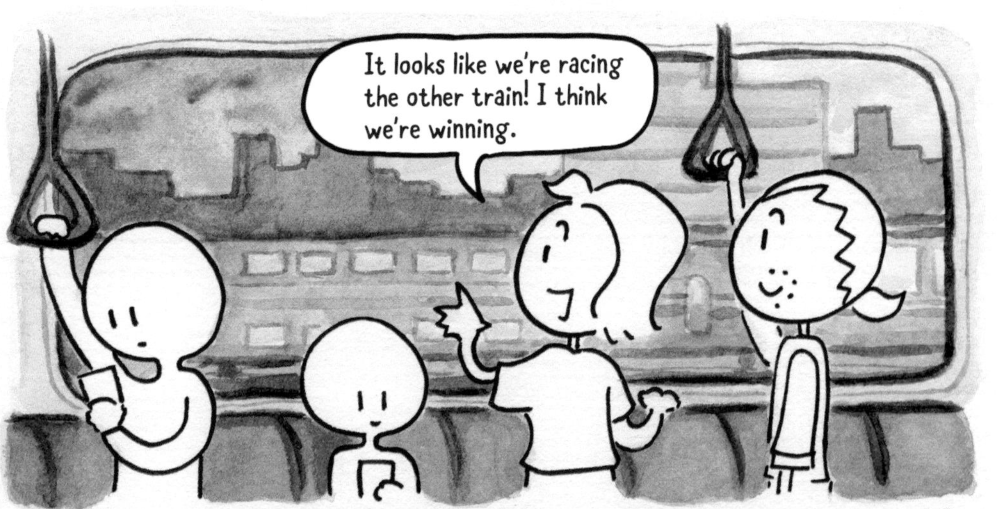
It looks like we're racing the other train! I think we're winning.

After dropping off my bags at the hotel, we met up with Connor's brother, Mason, and our friends Takuya and Satoko.

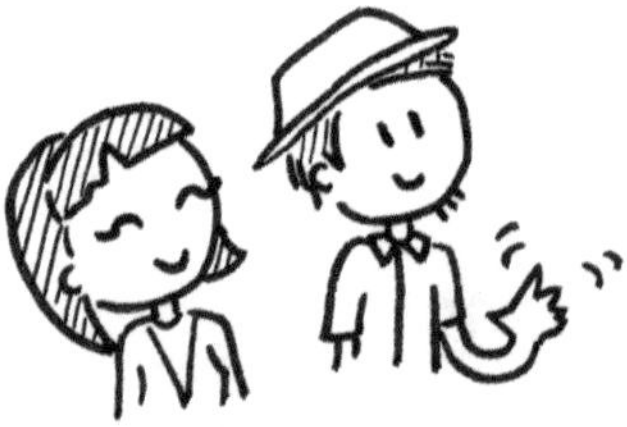

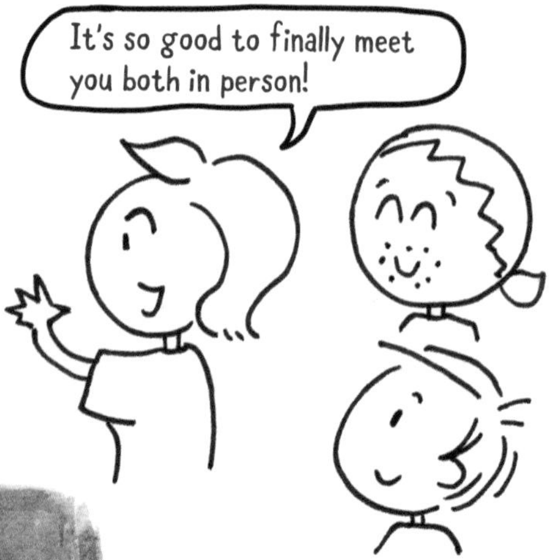
It's so good to finally meet you both in person!

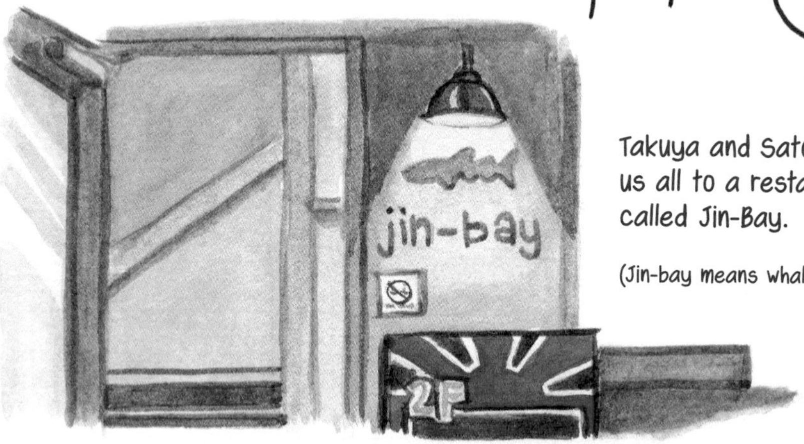
jin-bay
2F

Takuya and Satoko took us all to a restaurant called Jin-Bay.

(Jin-bay means whale shark)

While we waited for our food to be served, Takuya quizzed me on my understanding of Japanese.

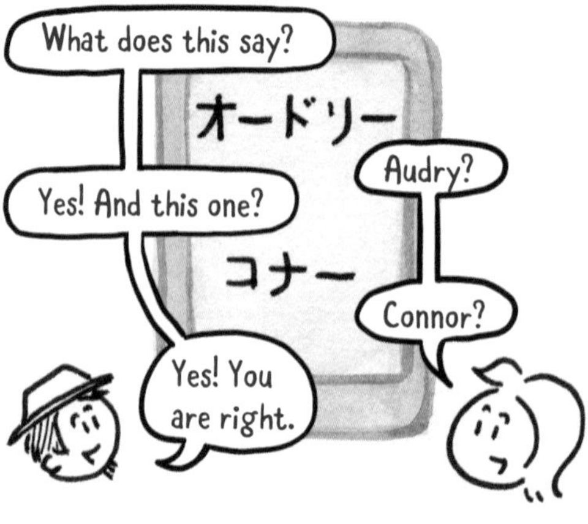
What does this say?
オードリー
Audry?
Yes! And this one?
コナー
Connor?
Yes! You are right.

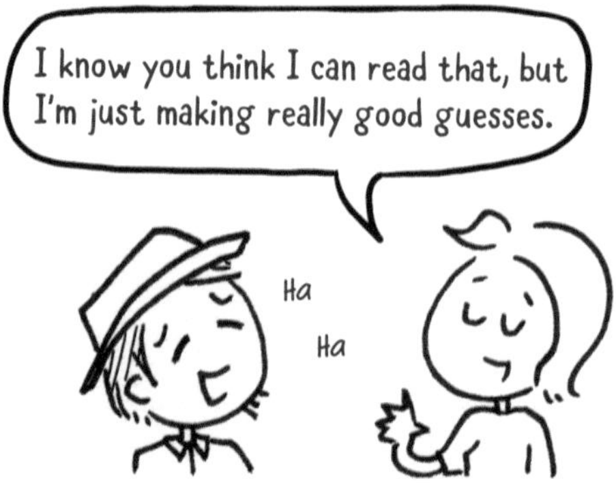
I know you think I can read that, but I'm just making really good guesses.
Ha
Ha

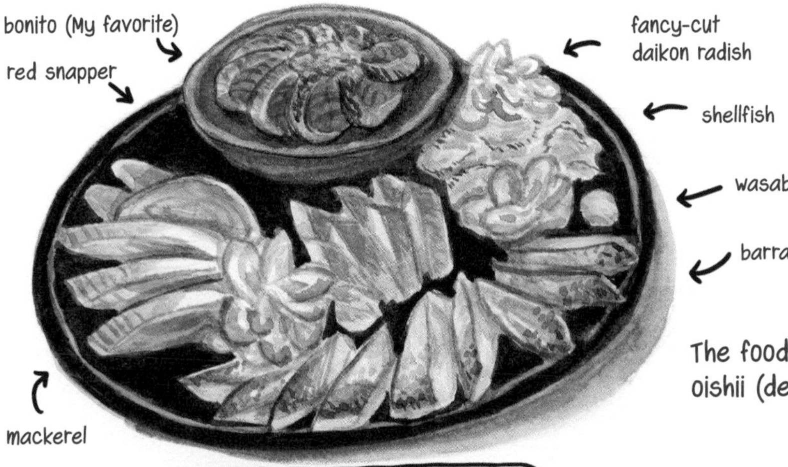
bonito (My favorite)
red snapper
fancy-cut daikon radish
shellfish
wasabi
barracuda
mackerel

The food was oishii (delicious)!

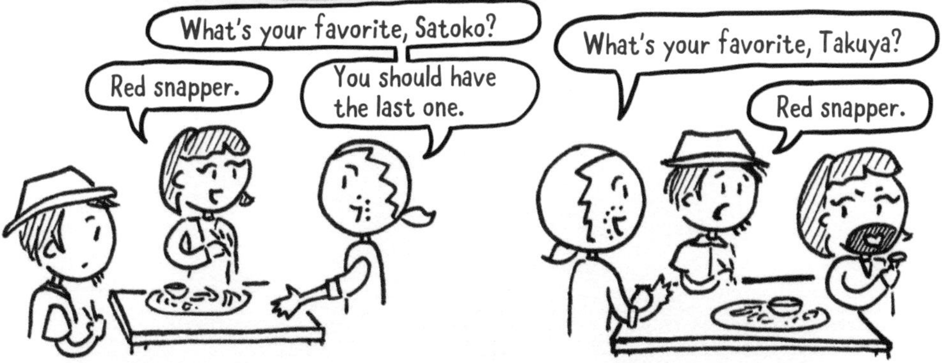
What's your favorite, Satoko?
Red snapper.
You should have the last one.
What's your favorite, Takuya?
Red snapper.

I was tired after dinner, so Connor and I said our goodbyes and walked back to our hotel. While getting ready for bed I encountered one of the complicated toilets I had heard existed in Japan.

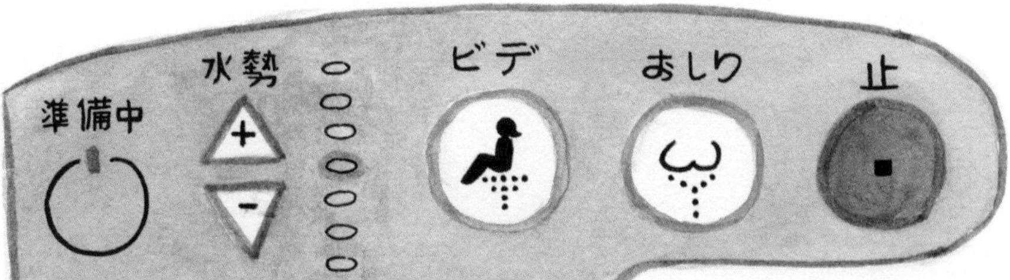
準備中
水勢
ビデ
おしり
止

It made waterfall sounds whenever someone sat on the seat.

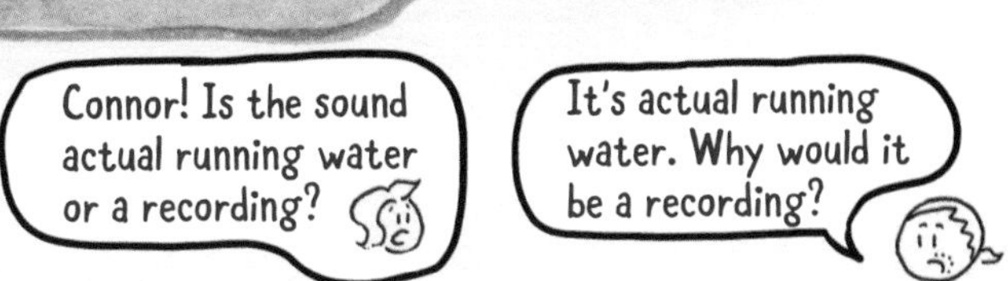
Connor! Is the sound actual running water or a recording?
It's actual running water. Why would it be a recording?

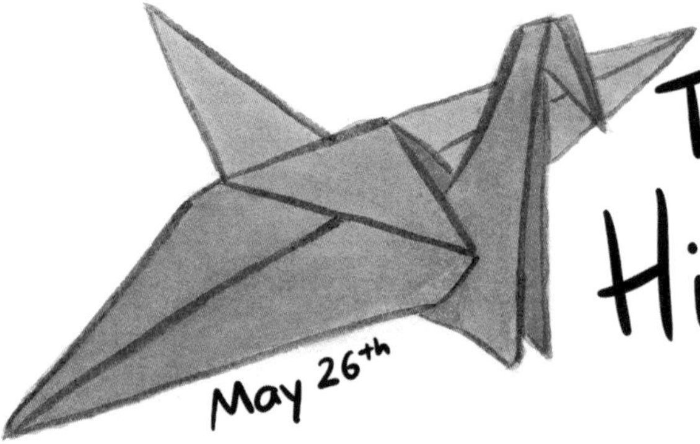

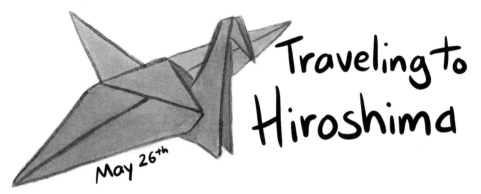

# Traveling to Hiroshima

May 26th

Knowing that we were going to be on the shinkansen (bullet train) for most of the day, we each bought an ekiben (station bento box).

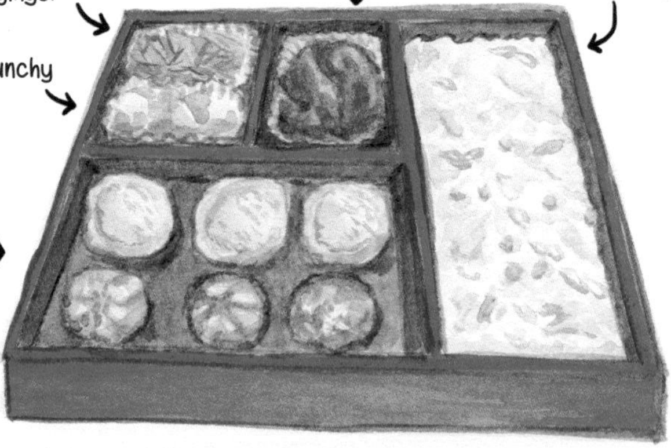

breaded chicken
ginger
peas, rice, and egg
no idea—a crunchy vegetable
meaty dumplings


While waiting for our train I observed that when each shinkansen left the station, a conductor would put their head out of the window and salute.

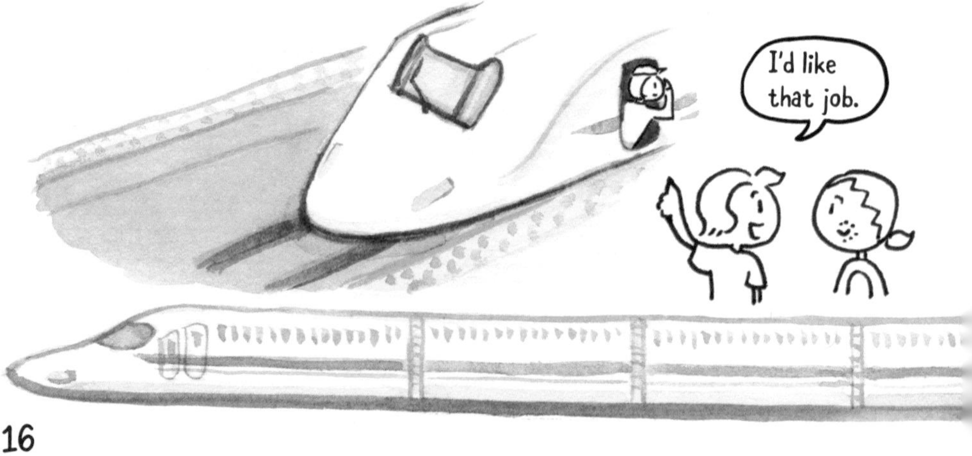

I'd like that job.

Satoko's Shinkansen Top Tip:

When going south, sit on the right hand side of the train to see Mount Fuji.

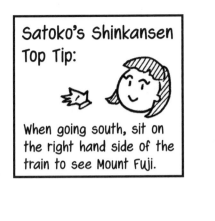

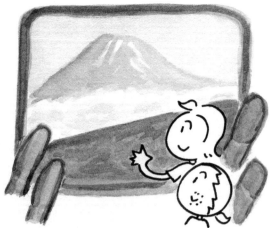

We transferred trains at:

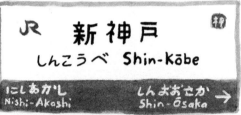

JR
新神戸
しんこうべ Shin-Kōbe
にしあかし
Nishi-Akashi
しんおおさか
Shin-Ōsaka

Fun fact: If a station has "shin" in its name, it means it's a shinkansen station.

Every station has a different tune that plays when a train arrives. Shin-Kobe's tune was "The Itsy Bitsy Spider."

## Other interesting shinkansen features:

A full row of seats can be rotated to face the opposite direction.

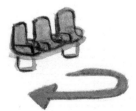

In the restroom there is a sensor that lowers the toilet seat for you.

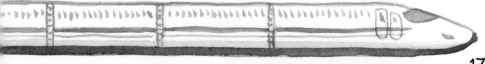

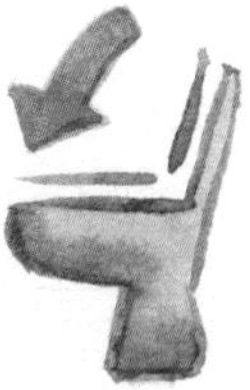

Our first stop in Hiroshima was the Peace Memorial Park, a tribute to those who died in the nuclear attack in 1945. Here we passed by the Children's Peace Monument, which features a girl holding up a paper crane. The monument's imagery is inspired by Sadako Sasaki, a girl who got leukemia ten years after the A-bomb fell. However, the monument is dedicated to all children who died due to the A-bomb.

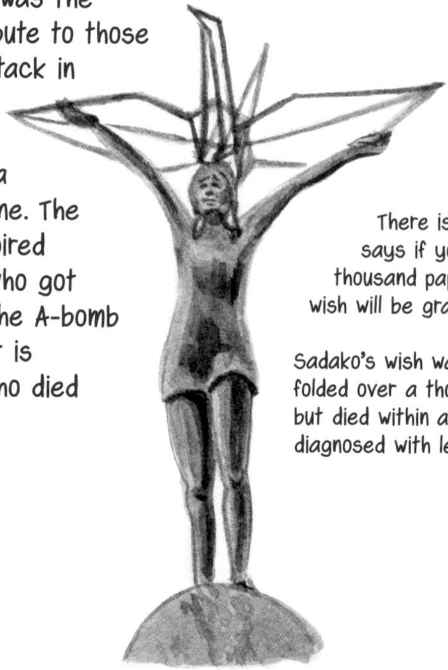

There is a legend that says if you fold one thousand paper cranes your wish will be granted.

Sadako's wish was to live. She folded over a thousand cranes, but died within a year of being diagnosed with leukemia.

Next we walked to the Hiroshima Peace Memorial Museum. The main building was closed for renovations, but there was a smaller exhibit in the east building. It was powerful to be reminded how the bomb affected ordinary people's lives.

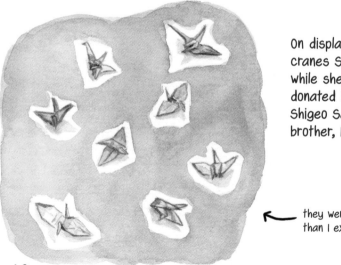

On display were some of the cranes Sadako Sasaki folded while she was sick. They were donated by Sadako's father, Shigeo Sasaki, and her brother, Masahiro Sasaki.

they were much smaller than I expected

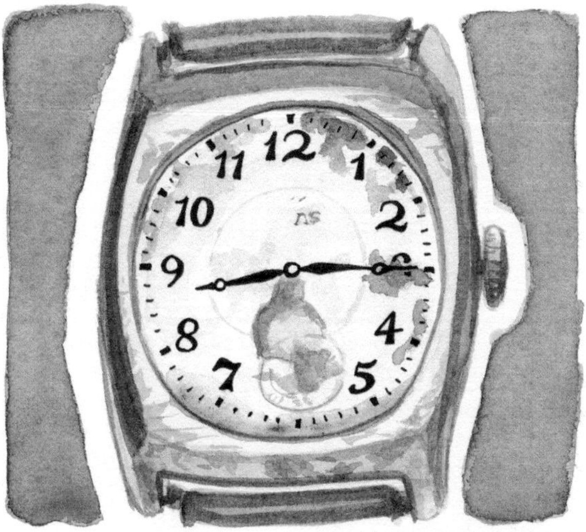
ns

There was a watch that stopped when the bomb fell: 8:15 AM on August 6th, 1945. It was donated by its wearer, Akito Kawagoe, who survived.

There was a tricycle that belonged to a boy named Shinichi Tetsutani. The three-year-old was riding it when the bomb exploded. He died later that night. It was donated by Shinichi's father, Nobuo Tetsutani.

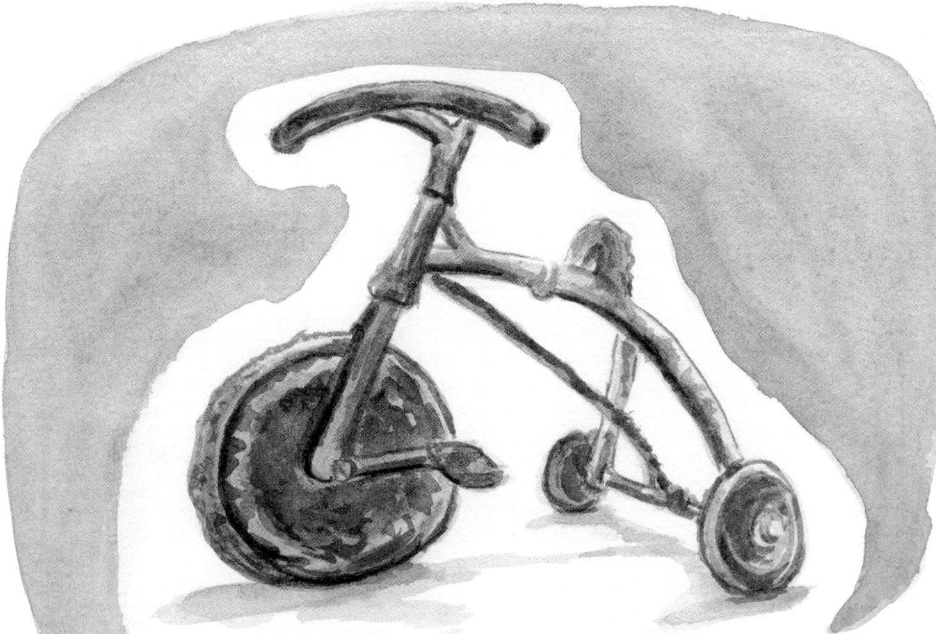

After leaving the museum, we walked over to the Cenotaph.

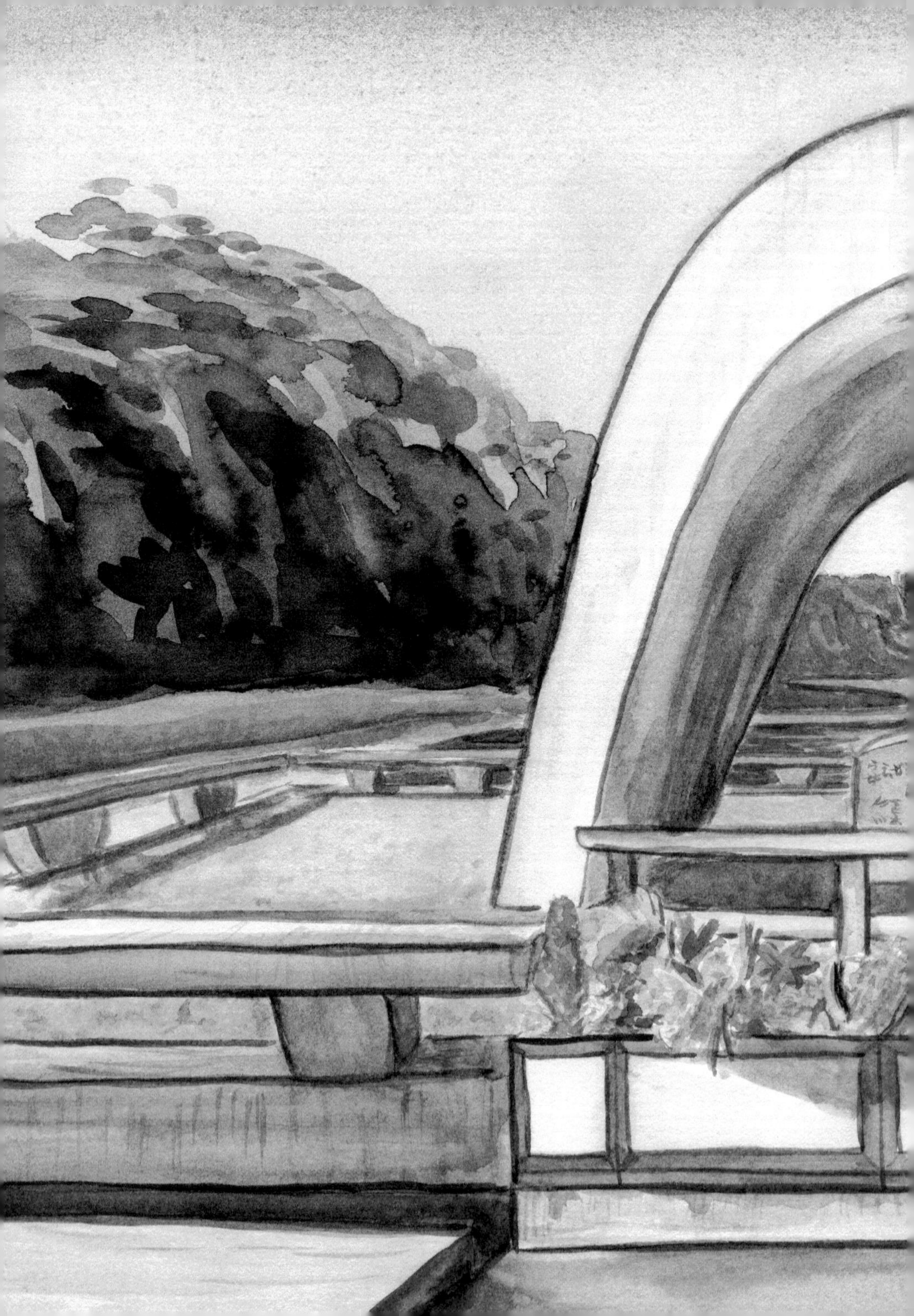

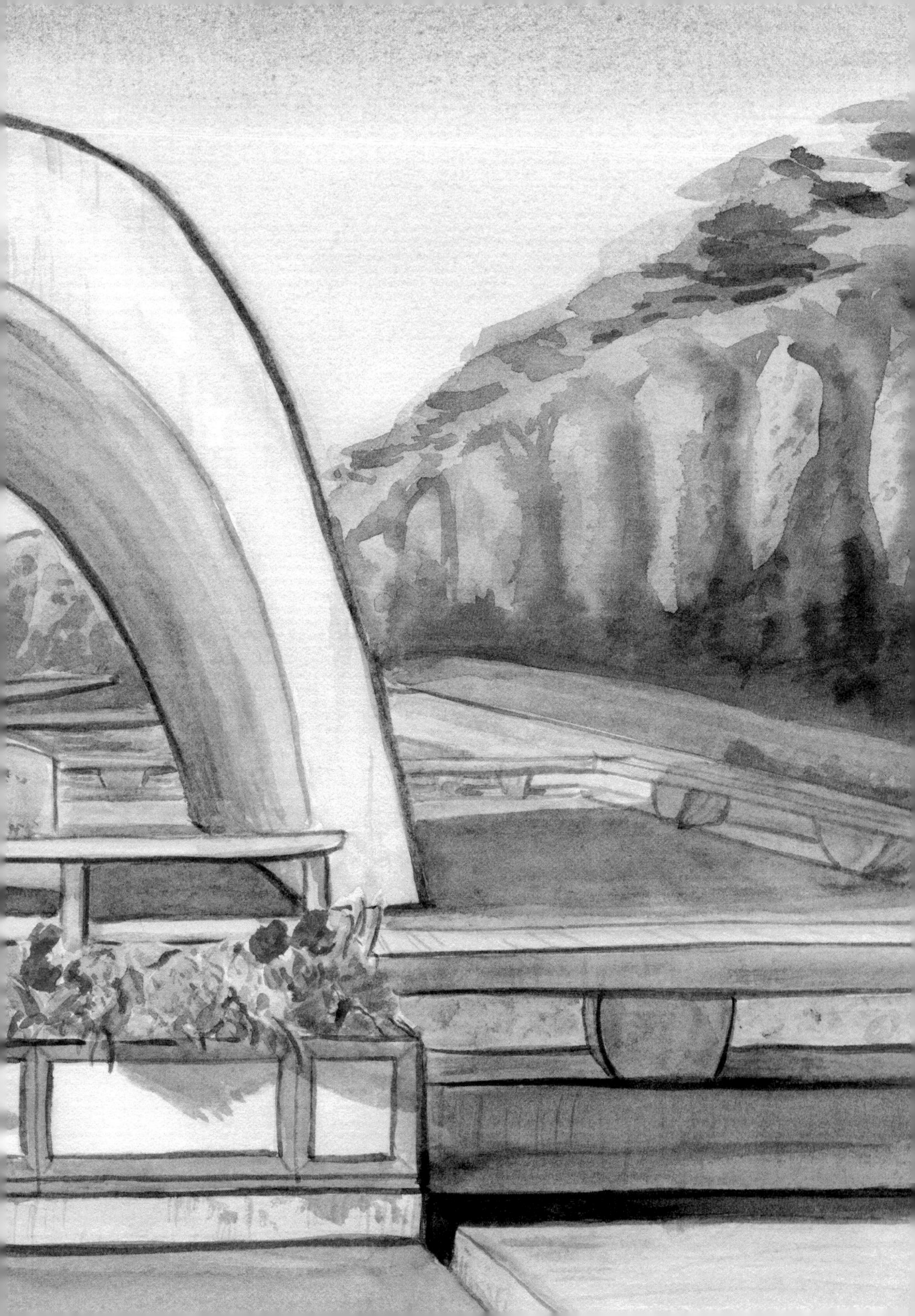

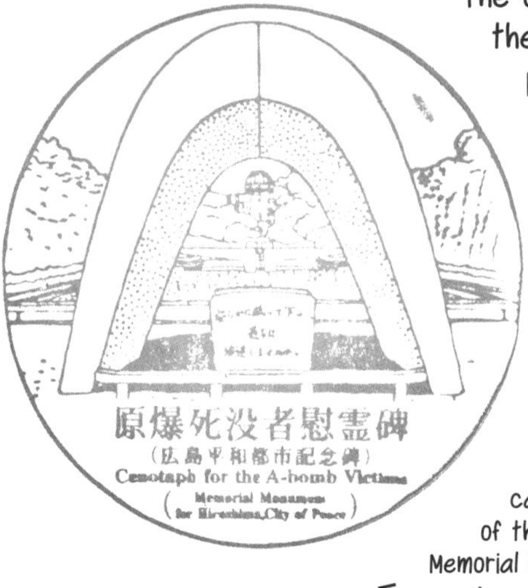
原爆死没者慰霊碑
(広島平和都市記念碑)
Cenotaph for the A-bomb Victims
(Memorial Monument for Hiroshima,City of Peace)

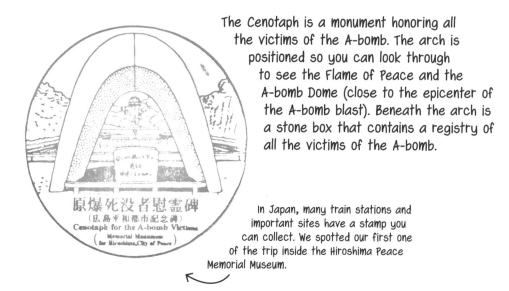

The Cenotaph is a monument honoring all the victims of the A-bomb. The arch is positioned so you can look through to see the Flame of Peace and the A-bomb Dome (close to the epicenter of the A-bomb blast). Beneath the arch is a stone box that contains a registry of all the victims of the A-bomb.

In Japan, many train stations and important sites have a stamp you can collect. We spotted our first one of the trip inside the Hiroshima Peace Memorial Museum.

The Flame of Peace burns on a pedestal that represents a pair of hands opening upward.

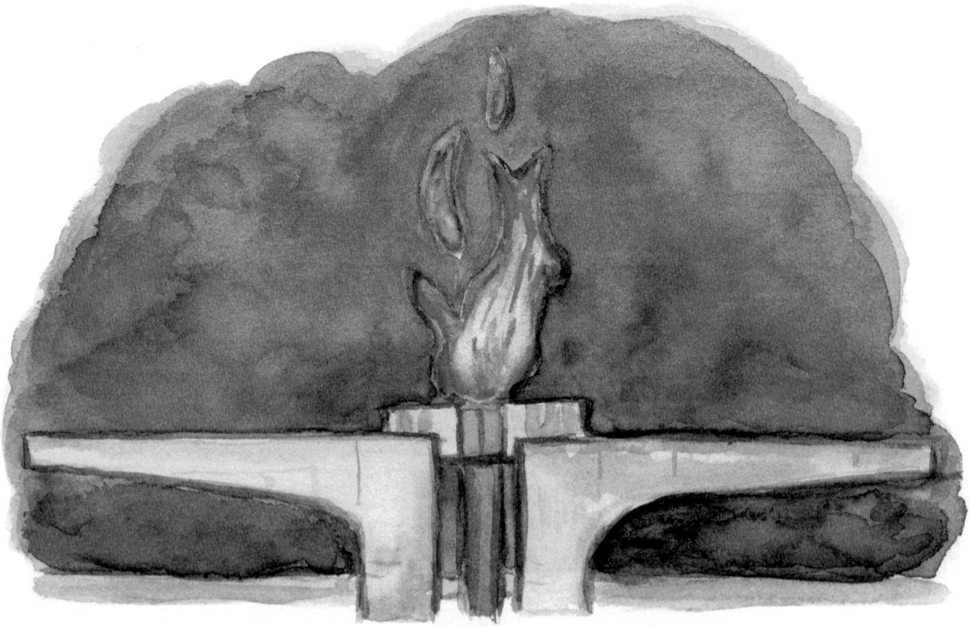

Burning continuously since it was lit on August 1, 1964, the flame will be extinguished when there are no more nuclear weapons in the world.

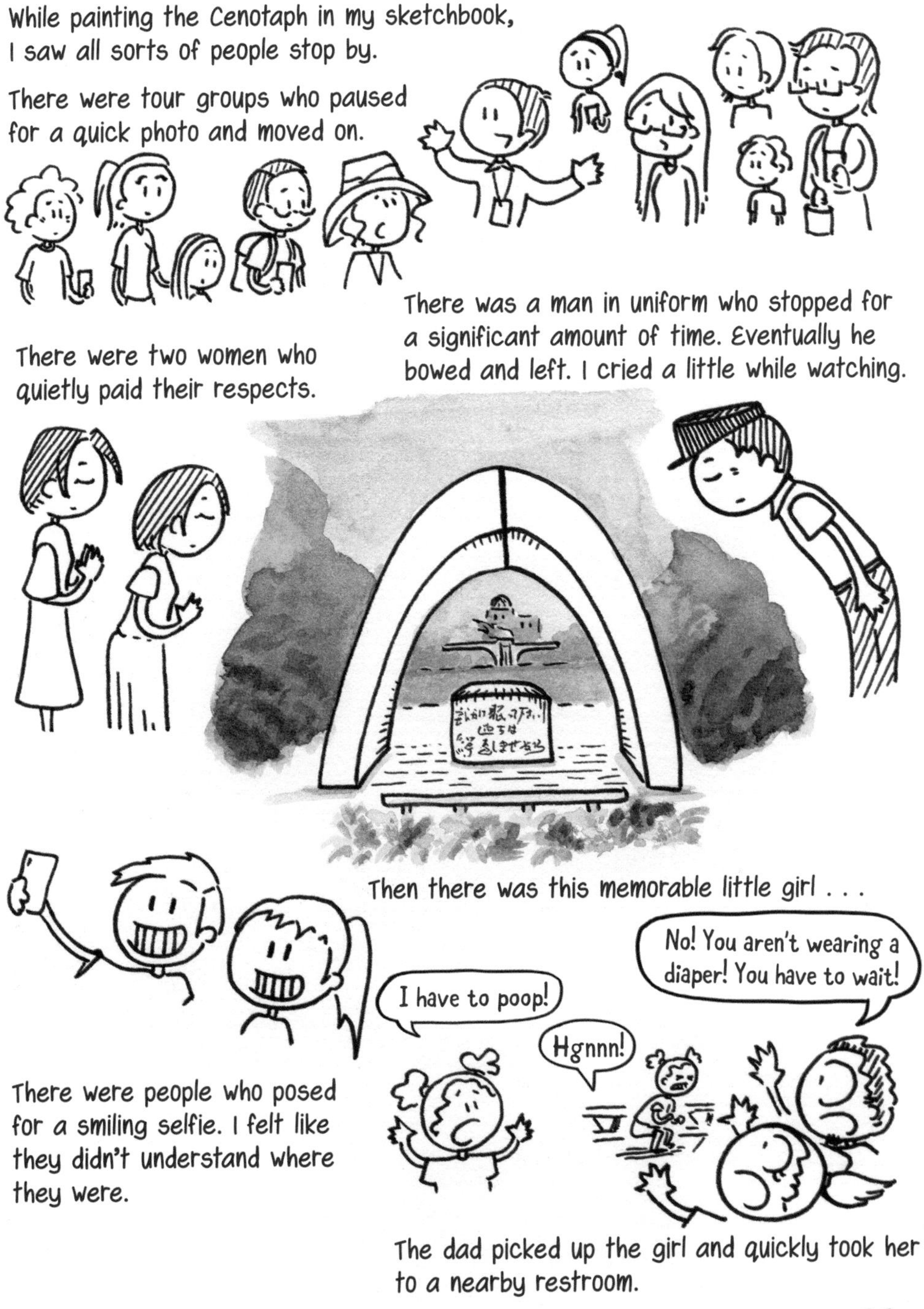
While painting the Cenotaph in my sketchbook, I saw all sorts of people stop by.
There were tour groups who paused for a quick photo and moved on.
There were two women who quietly paid their respects.
There was a man in uniform who stopped for a significant amount of time. Eventually he bowed and left. I cried a little while watching.
There were people who posed for a smiling selfie. I felt like they didn't understand where they were.
Then there was this memorable little girl . . .
I have to poop!
No! You aren't wearing a diaper! You have to wait!
Hgnnn!
The dad picked up the girl and quickly took her to a nearby restroom.

Before leaving the Peace Memorial Park, we stopped by the iconic A-bomb (Genbaku) Dome. Because the building was almost directly beneath the blast, the dome and many of the walls survived. Sadly, none of the people who had been inside the building lived through the initial blast.

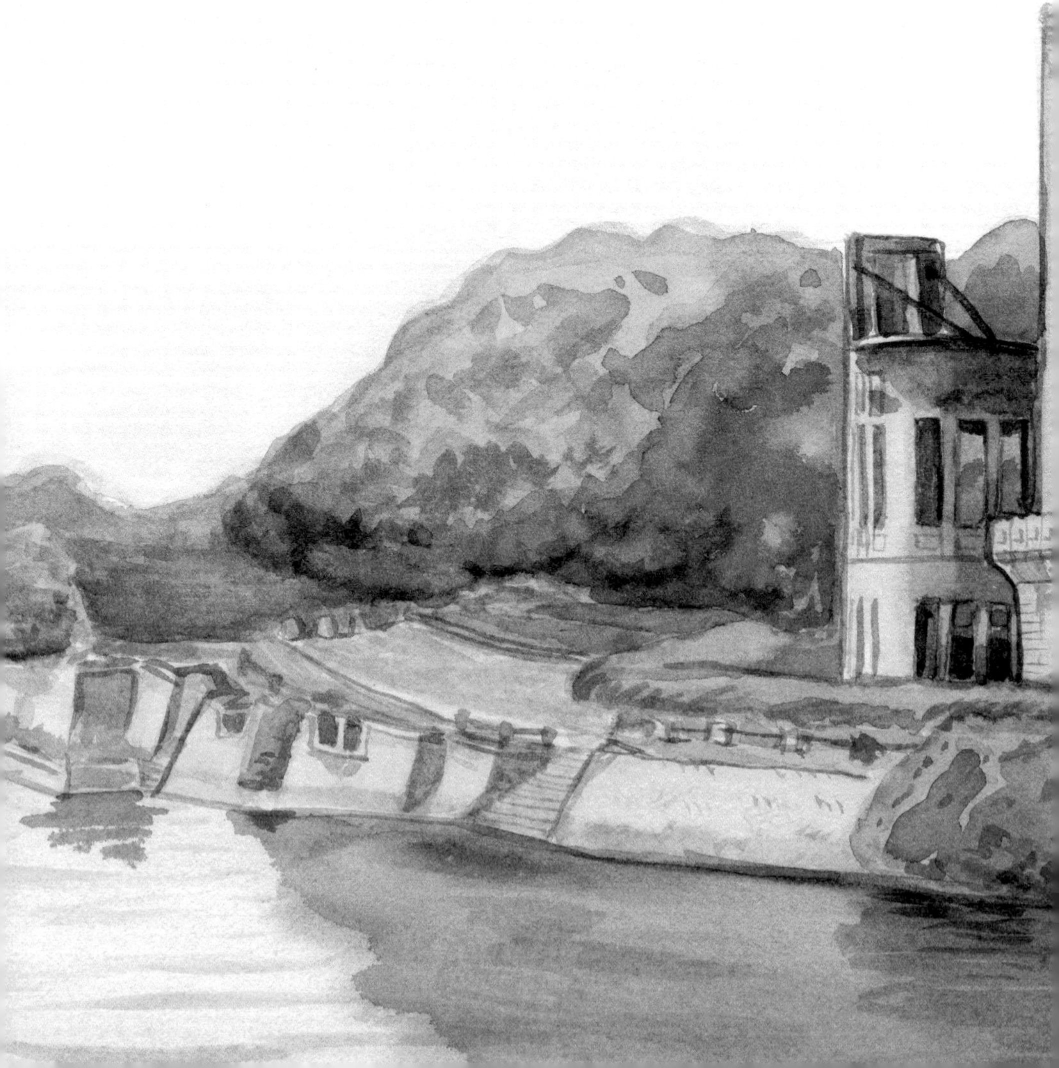

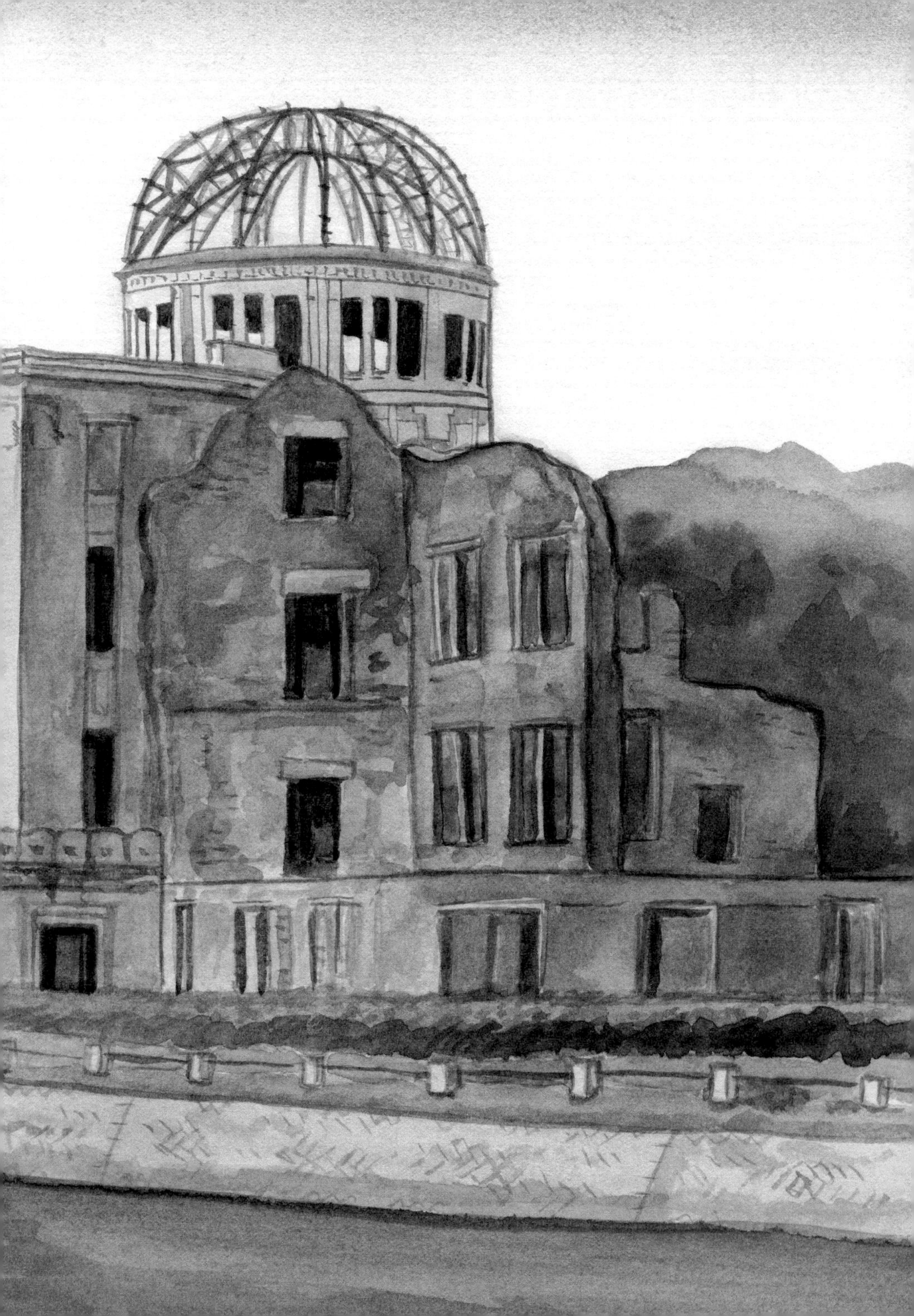

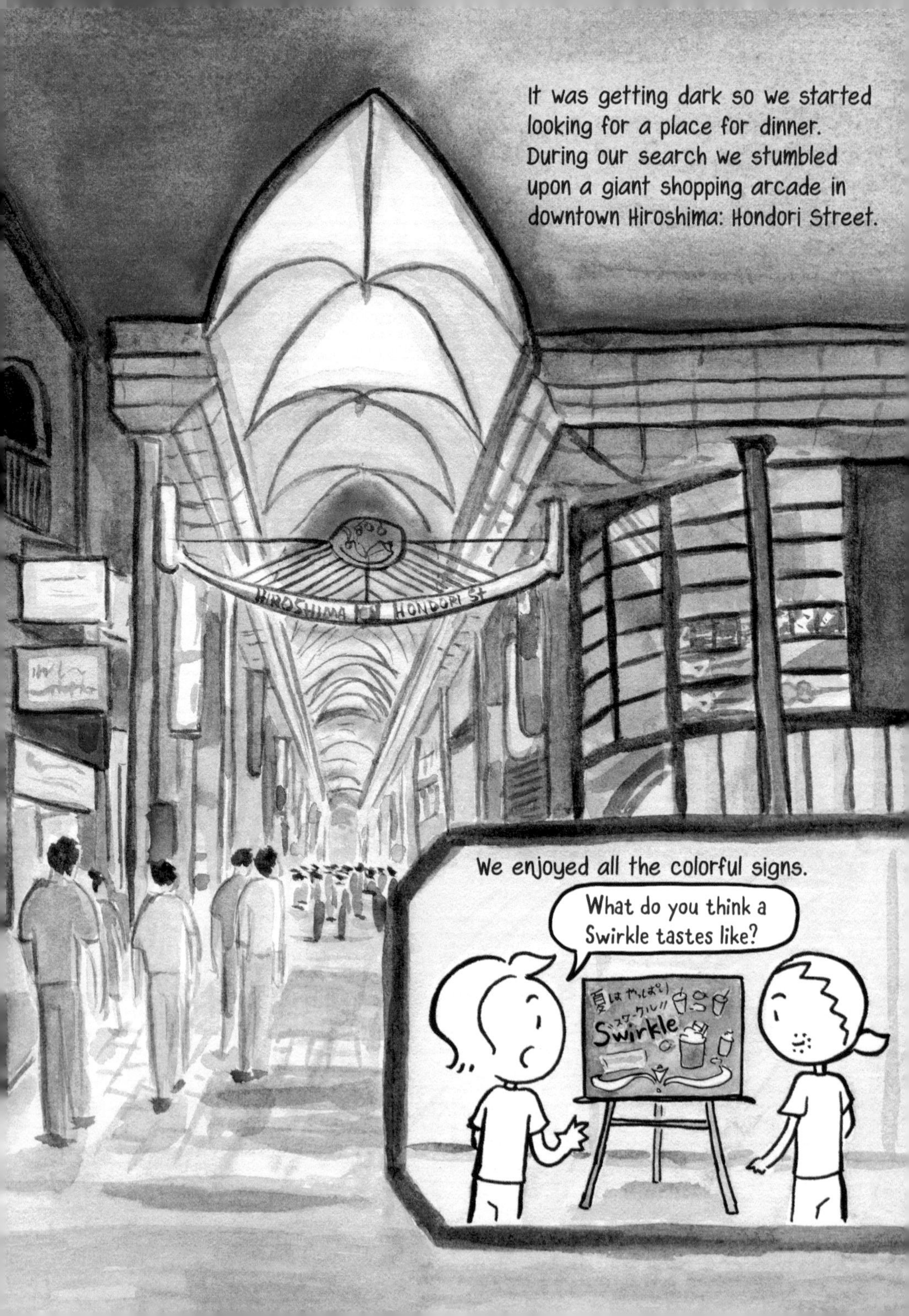
It was getting dark so we started looking for a place for dinner. During our search we stumbled upon a giant shopping arcade in downtown Hiroshima: Hondori Street.
HIROSHIMA HONDORI St
We enjoyed all the colorful signs.
What do you think a Swirkle tastes like?
夏はやっぱり
スワークル!!
Swirkle

Connor and I eventually made our way to a building supposedly full of okonomiyaki (savory pancake) restaurants. Although there were many options to choose from, the elevator doors opened directly in front of one that had two spots free.

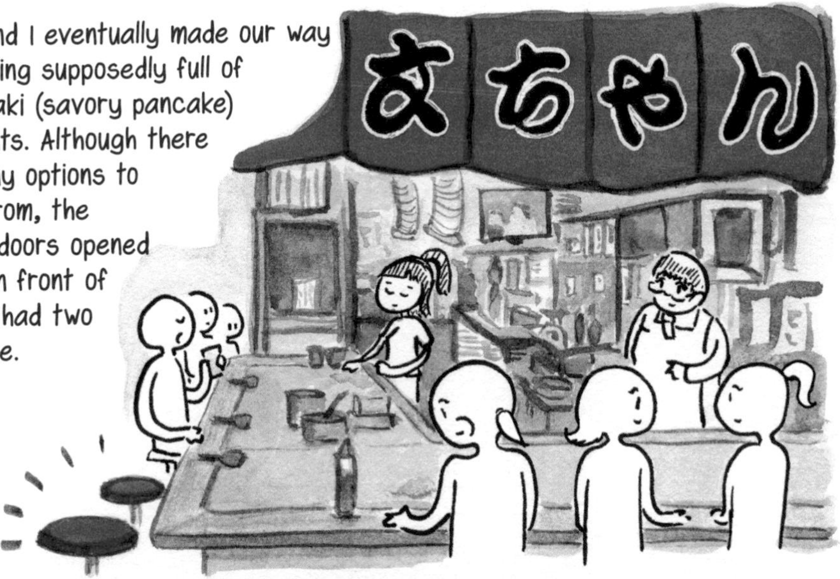
まちゃん

There are several styles of okonomiyaki. In Hiroshima, cabbage and noodles are layered on top of thin batter.
Then an egg is placed on top.

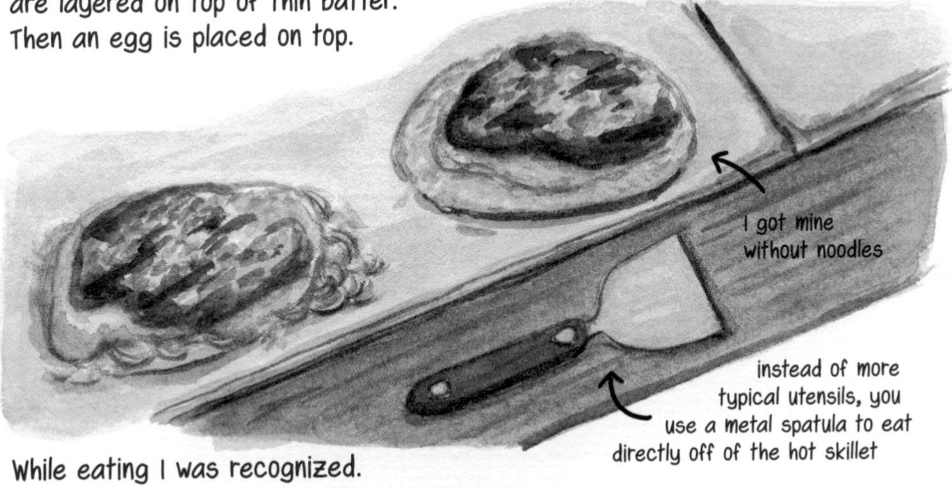
I got mine without noodles
instead of more typical utensils, you use a metal spatula to eat directly off of the hot skillet

While eating I was recognized.

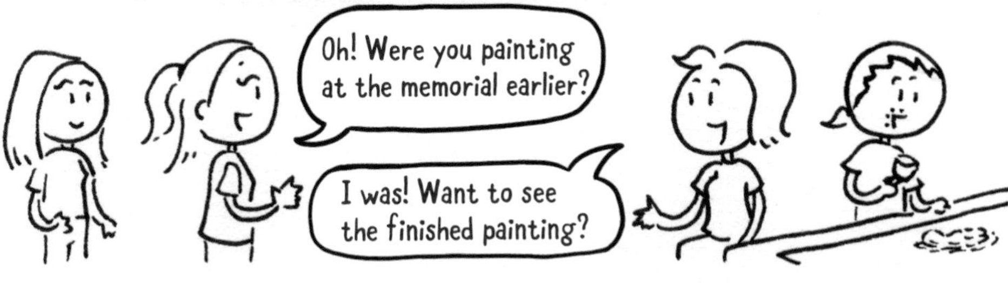
Oh! Were you painting at the memorial earlier?
I was! Want to see the finished painting?

# Day Trip to Miyajima

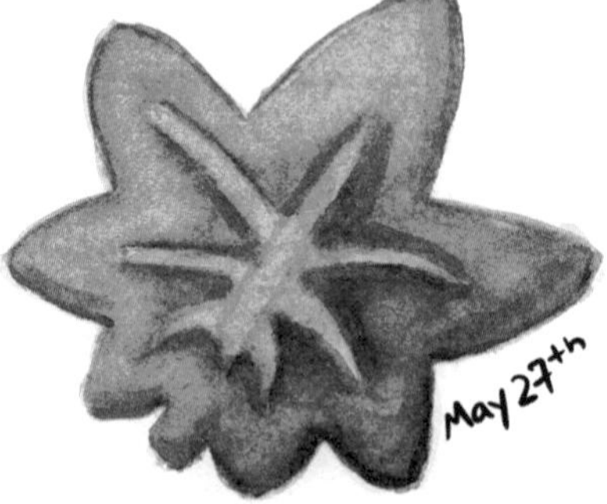
May 27th

Connor and I got up early so we could spend as much time as possible at Miyajima, an island near Hiroshima. Although it's better known as Miyajima, the true name of the island is Itsukushima. Miyajima means "shrine island" in Japanese.

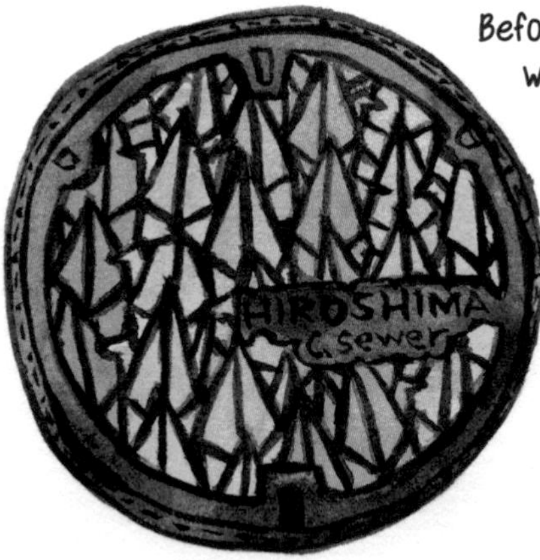
HIROSHIMA
C.Sewer

Before coming to Japan, I'd heard that there were decorative manhole cover designs in the different cities. I was excited to see my first one during our walk to our starting point of the day, Hiroshima Station.

We got off at Miyajimaguchi Station. I was pleased to find the station stamp.

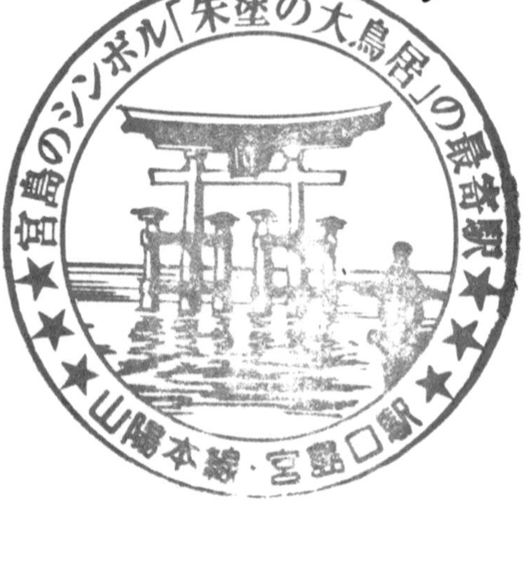
宮島のシンボル「朱塗の大鳥居」の最寄駅
山陽本線・宮島口駅

I stopped by the bathroom. When I sat down, a recording of rushing water and chirping played. It was like being in the middle of a pond.

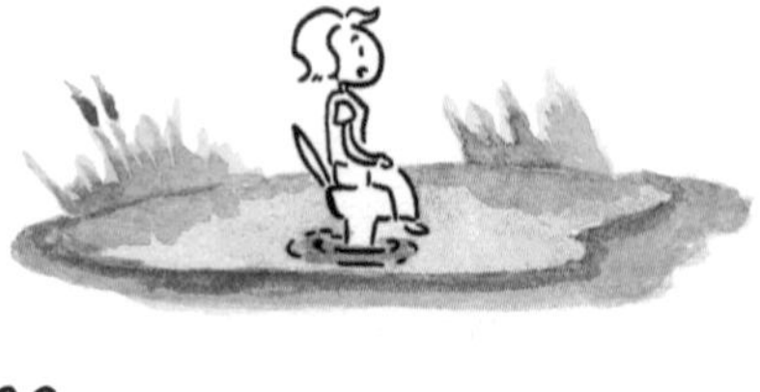

Between the train station and the ferry building was an interesting statue. Later I learned it was modeled on a bugaku (court dance) called The Prince of Lanling which is still performed at Itsukushima Shrine on Miyajima. The masked character is based on Ran Ryou-ou, a Chinese prince, who was known to have a beautiful face. When going into battle he would hide his beauty underneath a frightening mask.

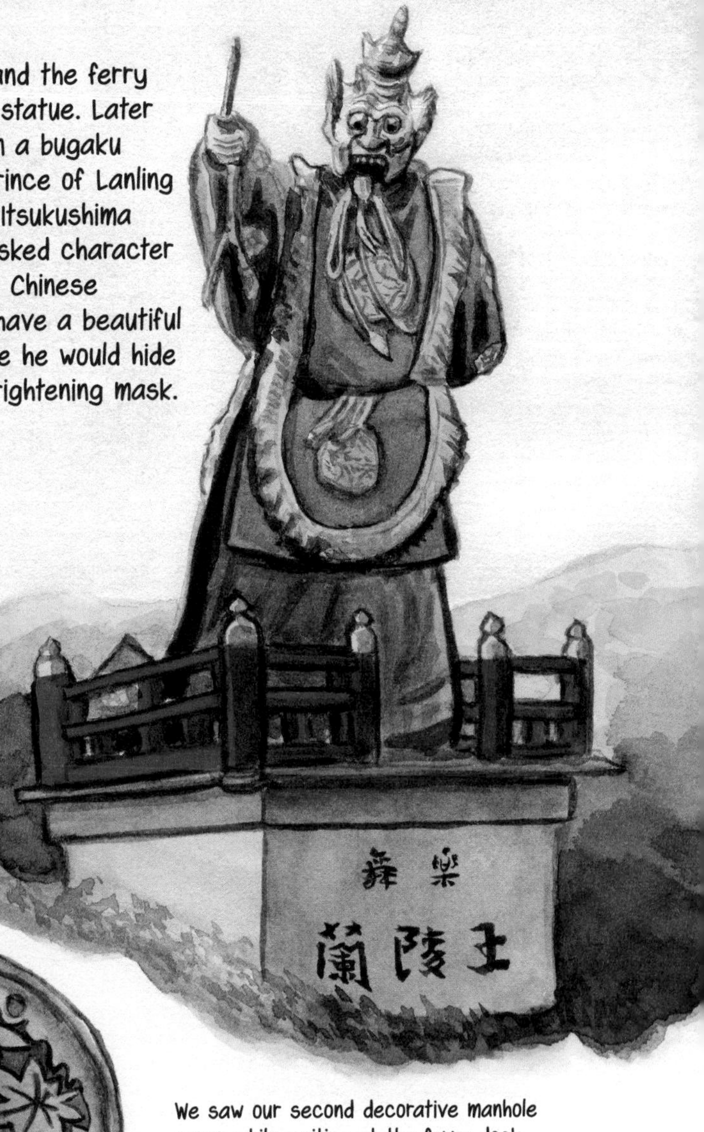
舞楽
蘭陵王

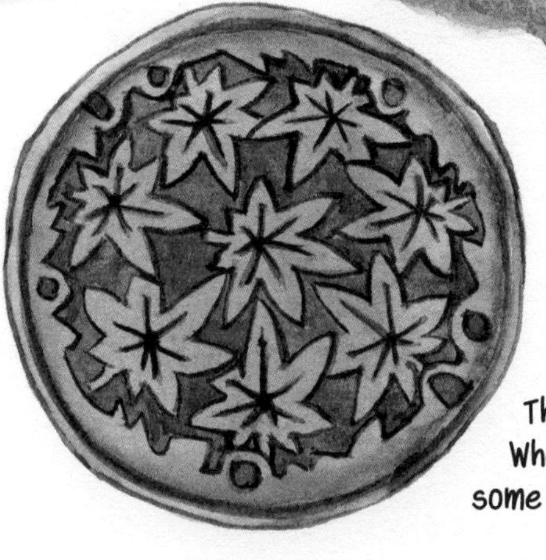

We saw our second decorative manhole cover while waiting at the ferry dock to go to Miyajima.

The ferry was quick and pleasant. When we got off we immediately met some of the locals . . .

There are Sika deer all over the island!

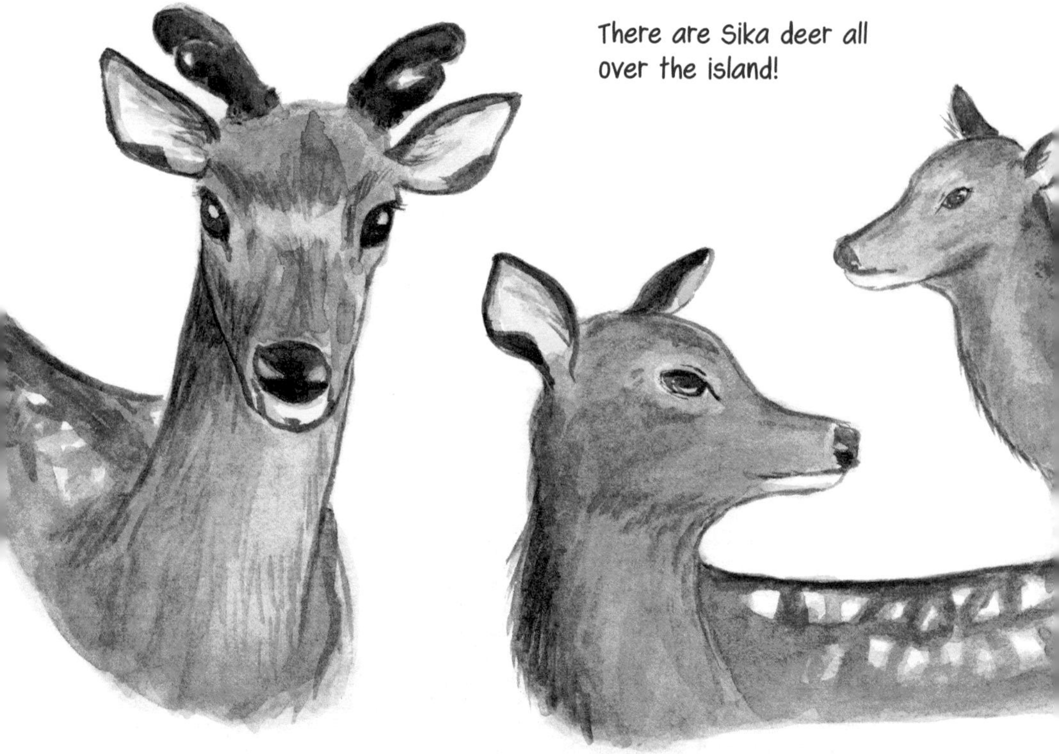

They all make squeaks that sound like a balloon deflating, and most of the adults have spots on their coats.

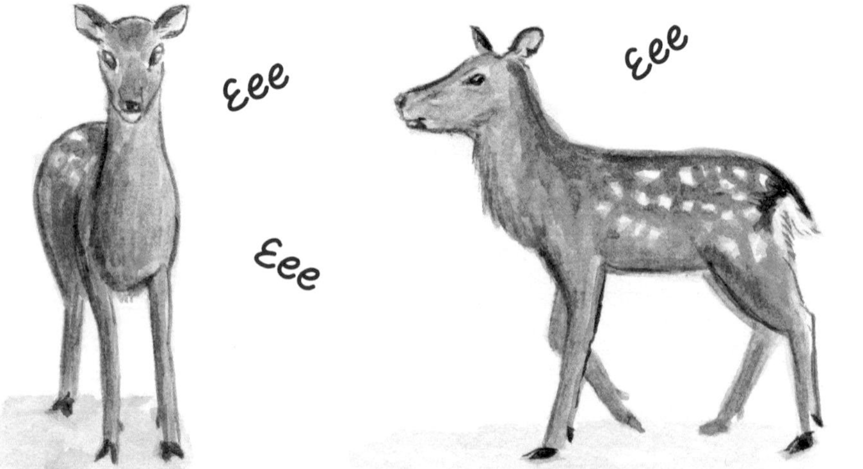
Eee
Eee
Eee

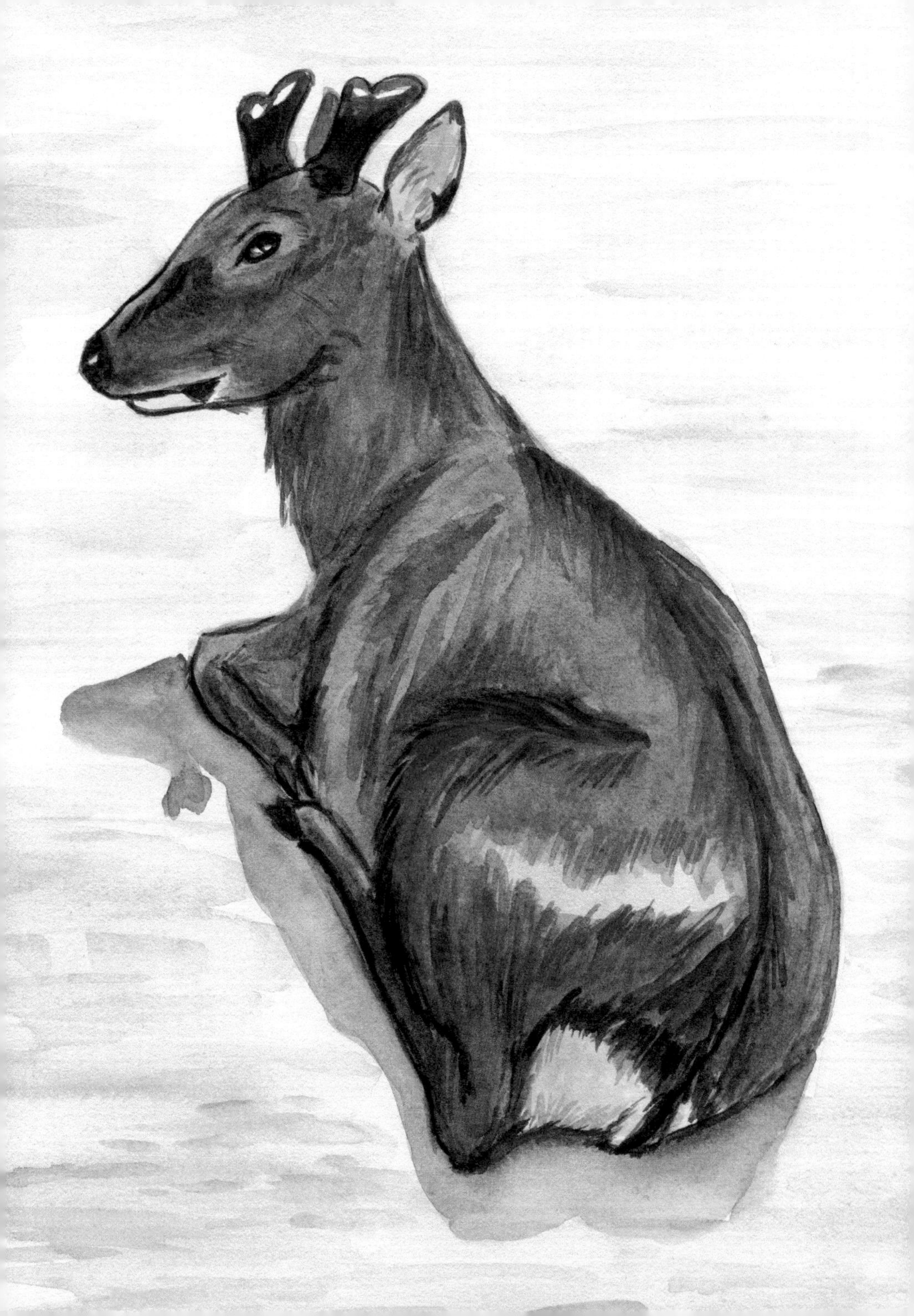

The deer were all highly attuned to certain noises. . . .

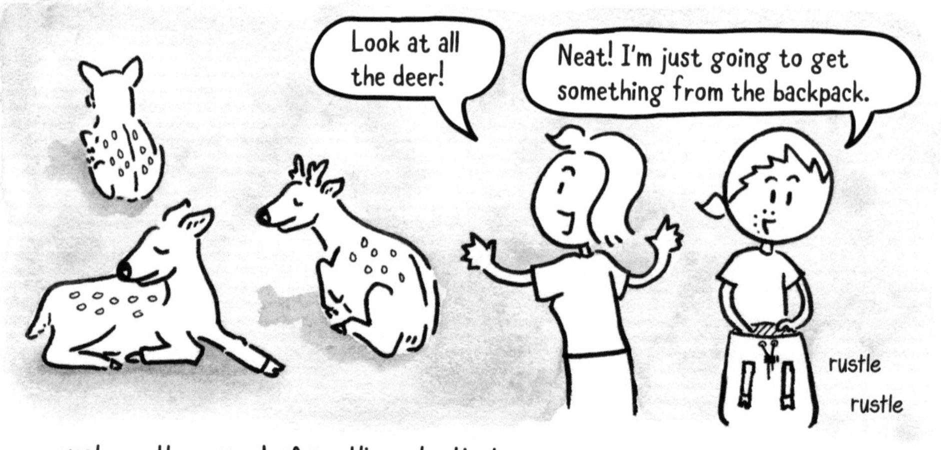
Look at all the deer!
Neat! I'm just going to get something from the backpack.
rustle
rustle

. . . such as the sound of rustling plastic bags.

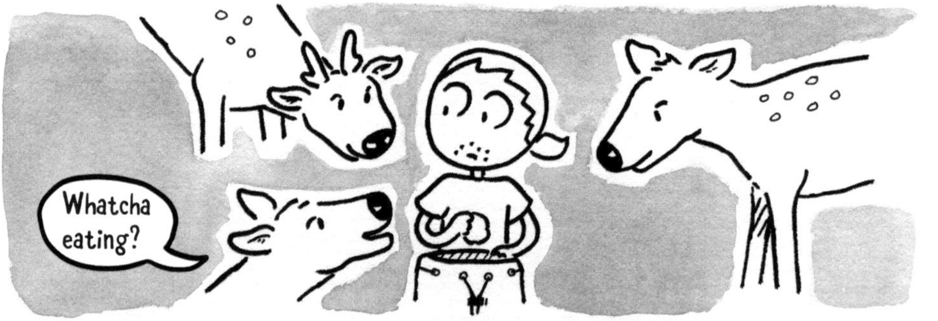
Whatcha eating?

There are signs all over Miyajima saying not to feed the deer. That doesn't mean they won't help themselves.

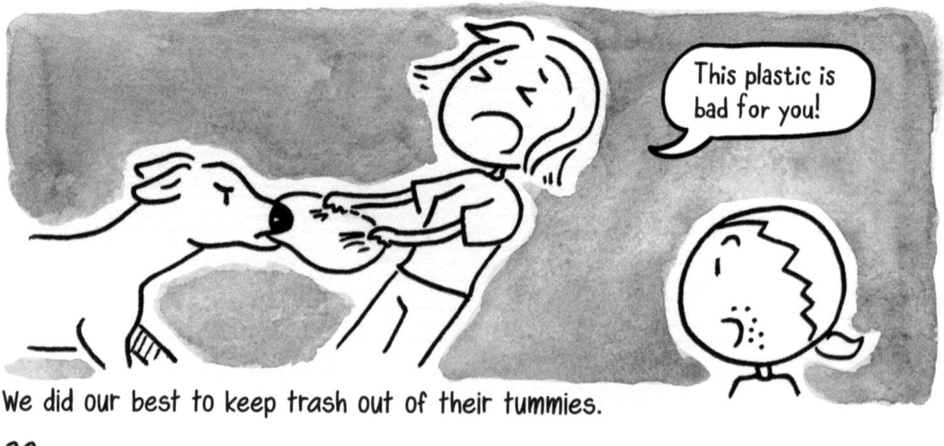
This plastic is bad for you!

We did our best to keep trash out of their tummies.

The deer were really sneaky about getting something to eat and I'm not surprised. It wasn't clear what food was available to them on the island.

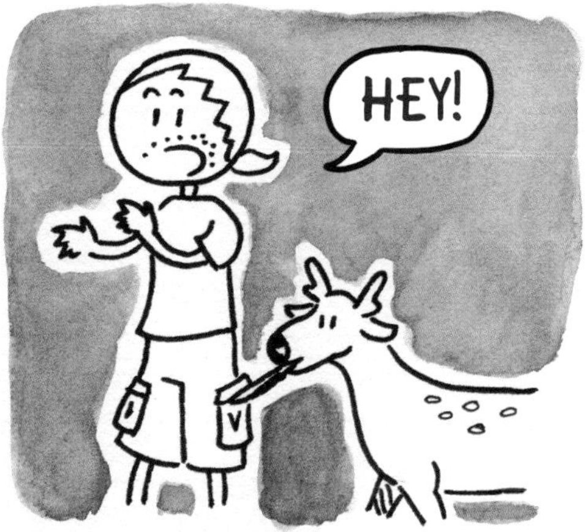
HEY!

The ultimate souvenir: a half-eaten map Connor wrestled back out of a deer's mouth.

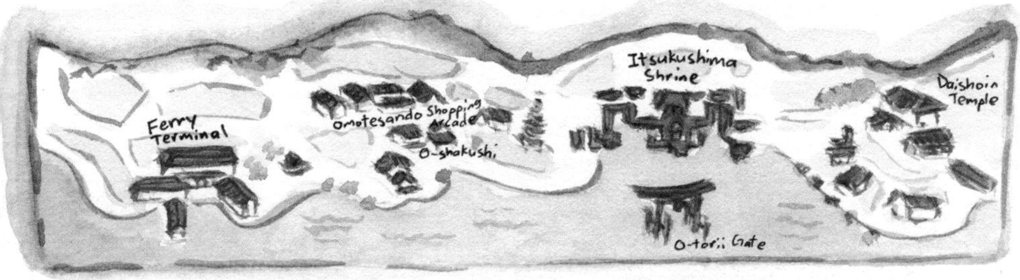
Itsukushima Shrine
Daishoin Temple
Ferry Terminal
Omotesando Shopping Arcade
O-shakushi
O-torii Gate

We observed that most deer on the island had rounded antlers.

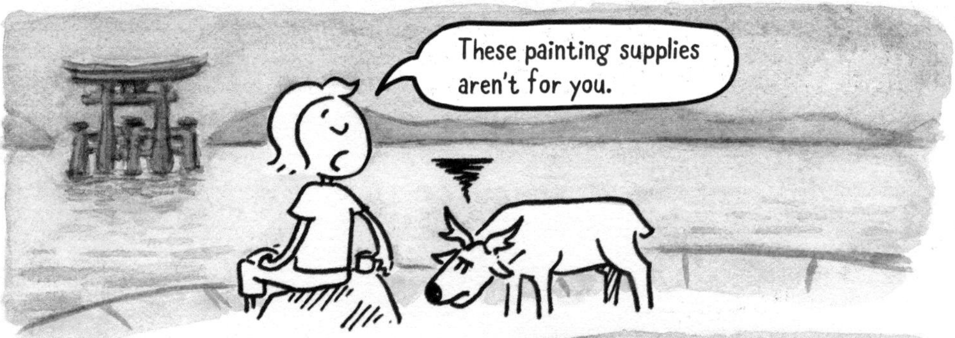
These painting supplies aren't for you.

However, while I was painting Itsukushima Shrine's famous O-Torii (Great Gate), I encountered the only one who still had pointy antlers.

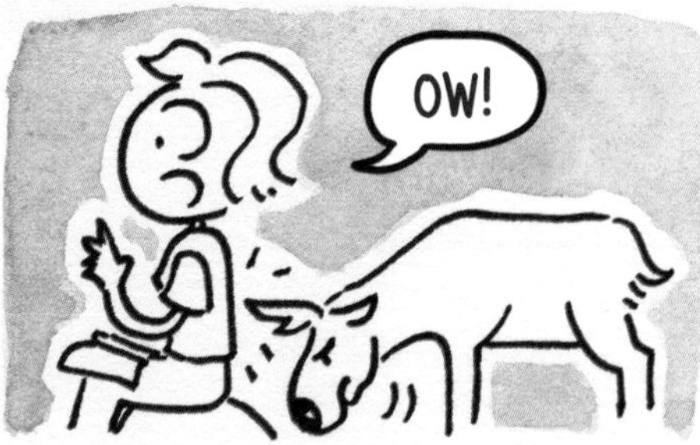
OW!

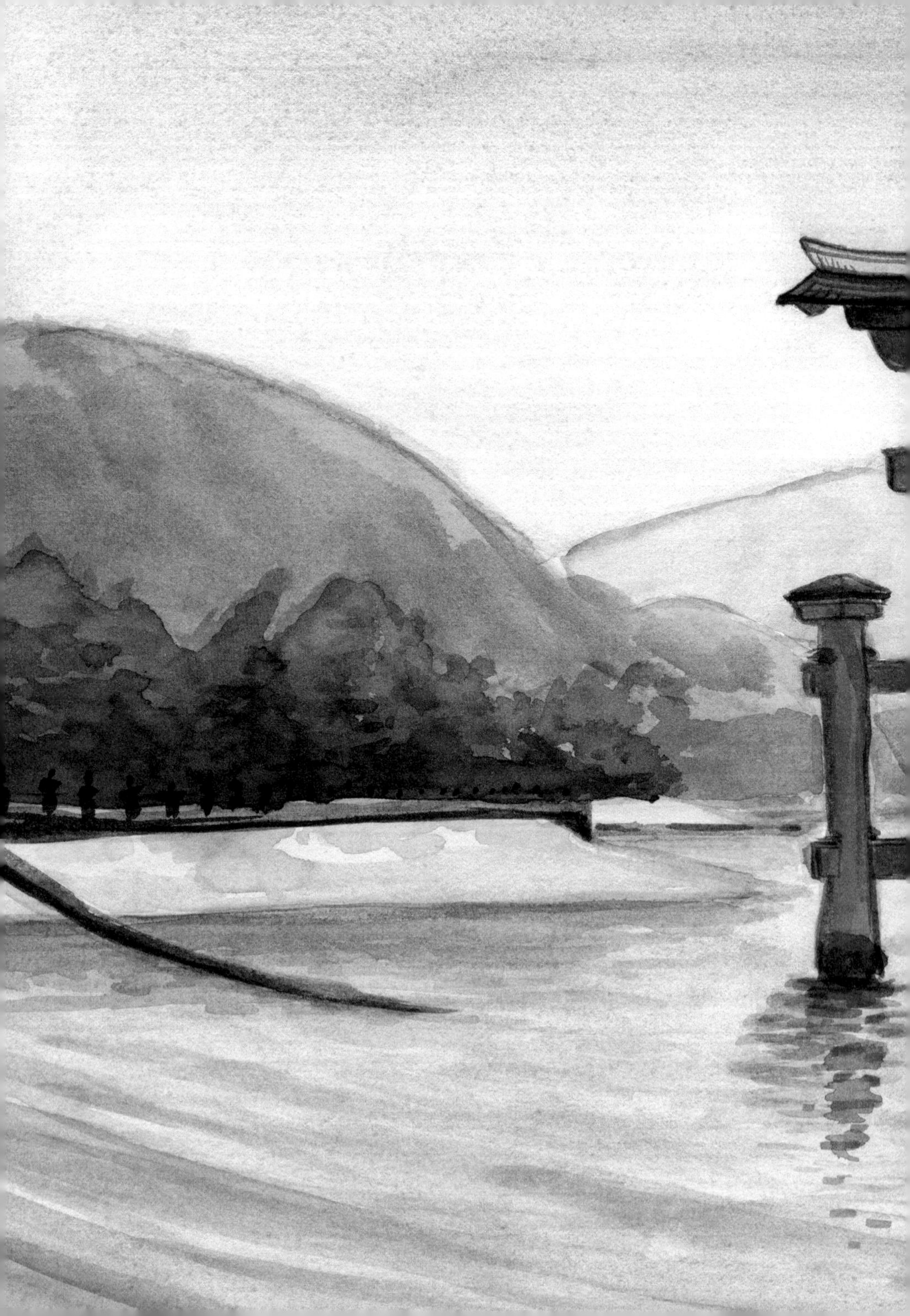

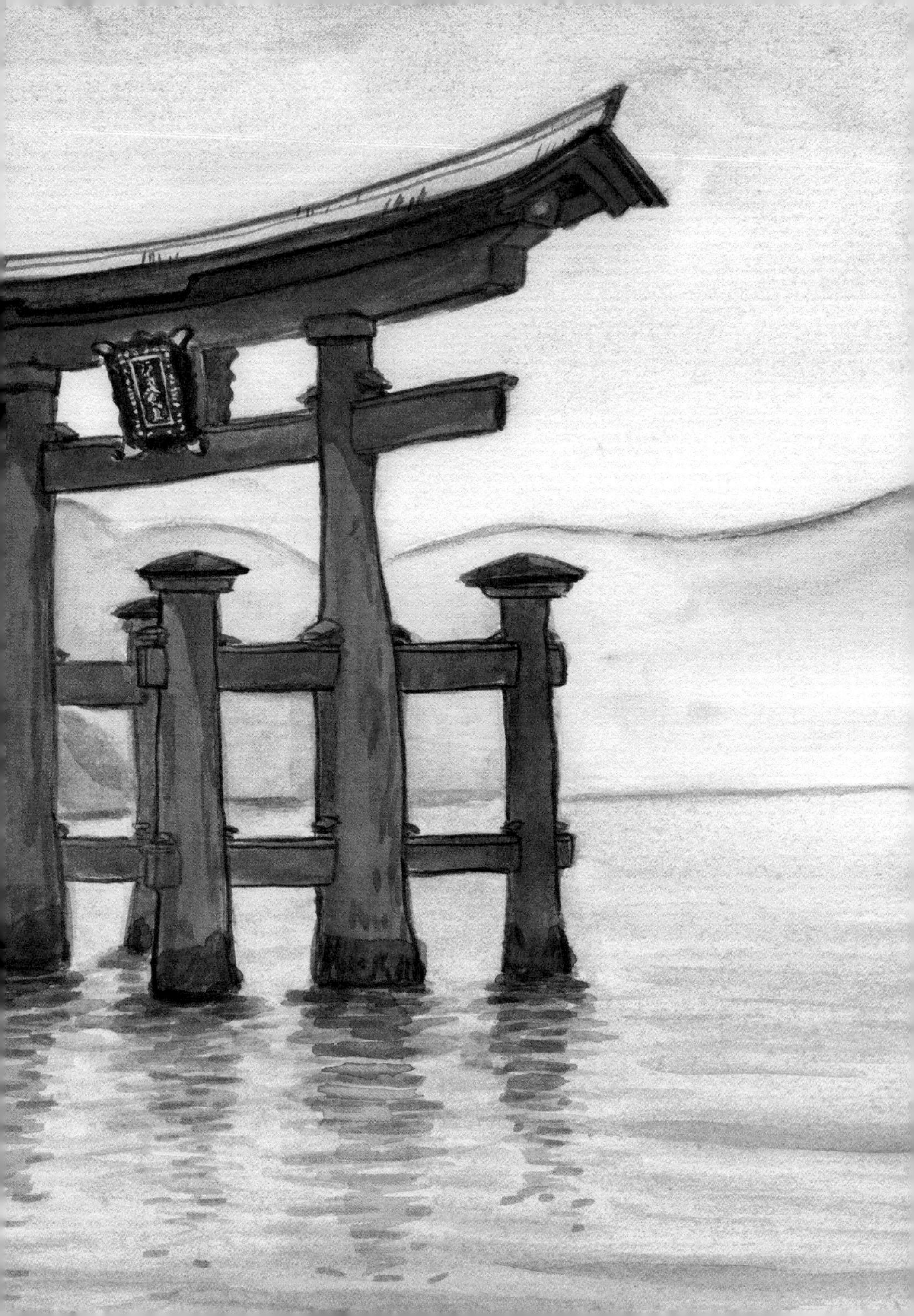

While I was painting, Connor noticed the tide was going out.

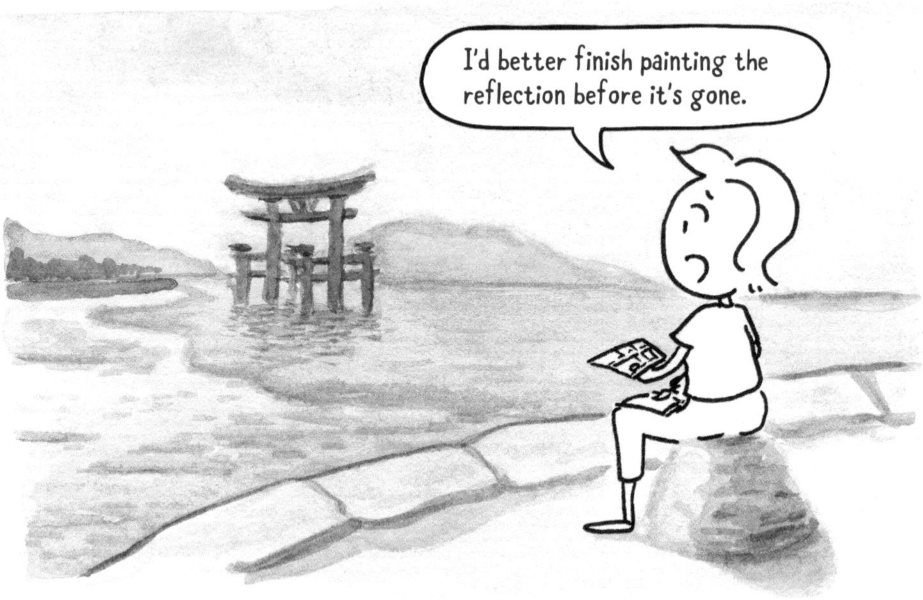
I'd better finish painting the reflection before it's gone.

The tide went out much faster than I expected which meant . . .

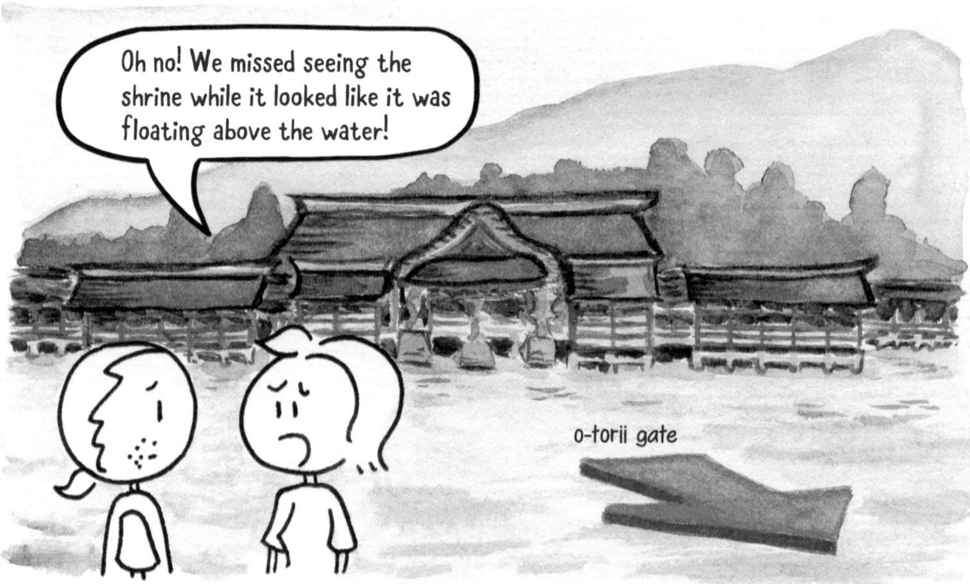
Oh no! We missed seeing the shrine while it looked like it was floating above the water!
o-torii gate

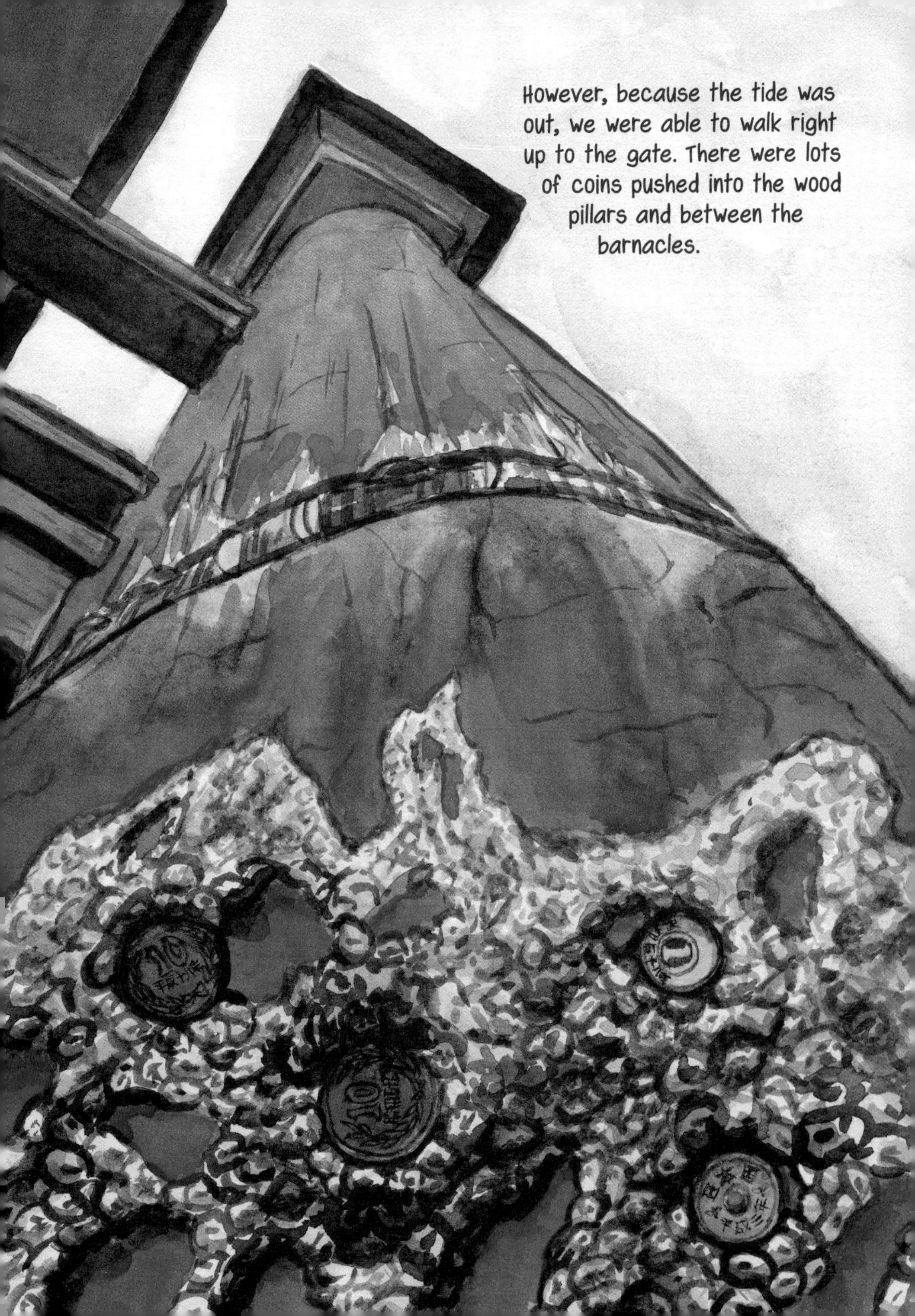
However, because the tide was out, we were able to walk right up to the gate. There were lots of coins pushed into the wood pillars and between the barnacles.

We decided to skip touring Itsukushima Shrine and went to Daisho-in Temple instead. The route wasn't very obvious, so we found ourselves walking up a narrow residential road.

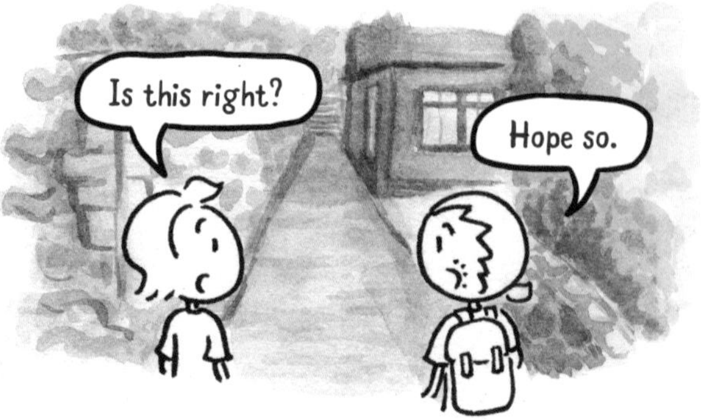

Is this right?
Hope so.


Eventually we found the entrance.

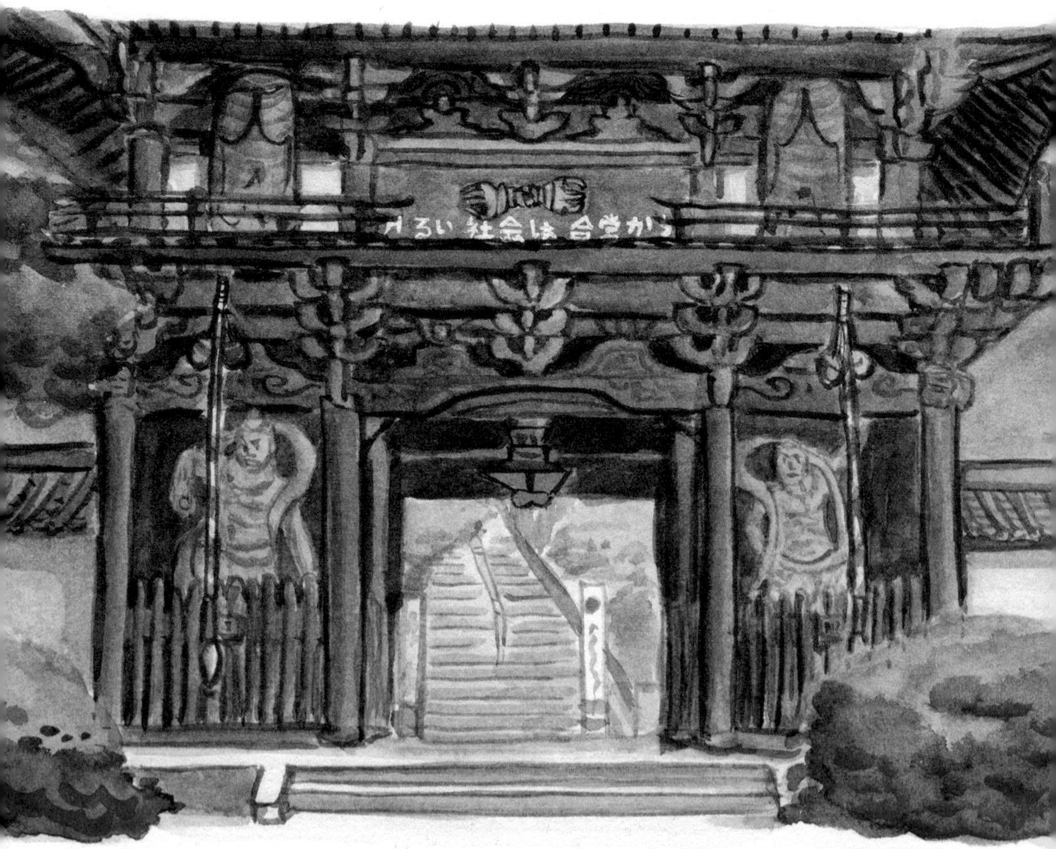

A monk named Kukai founded Daisho-in Temple in 806 AD. Kukai posthumously became known as Kobo Daishi. He is best recognized as the founder of the Shingon sect of esoteric Buddhism.

To enter you pass through a gate that's guarded by two statues known as "Nio".

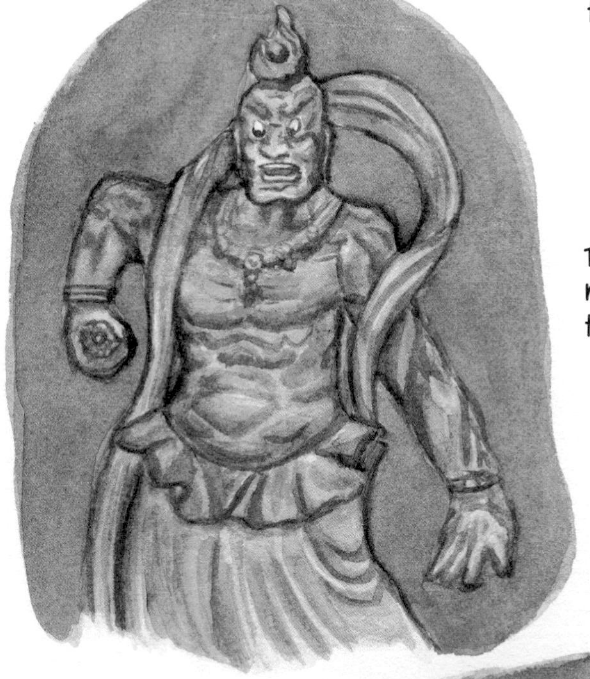

The statue on the left had its mouth open, while the one on the right had its mouth closed.

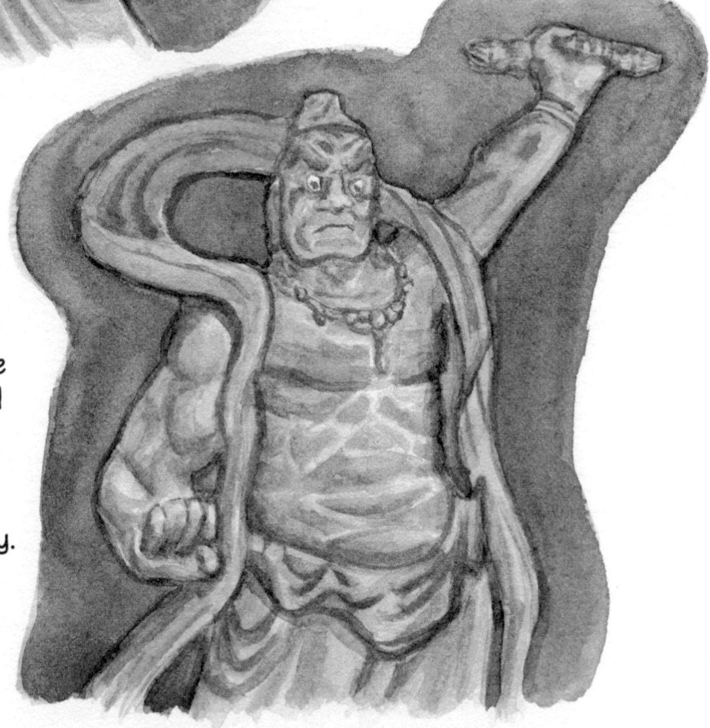

Later we learned that their mouths mimic the shape of the first and last letters in the Sanskrit alphabet, which represent birth and death respectively.

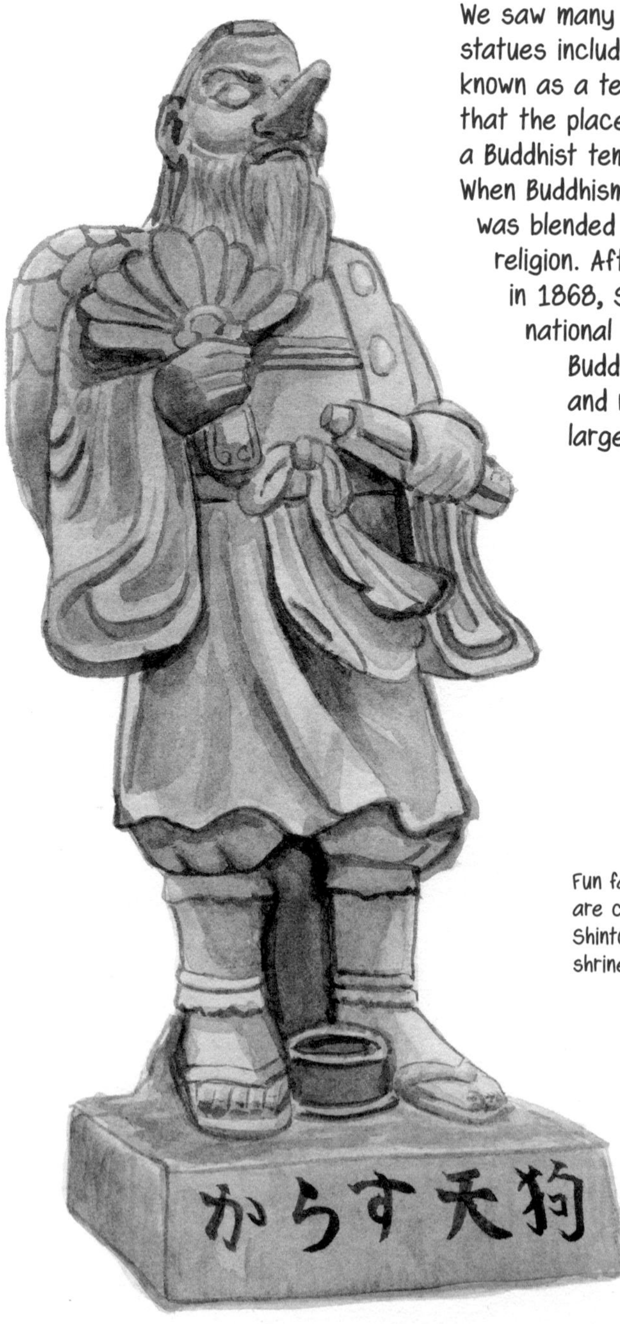
からす天狗

We saw many different types of statues including one of a Shinto god known as a tengu. Later, I realized that the placement of a Shinto god in a Buddhist temple was a little unusual. When Buddhism arrived in Japan, it was blended with the native Shinto religion. After the Meiji Restoration in 1868, Shinto was declared the national religion. As a result, Buddhist and Shinto icons and religious sites were largely separated.

Fun fact: Buddhist religious sites are called temples (tera) while Shinto religious sites are called shrines (jinja).

We encountered our first Jizo bosatsu (bodhisattva) statues while walking the temple grounds. A bodhisattva is someone who can reach nirvana, but has chosen not to in favor of helping out those who are suffering. Jizo are guardian deities. Most commonly they are guardians of children.

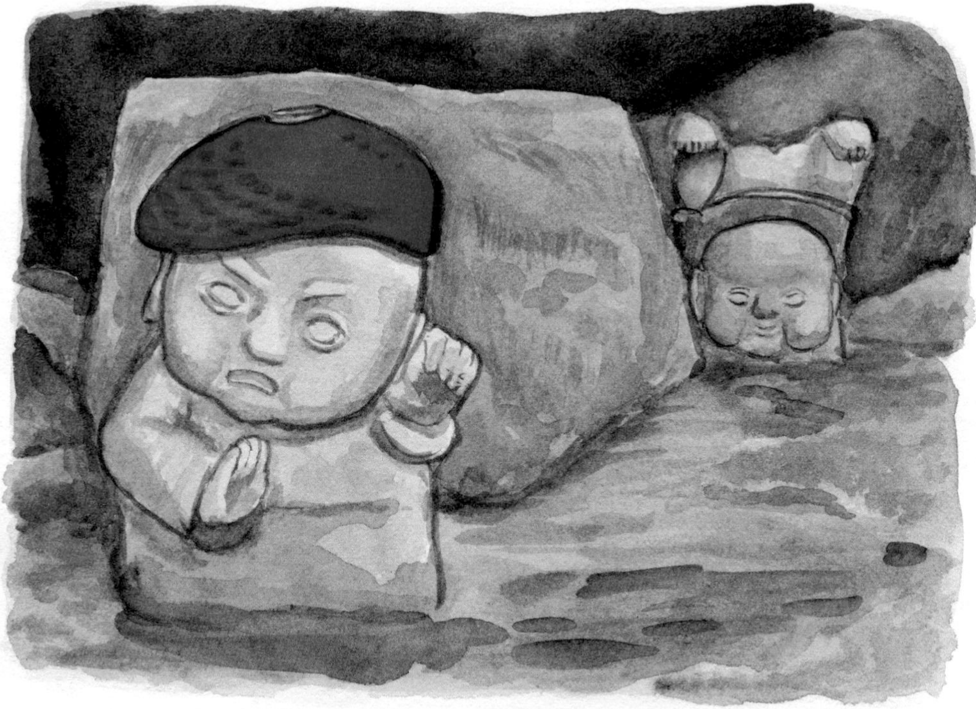

The main reason we chose to come to Daisho-in Temple was to see the lantern-filled Henjokutsu Cave. The entrance to the cave wasn't easy to locate.

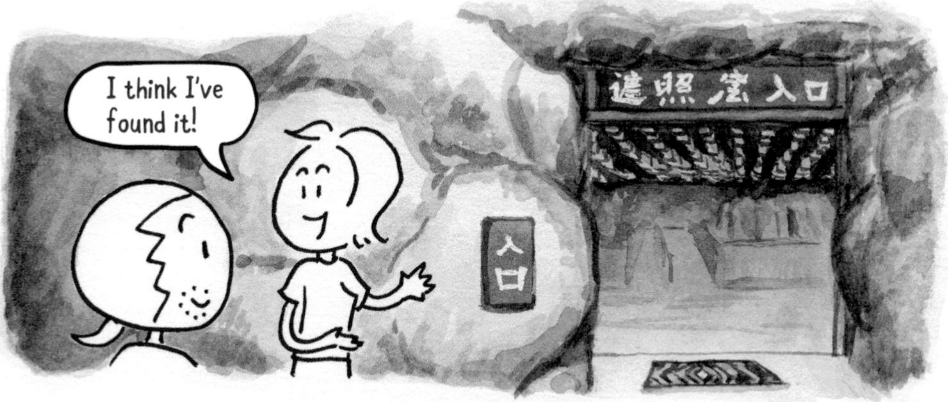
I think I've found it!
遍照窟入口
入口

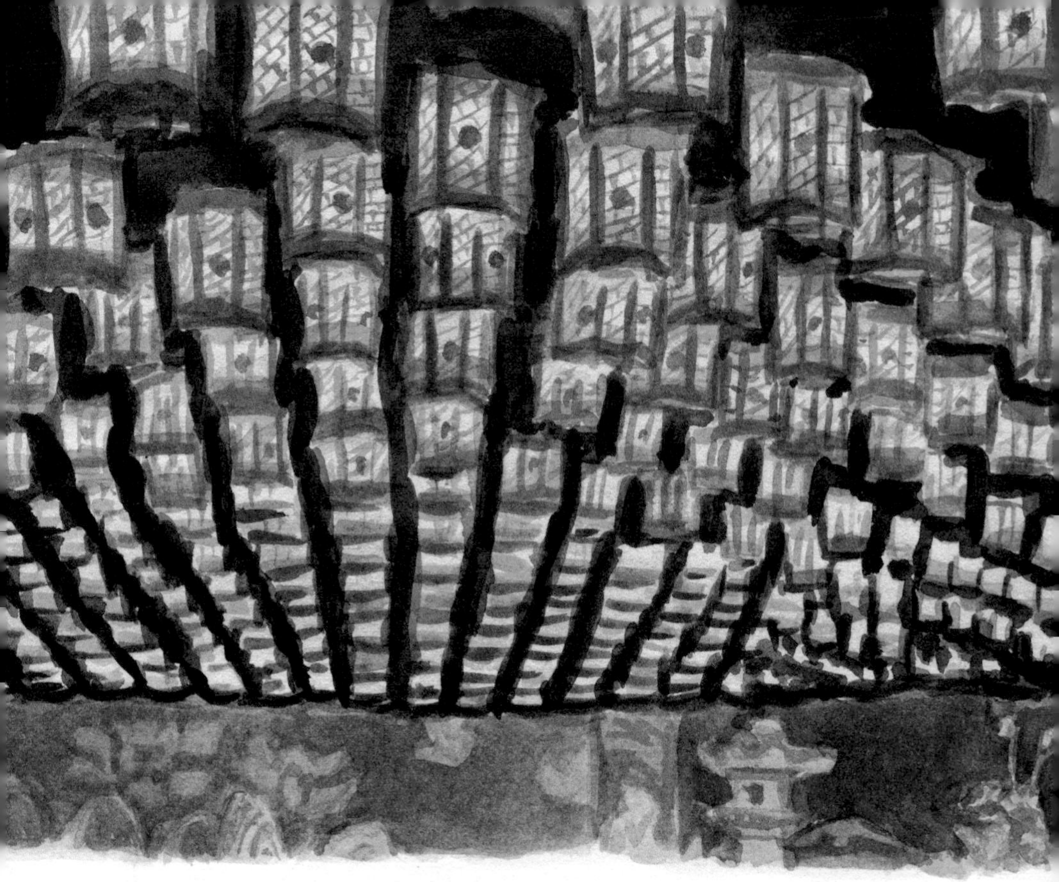

I loved the cave with its hundreds of lanterns. Housing 88 Buddhist icons representing the 88-temple Shikoku pilgrimage, it's believed that visiting this cave is the equivalent of doing the whole pilgrimage.

In the center of the cave was an artifact.

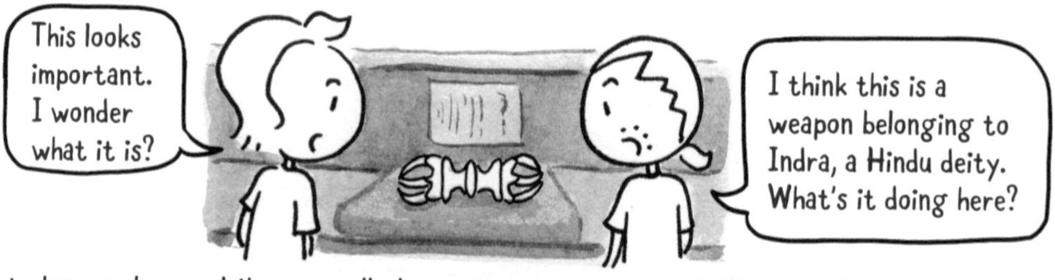
This looks important. I wonder what it is?
I think this is a weapon belonging to Indra, a Hindu deity. What's it doing here?

Later we learned it was called a vajra. Connor was right about it being Indra's weapon. It turns out that in some Buddhist sects the vajra symbolizes cutting off all human desires.

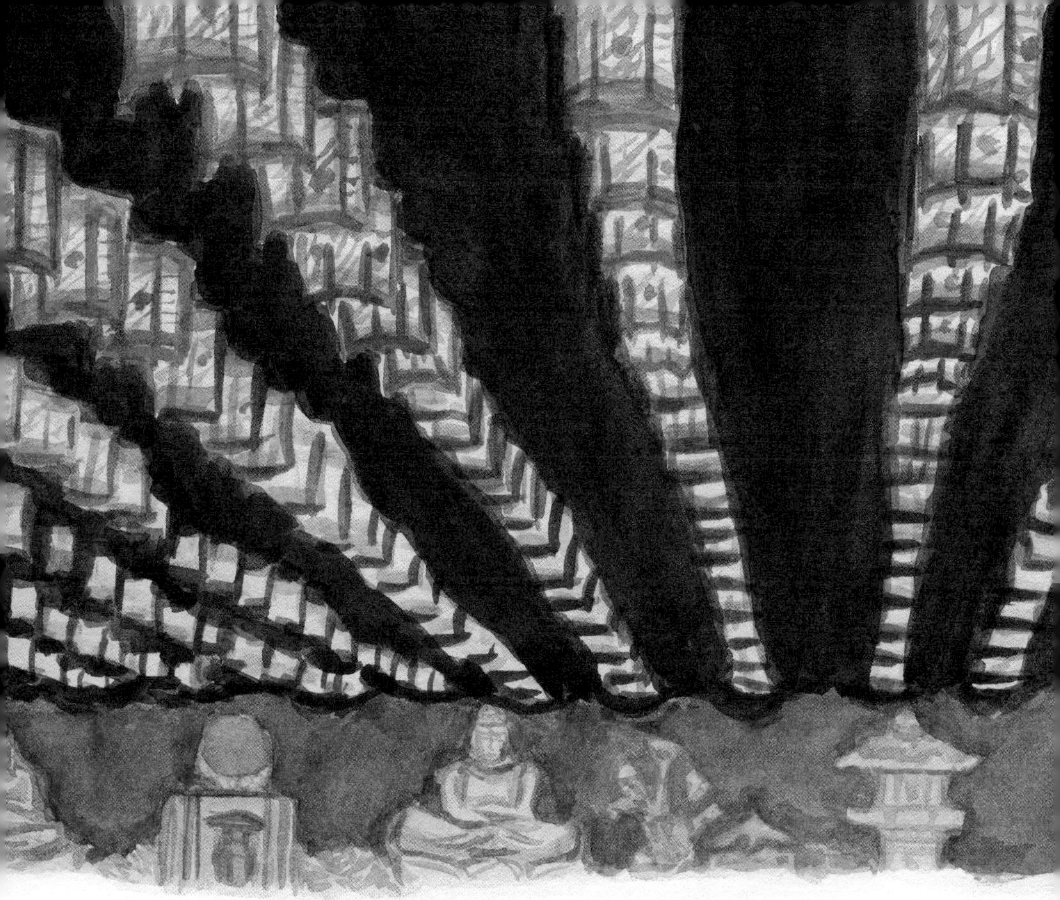

We walked past each of the icons, then sat in the back and took it all in.

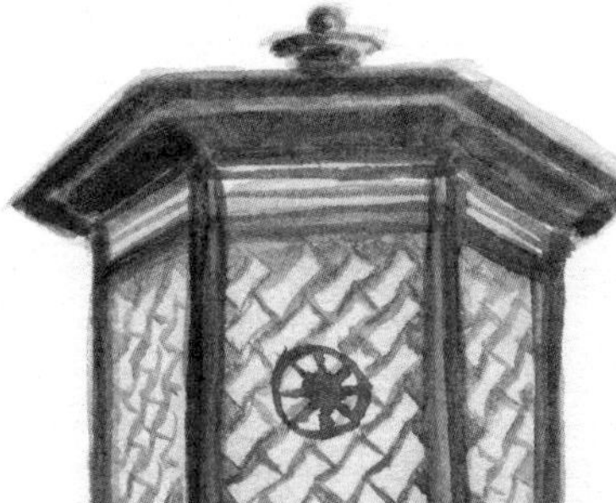

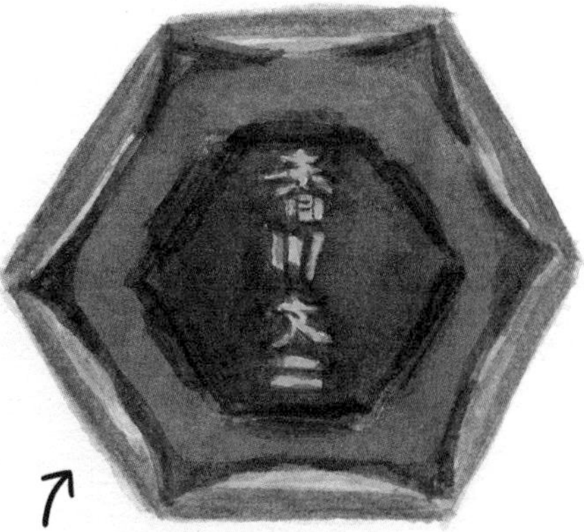

each lantern has something different written on the bottom of it

We headed back to the ferry, but not before visiting the Omotesando shopping arcade. We admired the O-Shakushi, or world's largest wooden rice scoop.

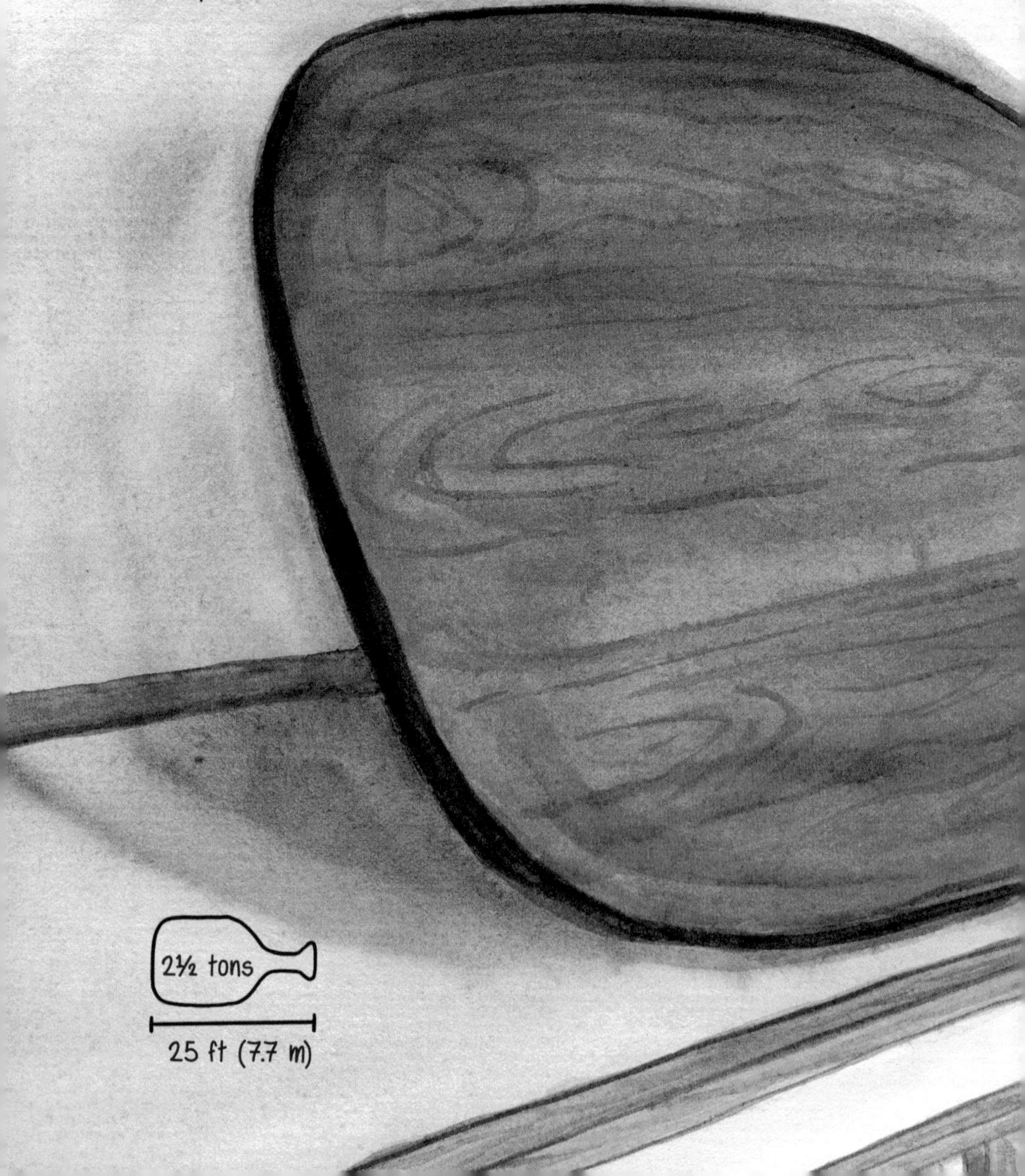
2½ tons
25 ft (7.7 m)

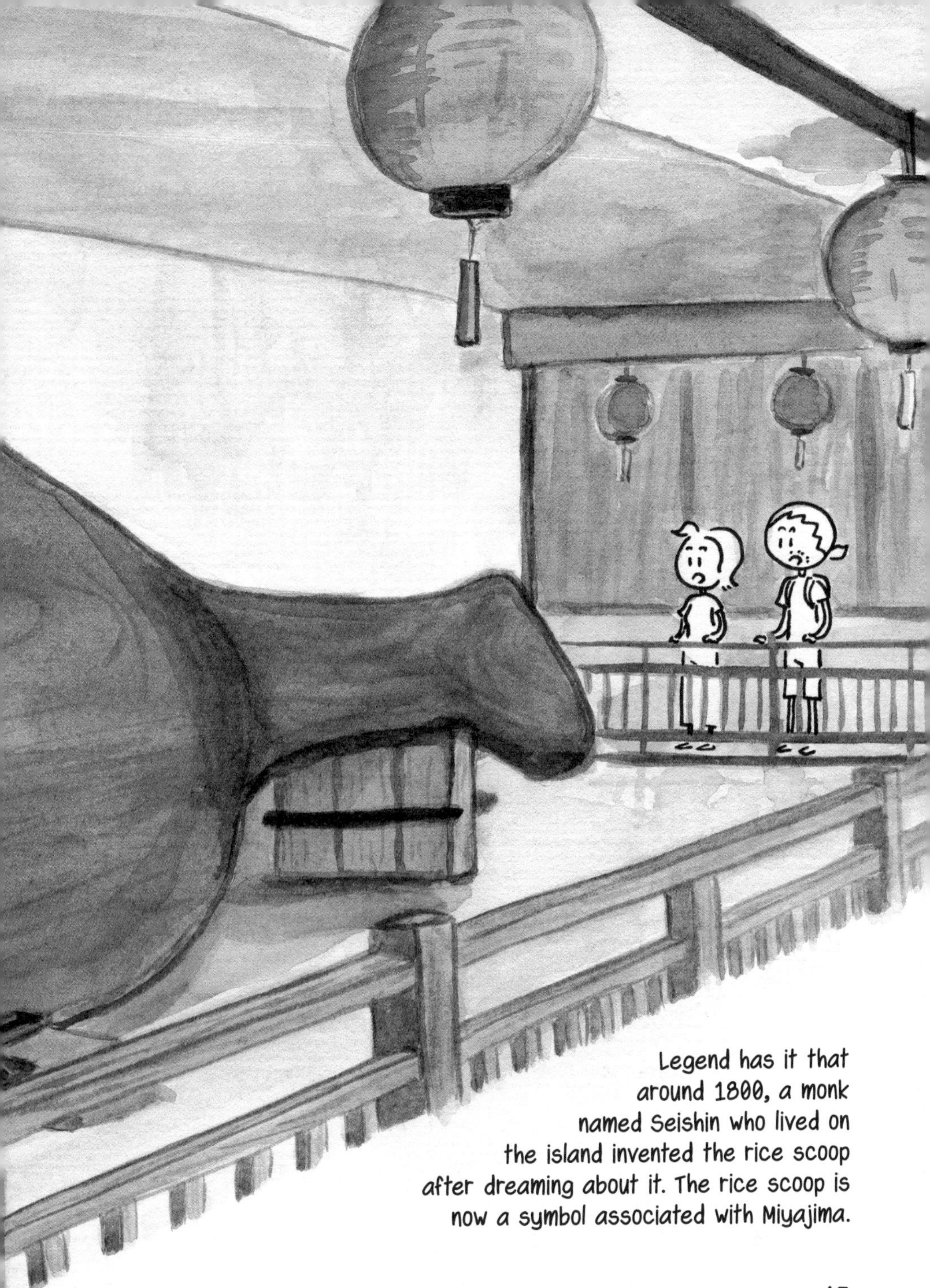

Legend has it that around 1800, a monk named Seishin who lived on the island invented the rice scoop after dreaming about it. The rice scoop is now a symbol associated with Miyajima.

Another symbol of Miyajima is the momiji manju, a small, maple leaf-shaped cake. Maple leaves are strongly associated with Miyajima because of the many maple trees on the island that change color in the fall.

adzuki bean paste is the classic flavor ↙

tastes sweet ↗

We tried momiji manju from several vendors. Traditional manju is steamed, but my favorite came from a vendor who deep-fried them. I was especially fond of the lemon flavor. Connor preferred the custard one.

Still hot!
↓

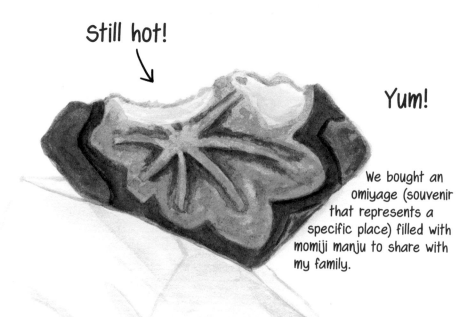

Yum!

We bought an omiyage (souvenir that represents a specific place) filled with momiji manju to share with my family.

We headed back to the Miyajima ferry building, which also had a stamp. At this point I realized that if I kept stamping in my sketchbook, I was going to run out of pages before the end of the trip.

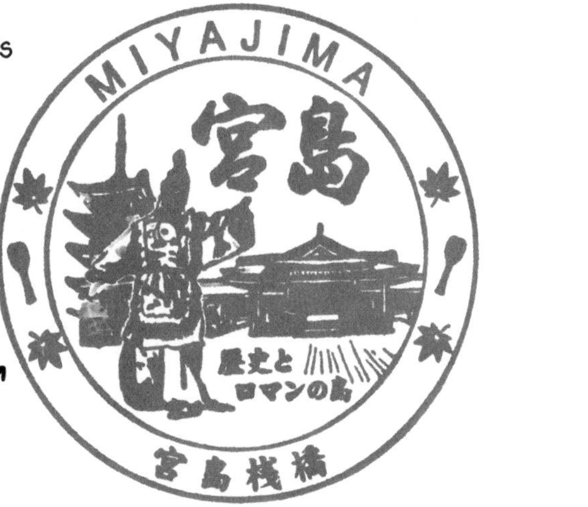
MIYAJIMA
宮島
歴史と
ロマンの島
宮島桟橋

rice scoop

maple leaf

Clearly I'm not the only one who has had this problem because it turns out there's a book available for collecting stamps.

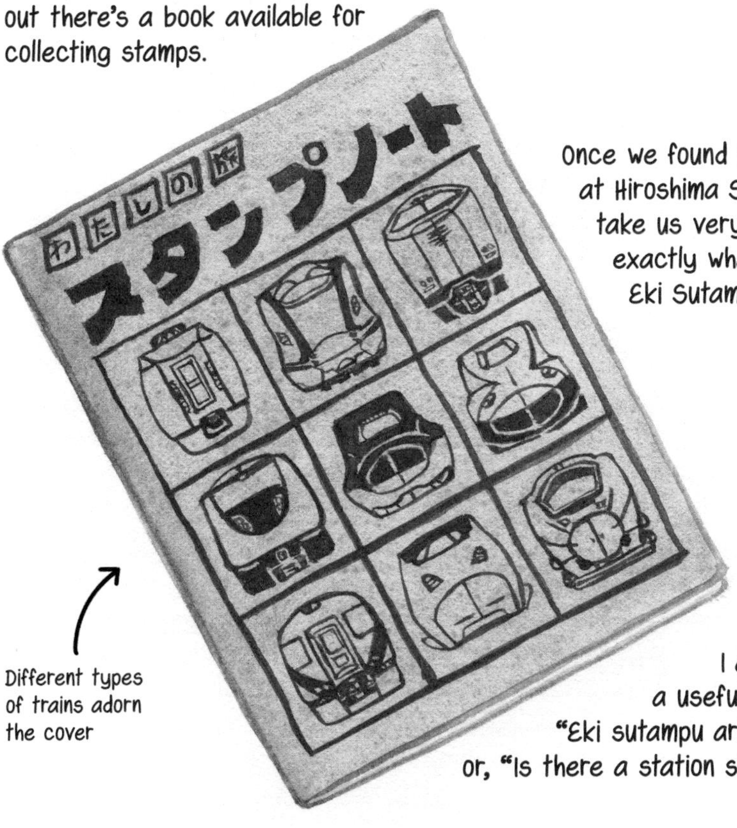
わたしの旅
スタンプノート

Once we found the bookstore at Hiroshima Station, it didn't take us very long to find exactly what I needed: an Eki Sutampu book.

Different types of trains adorn the cover

I also learned a useful phrase: "Eki sutampu arimasu ka?" or, "Is there a station stamp?"

From Hiroshima Station we walked to Hiroshima Castle. The original castle didn't survive the A-bomb and had to be rebuilt. However, a few trees on the castle grounds did manage to survive.

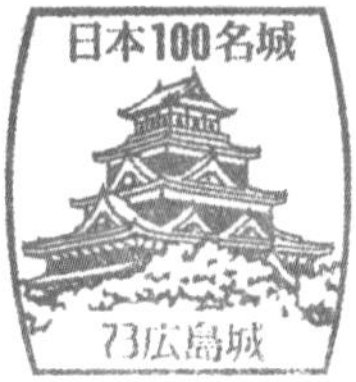
日本100名城
73広島城

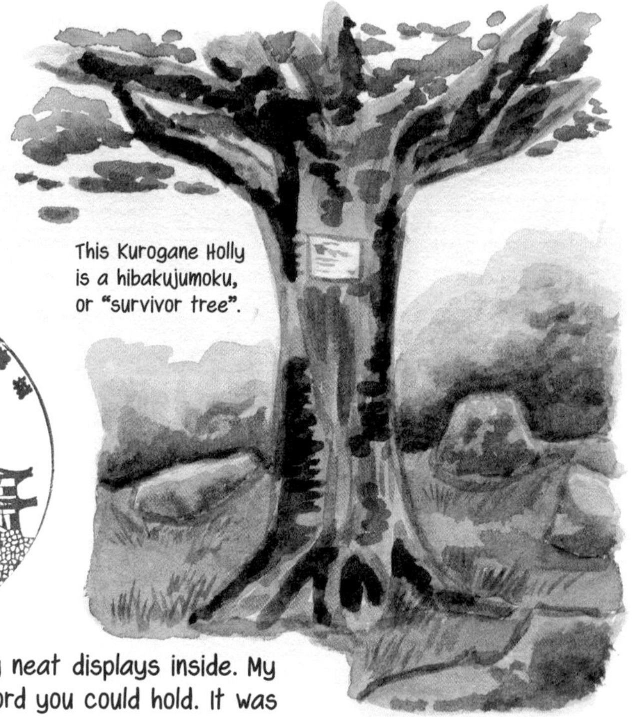
This Kurogane Holly is a hibakujumoku, or "survivor tree".

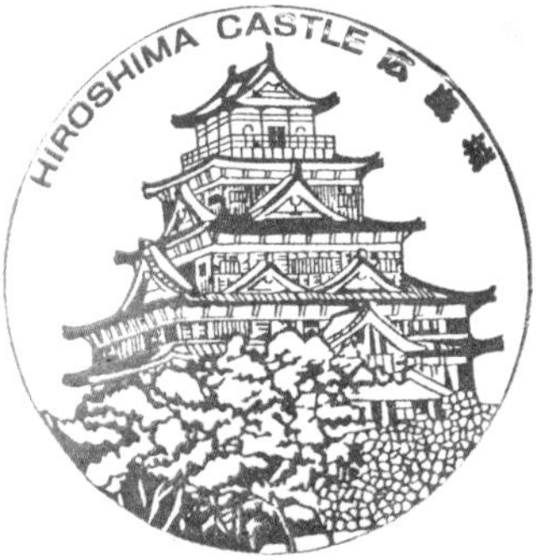
HIROSHIMA CASTLE 広島城

The castle had some really neat displays inside. My favorite was a samurai sword you could hold. It was quite heavy!

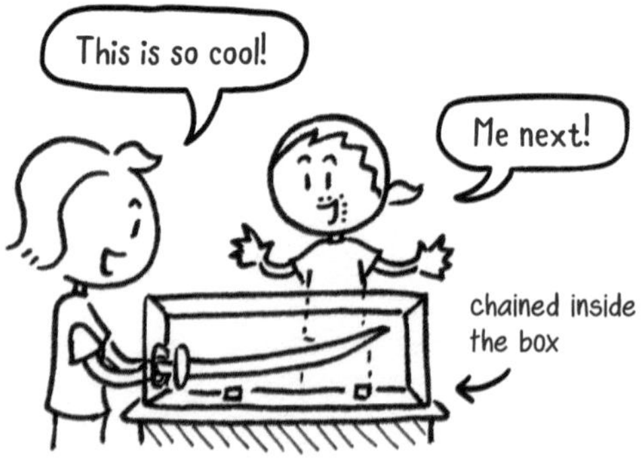
This is so cool!
Me next!
chained inside the box

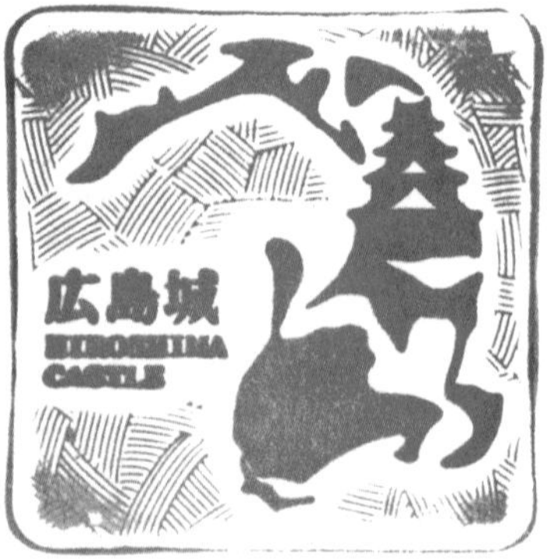
広島城
HIROSHIMA CASTLE

You're allowed to go to the top of the castle. Looking down we saw a big turtle swimming in the moat.

After the castle closed for the day, I sat outside and painted it. I didn't notice, but a man took some pictures of me while I was painting. He then gave Connor some candy.


tasted like
maple syrup

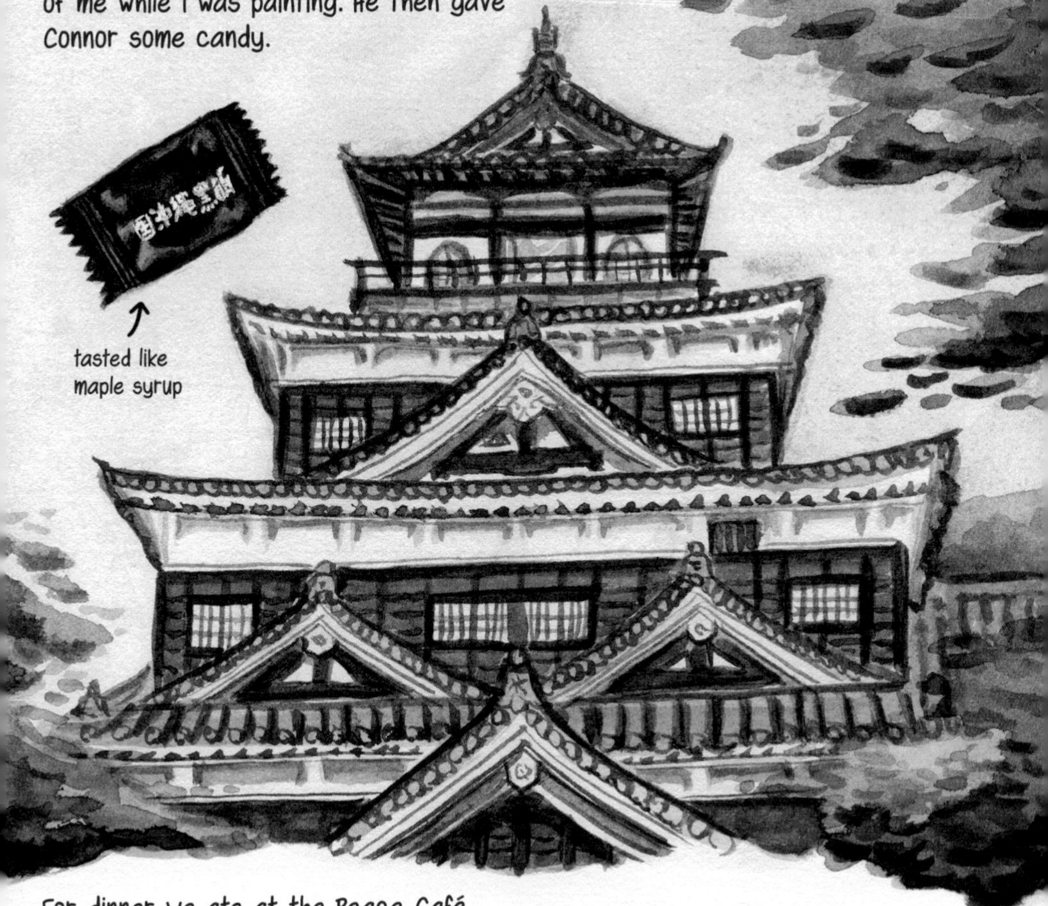

For dinner we ate at the Peace Café. I told the owner, Tim, that I'd been having trouble finding meals with vegetables in Japan. It turned out Tim had previously been a professor and had taken Japanese students on trips around the world. He shared some insights . . .

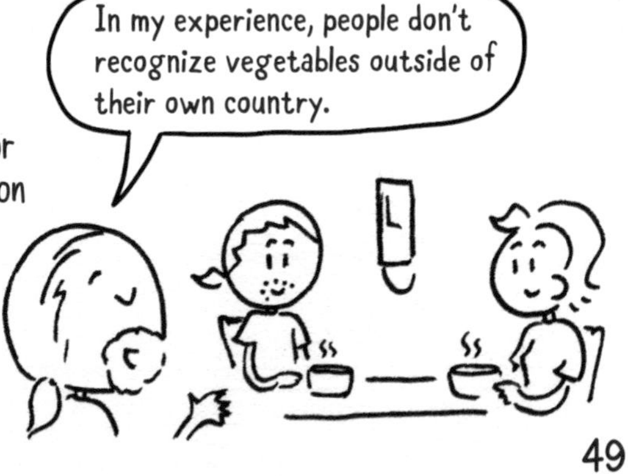
In my experience, people don't recognize vegetables outside of their own country.

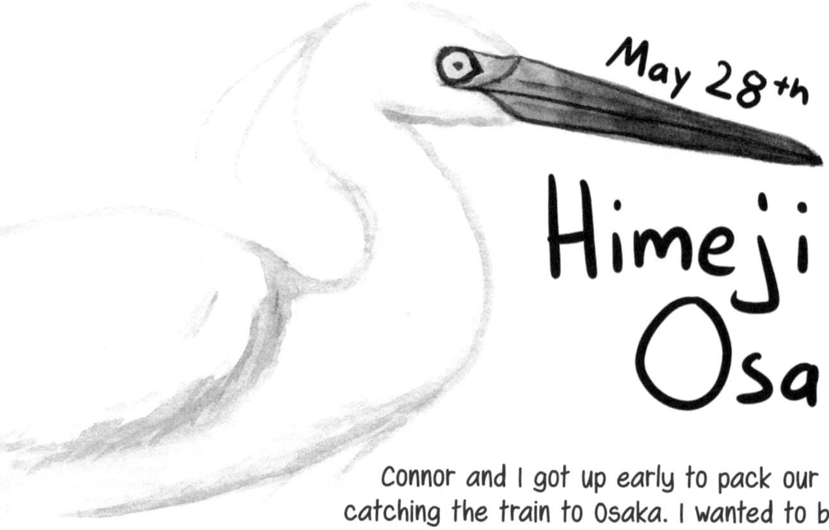

May 28th

# Himeji and Osaka

Connor and I got up early to pack our bags before catching the train to Osaka. I wanted to be sure to have time to visit Himeji along the way.

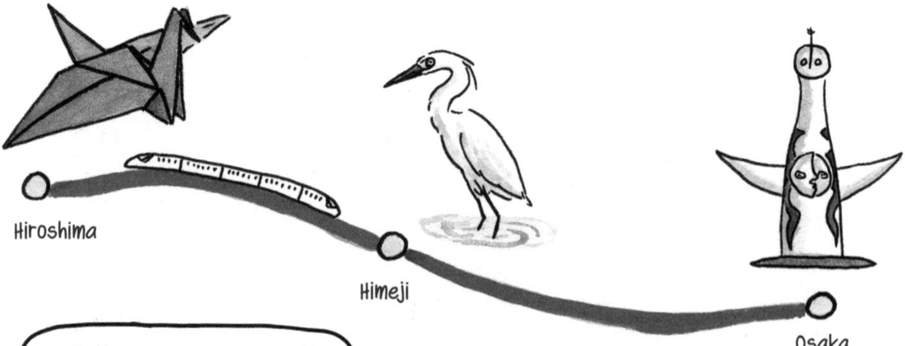
Hiroshima
Himeji
Osaka

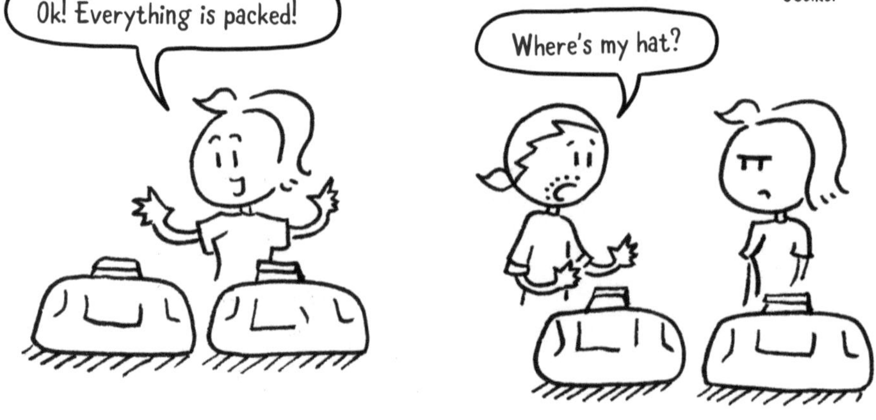
Ok! Everything is packed!
Where's my hat?

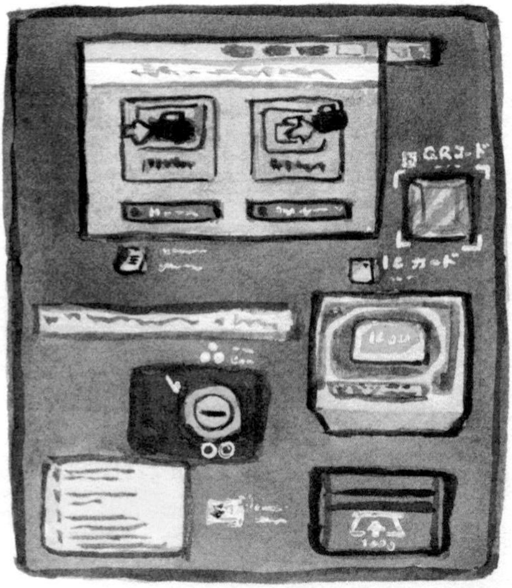

Even though Himeji Castle is down the street from the train station, we decided to use a coin locker to stash our bags. Coin lockers can be found at most train stations. We were able to fit our bags into a ¥500 locker.

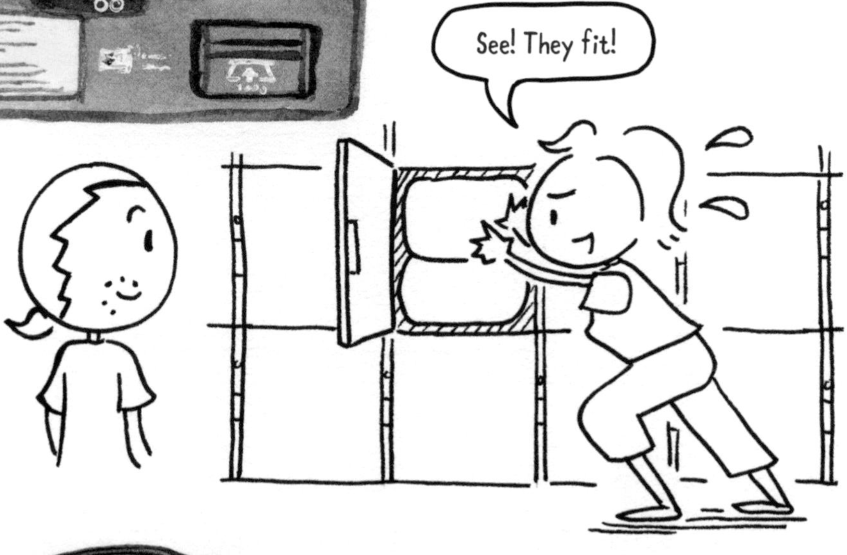
See! They fit!

A manhole and a utility cover decorated with white herons seen while walking towards the castle.

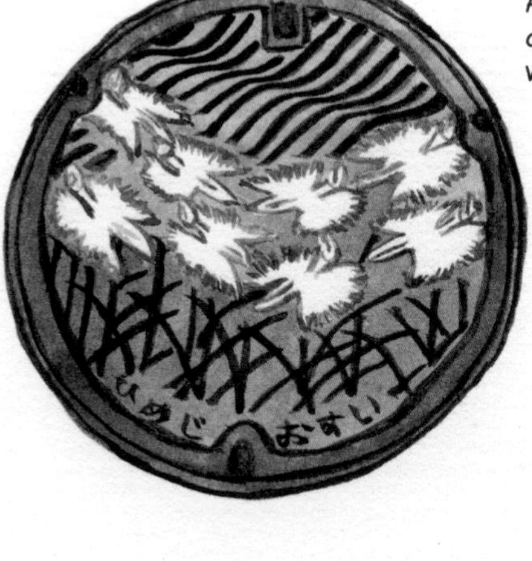
ひめじ
おすい

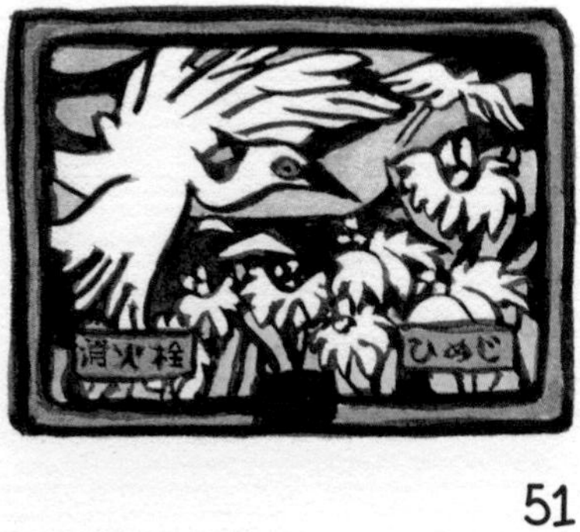
消火栓
ひめじ

Himeji Castle is supposed to resemble a bird taking flight. The castle is also known as Hakuru-jo (White Egret Castle) or Shirasagi-jo (White Heron Castle).

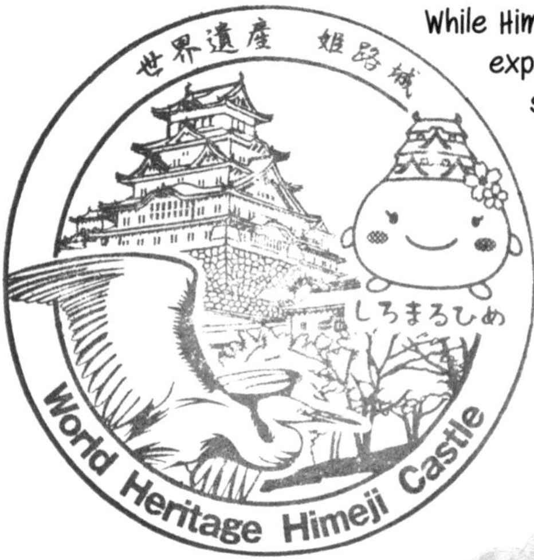
世界遺產　姫路城
しろまるひめ
World Heritage Himeji Castle

While Himeji Castle has been renovated and expanded over its lifetime, what makes it special is that it's one of the few original castles in Japan. Most other Japanese castles have been rebuilt due to wars, fire, earthquakes, or other natural disasters.

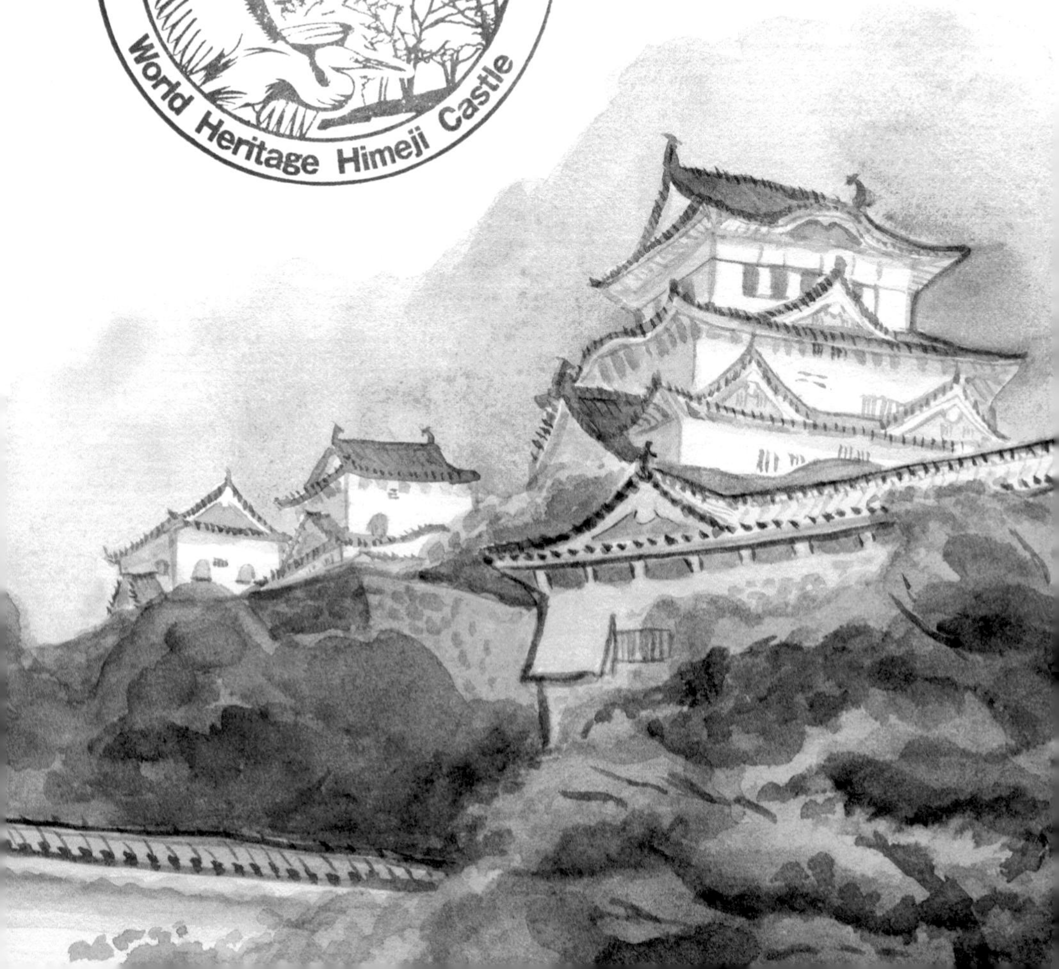

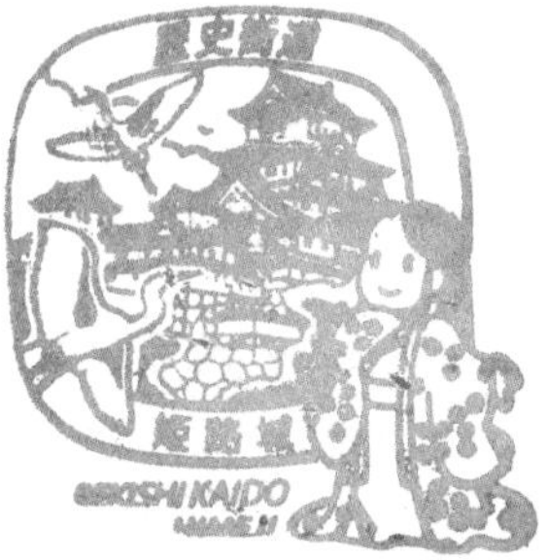

Roof ornaments in the shape of Shachihoko (carp with a tiger head) were added to the roof to help ward away fires. It was believed that Shachihoko could summon rain.

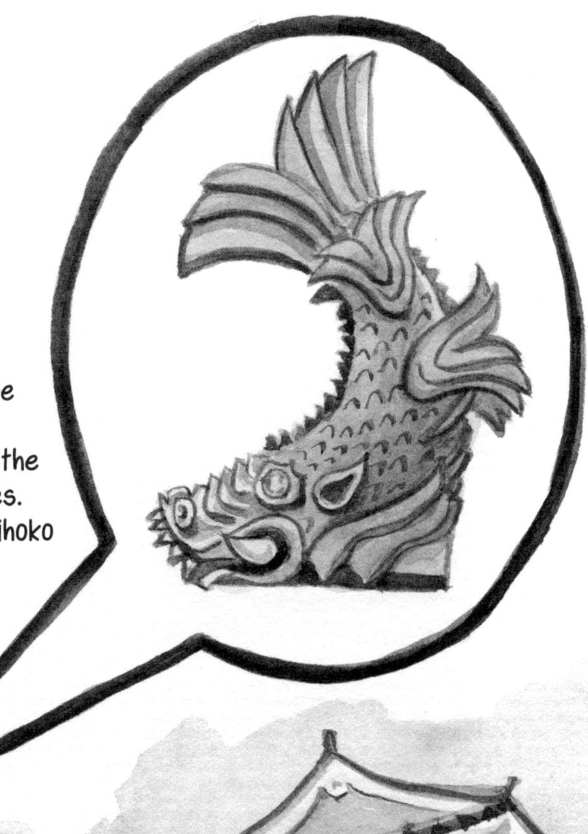

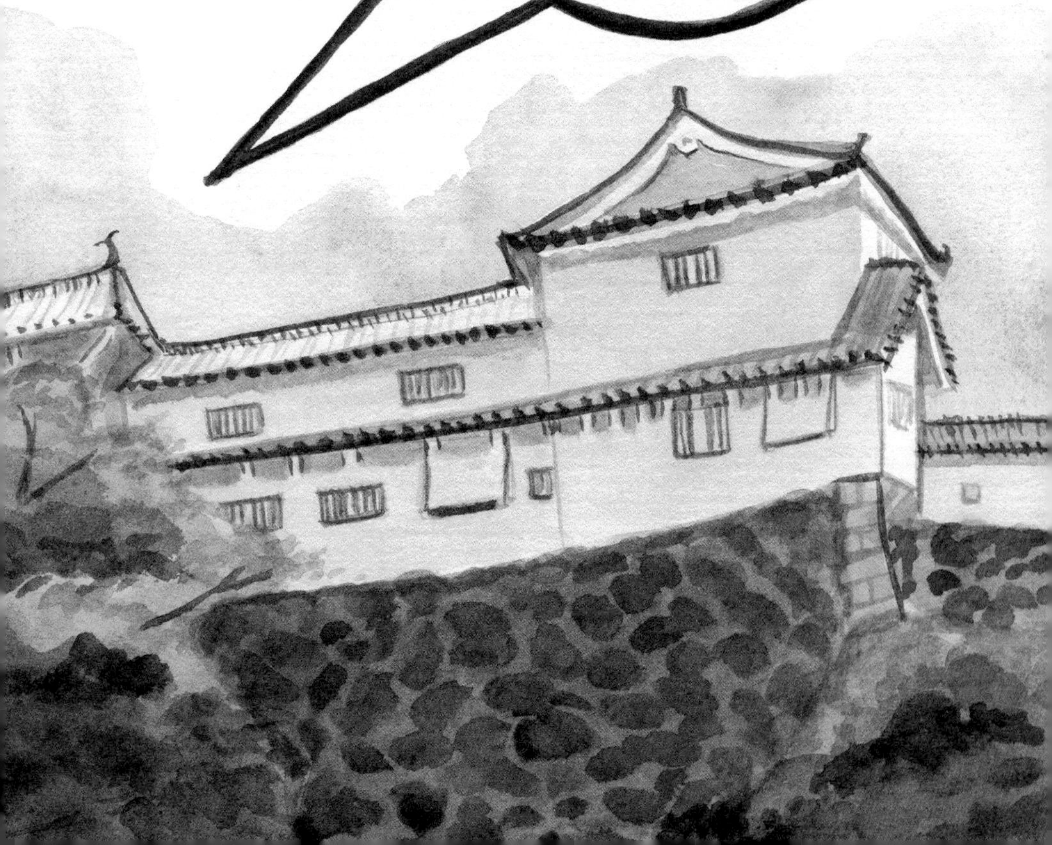

It is possible to go into the castle, but after reading reviews about long queues, we opted to walk the grounds instead. While exploring, we spotted roof tiles with the kamon (family crest) of the Sakakibara samurai clan. The diverse number of kamon found around Himeji Castle are a testament to how many families have occupied it over the years.

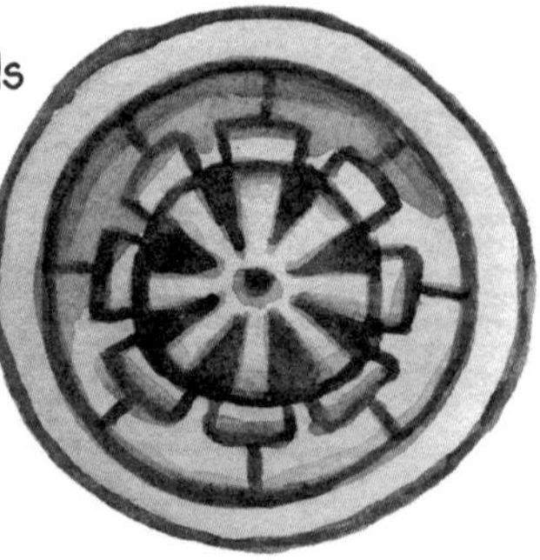

Before leaving the castle, we walked the perimeter, following the path of the moat.

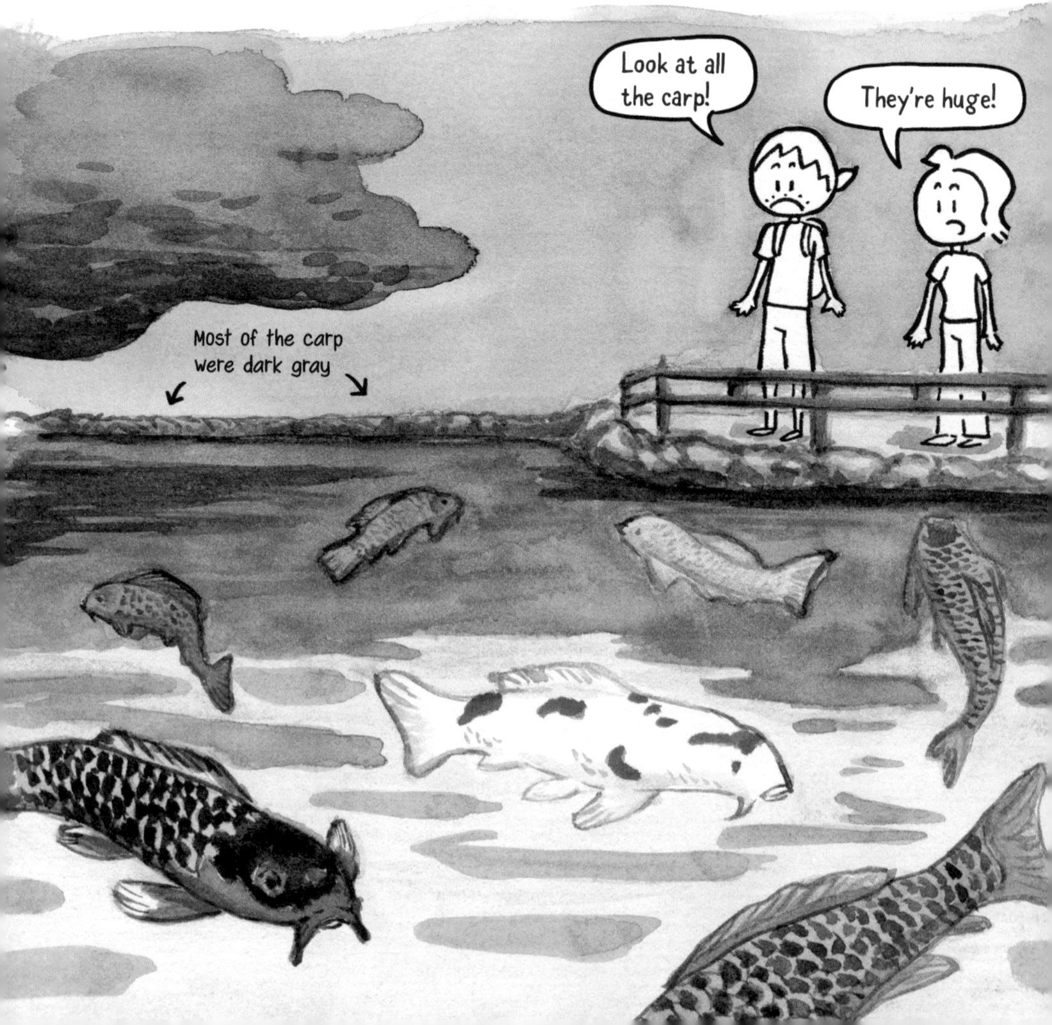
Look at all the carp!
They're huge!
Most of the carp were dark gray

We picked our bags back up from Himeji Station and caught the train to Osaka without a problem. Osaka was harder to navigate and we couldn't find our accommodation. Thankfully, we got help from several people.

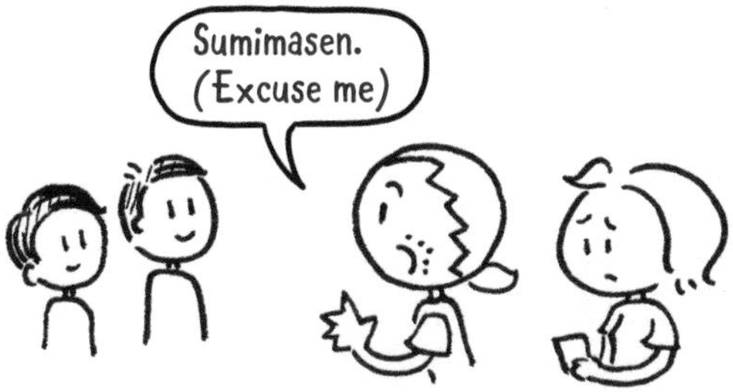
Sumimasen.
(Excuse me)

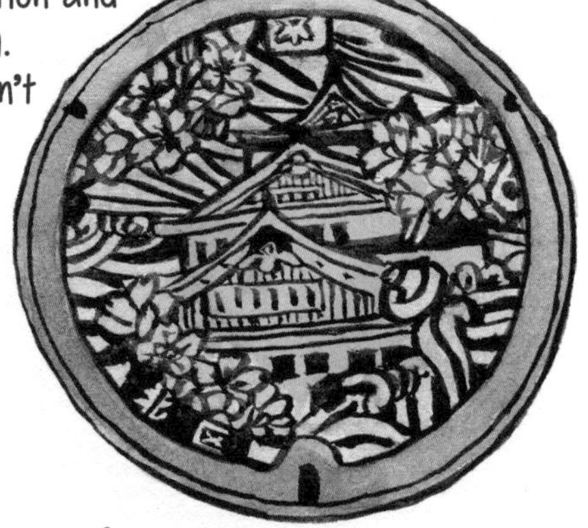

manhole cover seen while wandering around Osaka

After dropping off our bags and returning to the train station to go to Expo Park, we encountered another difficulty—we'd never come across a ticket machine like this one before. Usually we would select our destination before paying, but this machine didn't display any destination options. Compounding the problem was that

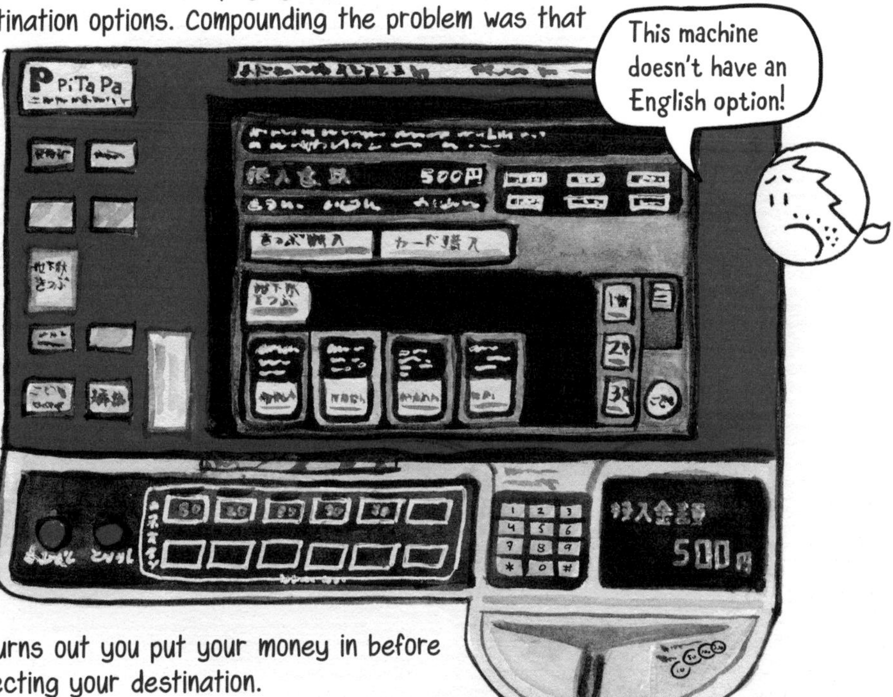
This machine doesn't have an English option!
PiTaPa
500円
500円

It turns out you put your money in before selecting your destination.

Expo Park was originally built for the 1970 World's Fair with the Tower of the Sun at its heart. I had seen pictures and thought the tower would be 20–30 feet (6–9 m) tall. I was surprised when I saw it in person, as it stands at an impressive 230 feet (70 m).

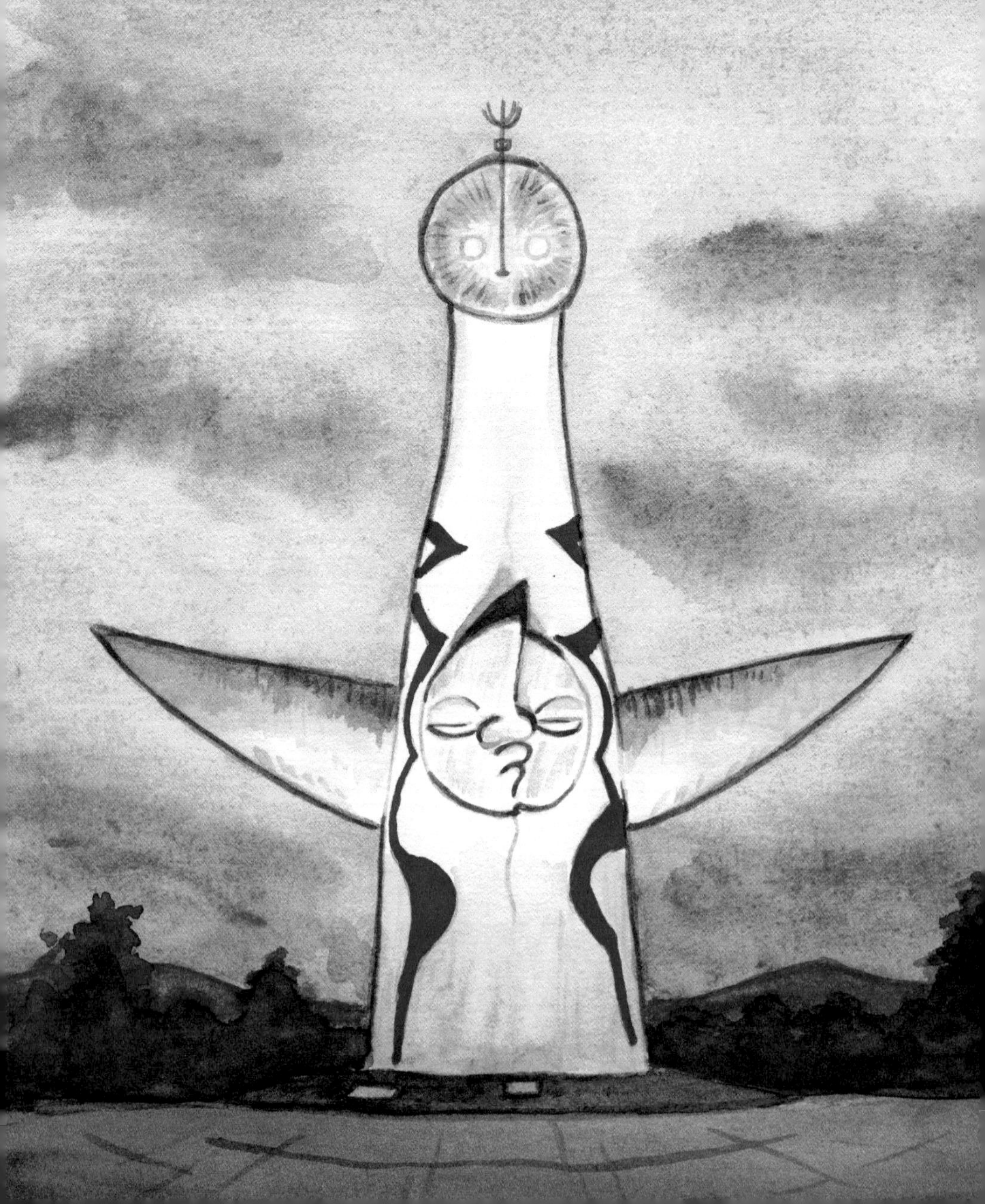

We came to Expo Park specifically to see the hotaru (fireflies). We were not disappointed.

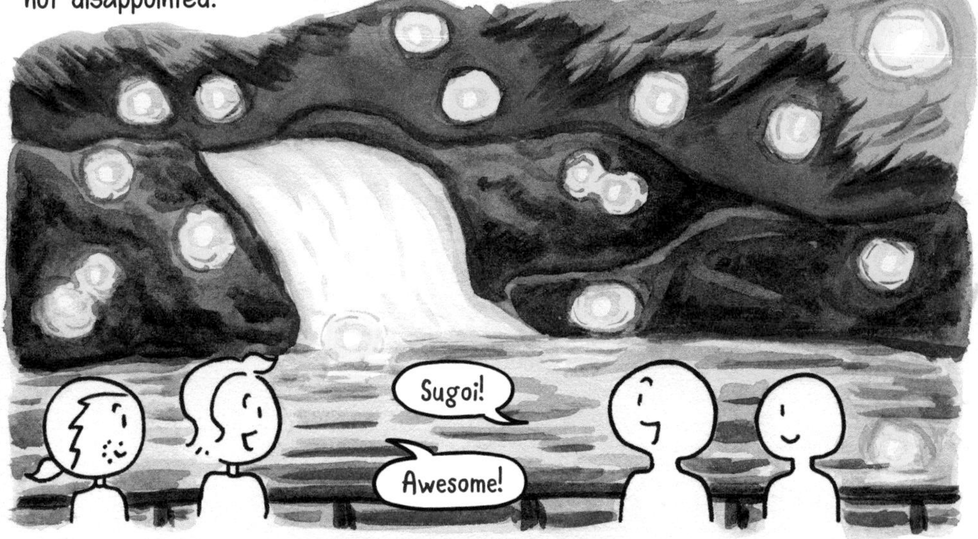
Sugoi!
Awesome!

Both the Genji-botaru (Luciola cruciata) and the Heike-botaru (Aquatica lateralis) firefly species were at the park. The larger Genji firefly is named after the Genji clan who defeated the Heike clan during the battle of Dannoura in 1185. This ended the Genpei War and marked the beginning of the Kamakura shogunate. The fireflies are said to be the souls of the soldiers who fell in battle.

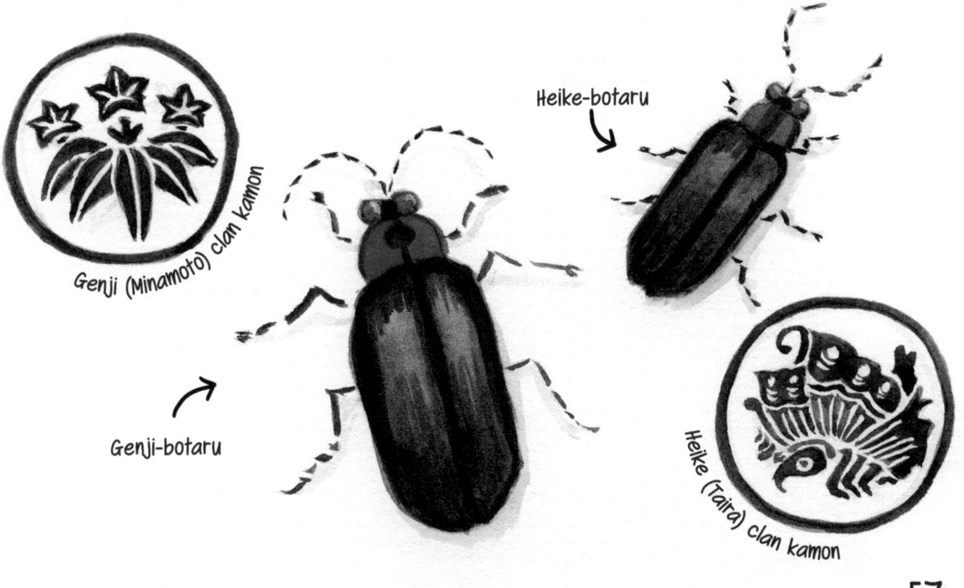
Genji (Minamoto) clan kamon
Heike-botaru
Genji-botaru
Heike (Taira) clan kamon

Getting back from Expo Park was frustrating as the route required a transfer that we didn't have to make before.

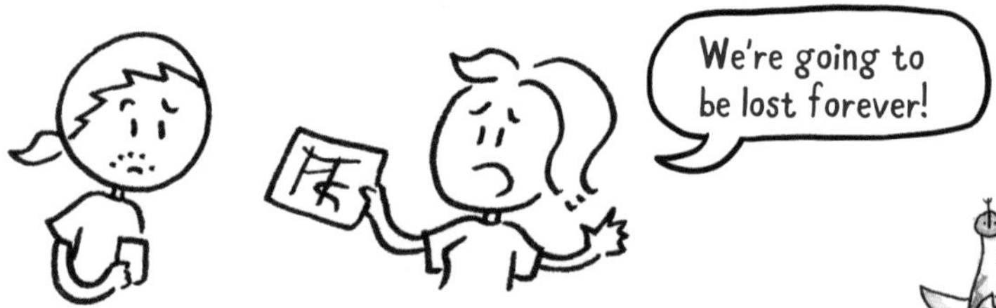

We're going to be lost forever!


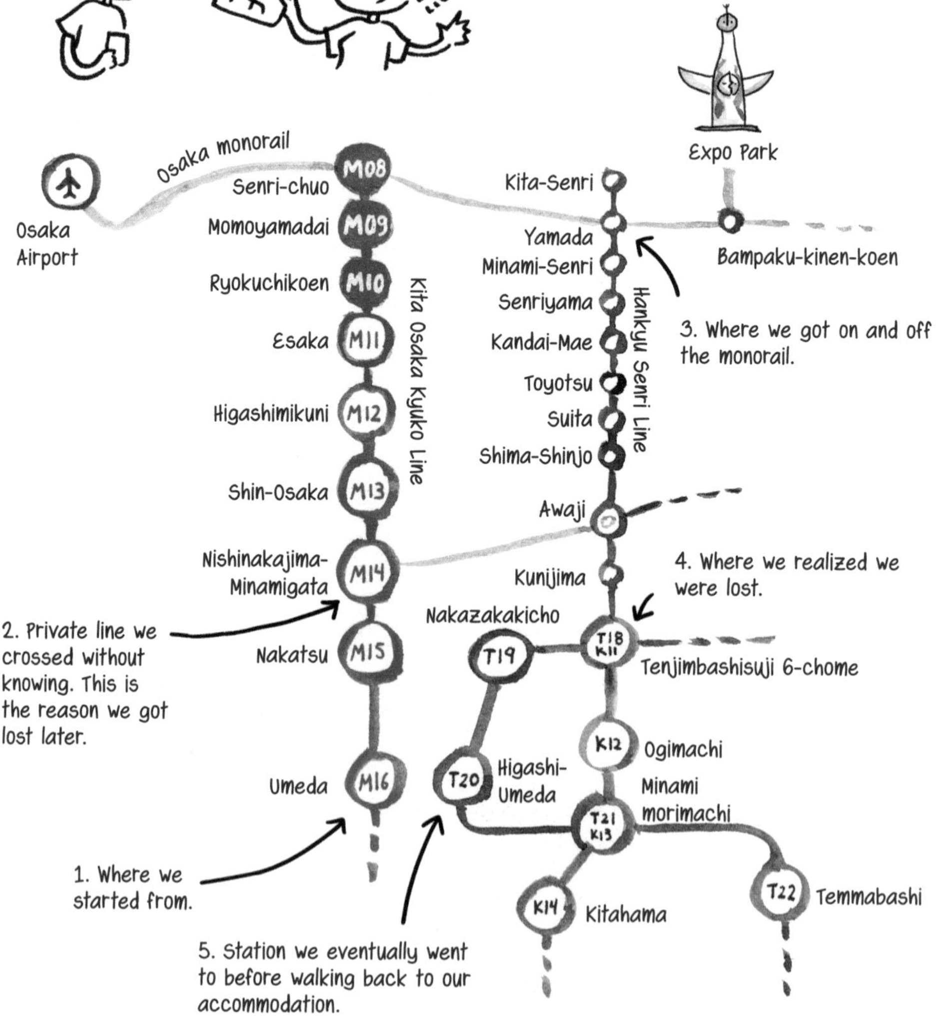

Expo Park
Osaka monorail
Osaka Airport
M08 Senri-chuo
M09 Momoyamadai
M10 Ryokuchikoen
M11 Esaka
M12 Higashimikuni
M13 Shin-Osaka
M14 Nishinakajima-Minamigata
M15 Nakatsu
M16 Umeda
Kita Osaka Kyuko Line
Kita-Senri
Yamada
Minami-Senri
Senriyama
Kandai-Mae
Toyotsu
Suita
Shima-Shinjo
Awaji
Kunijima
Hankyu Senri Line
Bampaku-kinen-koen
T18 K11 Tenjimbashisuji 6-chome
T19 Nakazakakicho
T20 Higashi-Umeda
K12 Ogimachi
T21 K13 Minami morimachi
K14 Kitahama
T22 Temmabashi
1. Where we started from.
2. Private line we crossed without knowing. This is the reason we got lost later.
3. Where we got on and off the monorail.
4. Where we realized we were lost.
5. Station we eventually went to before walking back to our accommodation.


We were exhausted by the time we got back to our room.

# Exploring Osaka

May 29th

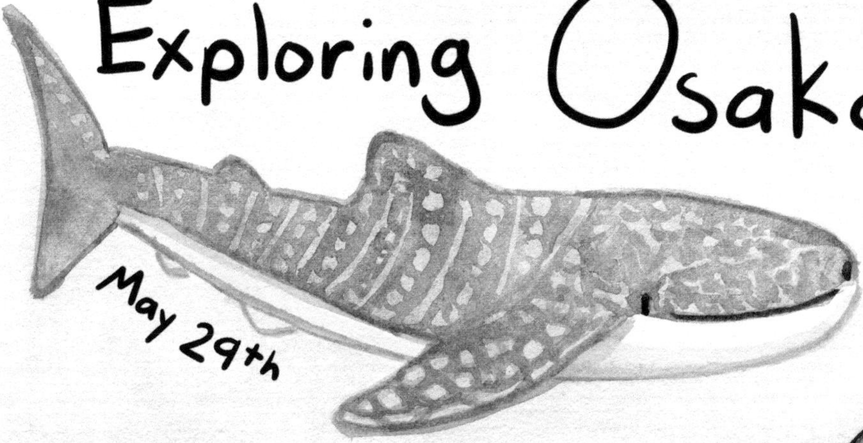

Connor's brother, Mason, was staying in Osaka, so he met us out in front of Kaiyukan Aquarium. There were windsocks still hanging up from Children's Day, a national holiday in Japan on May 5th.

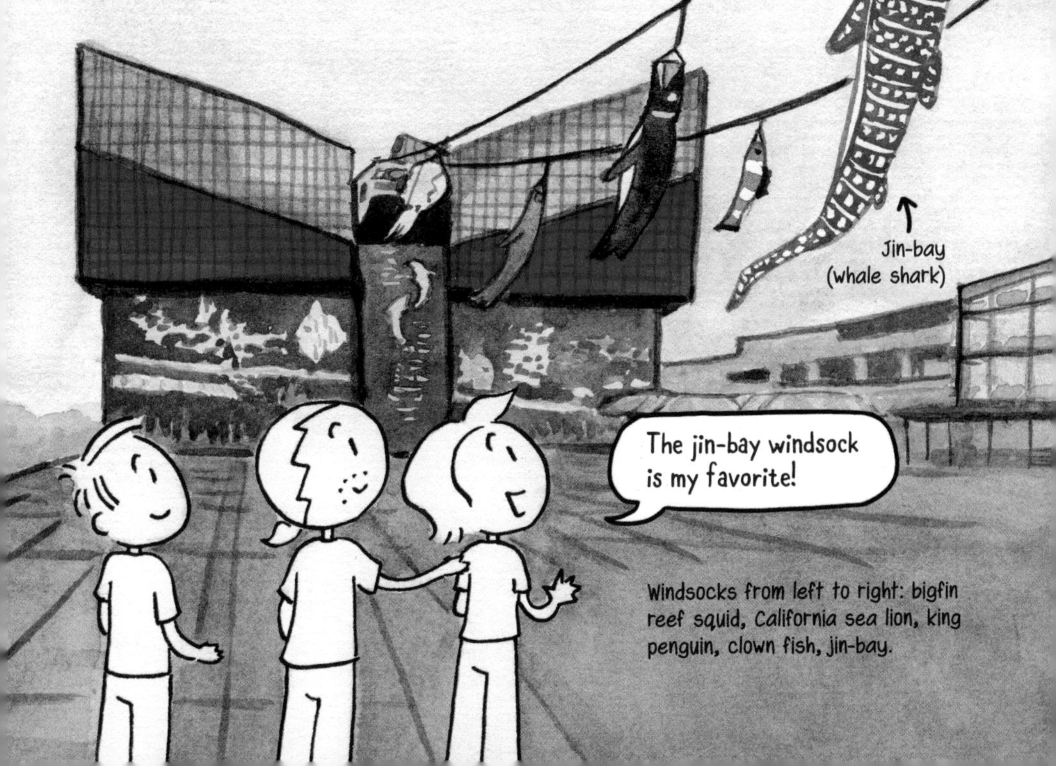
Jin-bay (whale shark)
The jin-bay windsock is my favorite!

Windsocks from left to right: bigfin reef squid, California sea lion, king penguin, clown fish, jin-bay.

The aquarium is set up in an innovative way. To start, you go through a tube shaped tank that allows fish and rays to swim all around you.

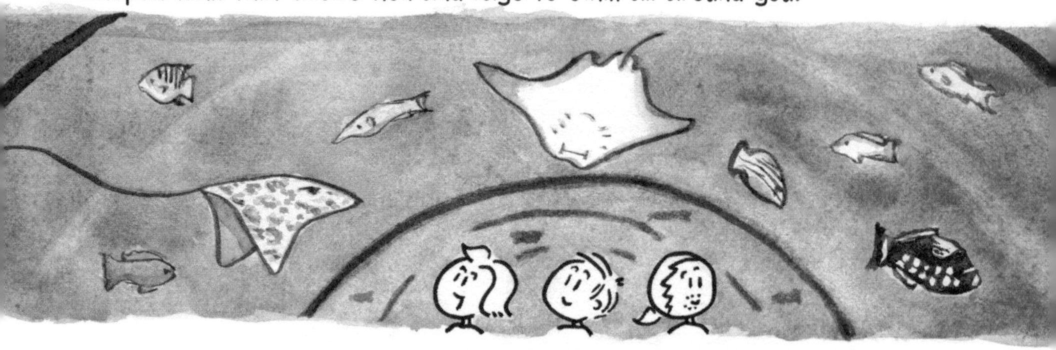

Then you take an elevator up to the eighth floor. The walkway spirals downwards around the perimeter of the building, leading you back to where you started. Along the route there are exhibits representing different parts of the world.

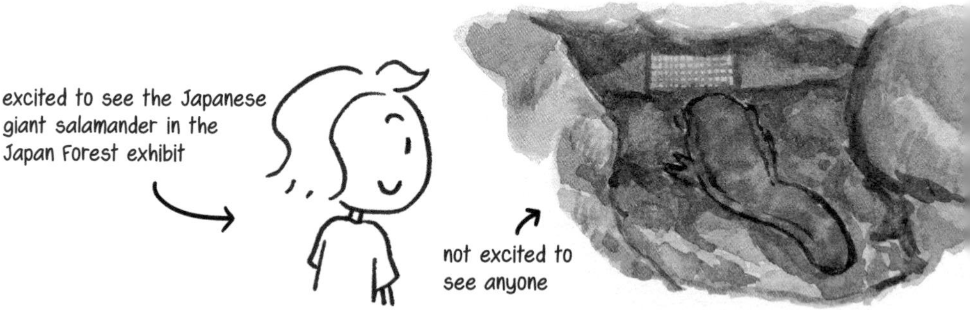
excited to see the Japanese giant salamander in the Japan Forest exhibit
not excited to see anyone

I'd previously seen a TV episode of River Monsters that talked about catching arapaima fish. I never thought I'd get to see one in person, but there were several in the Ecuador Rain Forest exhibit.

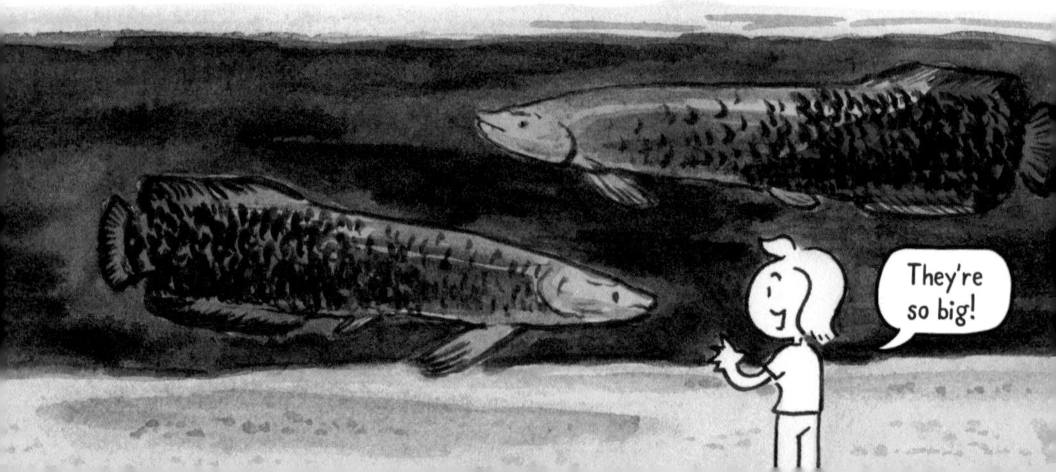
They're so big!

The main reason we came, though, was to see the

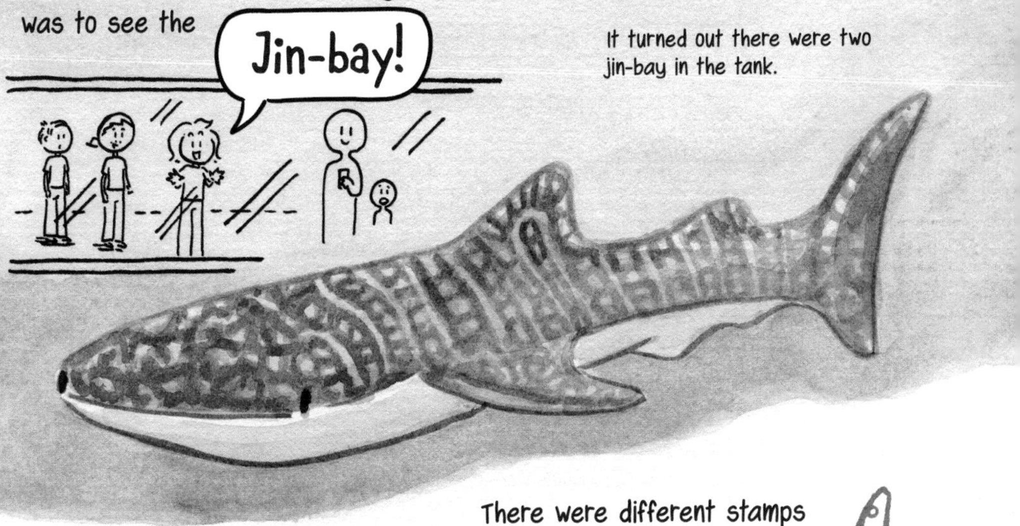
Jin-bay!

It turned out there were two jin-bay in the tank.

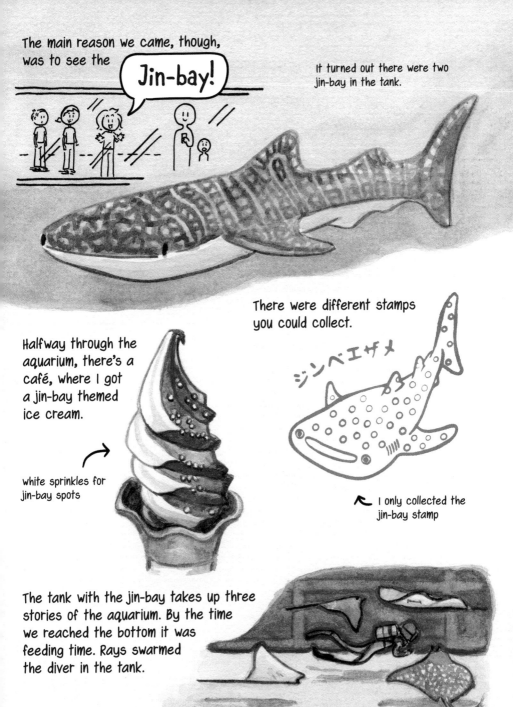

There were different stamps you could collect.

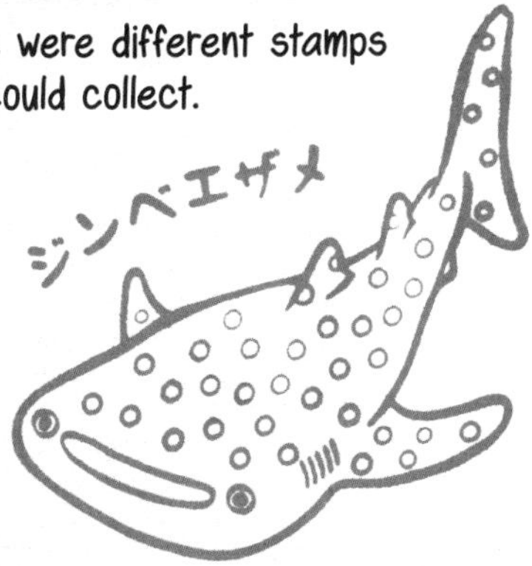
ジンベエザメ

I only collected the jin-bay stamp

Halfway through the aquarium, there's a café, where I got a jin-bay themed ice cream.

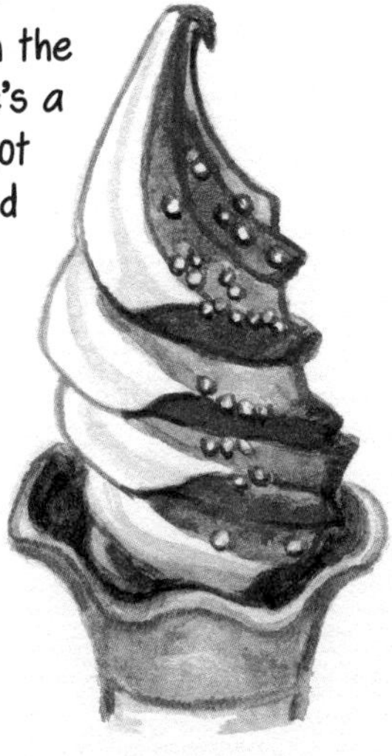

white sprinkles for jin-bay spots

The tank with the jin-bay takes up three stories of the aquarium. By the time we reached the bottom it was feeding time. Rays swarmed the diver in the tank.

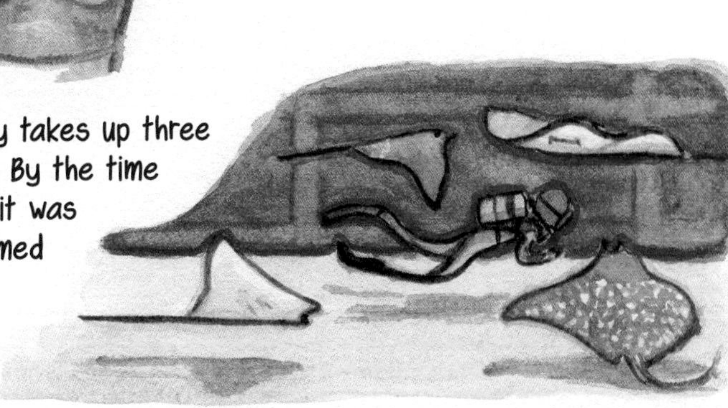

Past the giant tank was the Japan Deep exhibit, where you could see Japanese spider crabs.

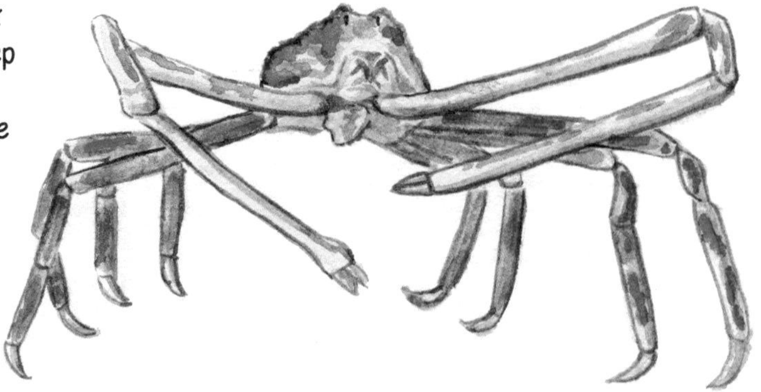

There was a new jellyfish exhibit. I really liked the tank with all the moon jellies.

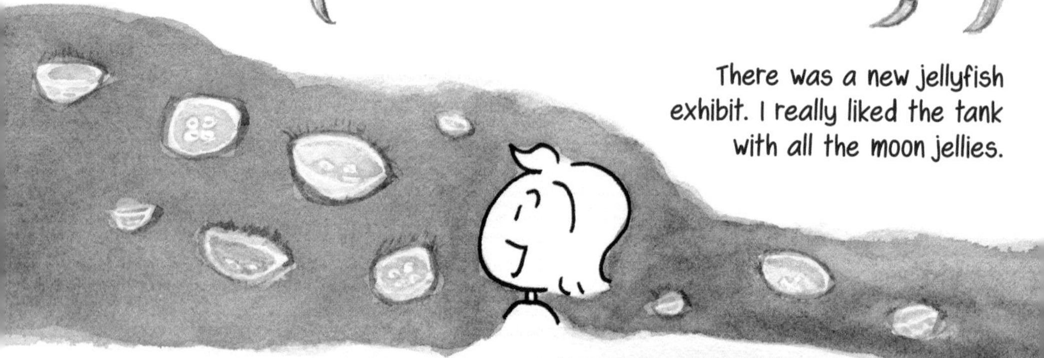

In the Arctic exhibit was a really relaxed seal.

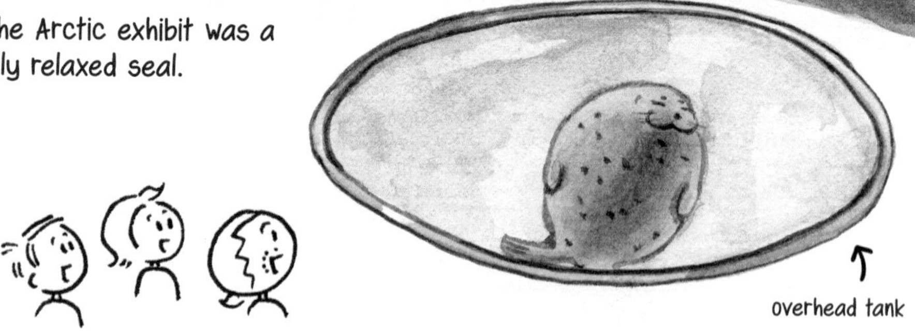
overhead tank

As with most places, the gift shop was located by the exit. Outside the shop was a silly toy machine that sold animals posed like people.

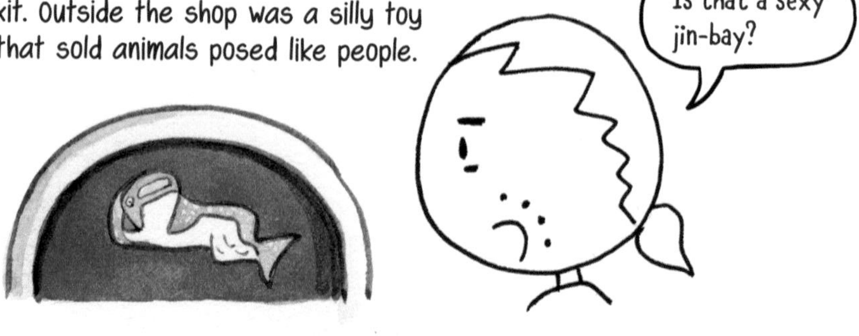
Is that a sexy jin-bay?

Before saying goodbye to each other, Mason, Connor, and I had Osaka-style okonomiyaki for lunch. The difference between Hiroshima and Osaka okonomiyaki is that in Osaka egg was mixed in with the rest of the ingredients, gluing everything together as it cooked.

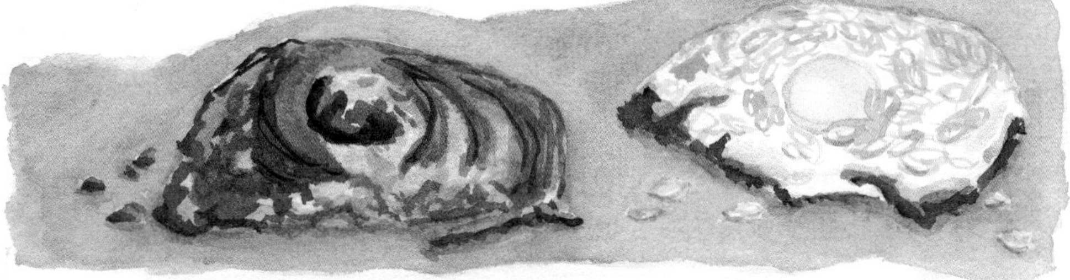

In the evening, Connor and I went to visit the Dotonbori district to see what all the fuss was about. We found it dirty and crowded, but the neon signs were amazing.

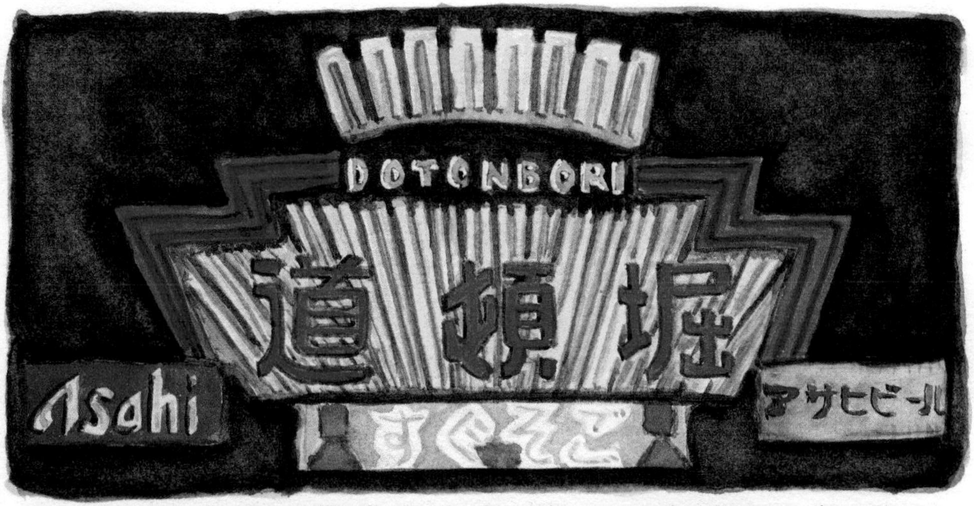
DOTONBORI
道頓堀
Asahi
アサヒビール

We got a drink so we could sit at a café while I painted the signs along the canal. While we sat, we noticed that there was a giant line nearby to buy a cheese-filled corn dog.

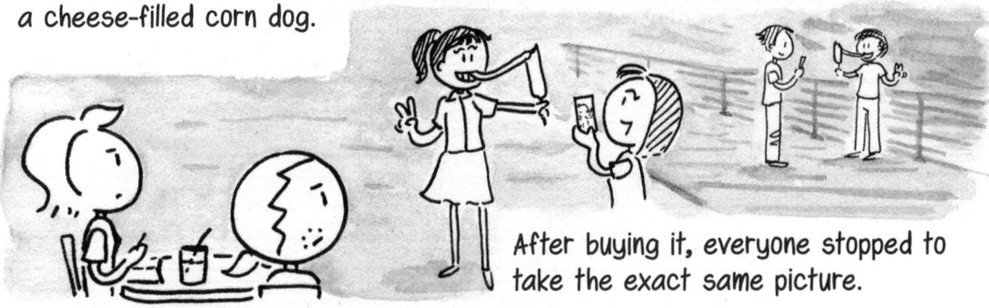

After buying it, everyone stopped to take the exact same picture.

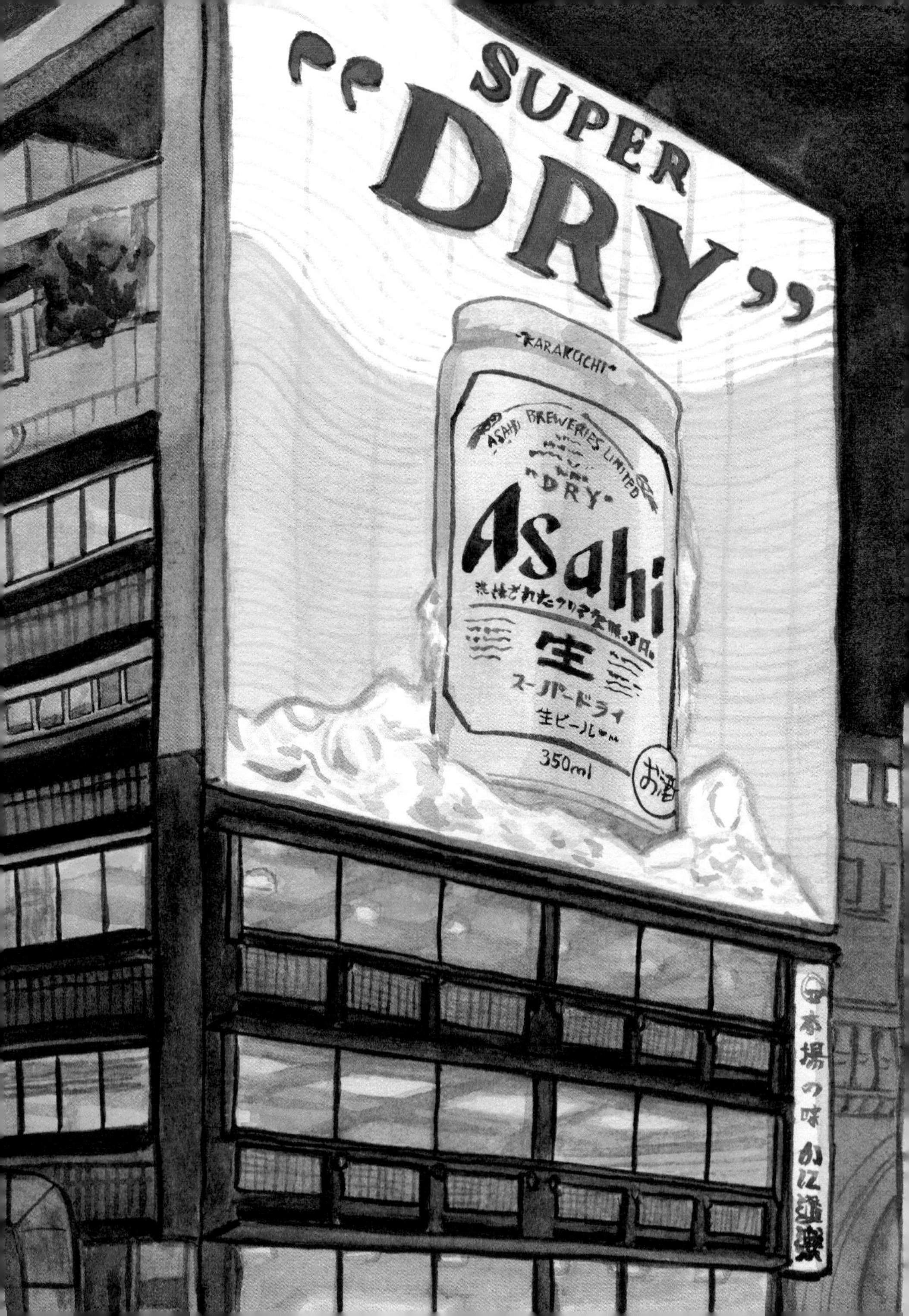
"SUPER DRY"
KARAKUCHI
ASAHI BREWERIES LIMITED
"DRY"
Asahi
生
スーパードライ
生ビール
350ml
お酒
本場の味 かに道楽

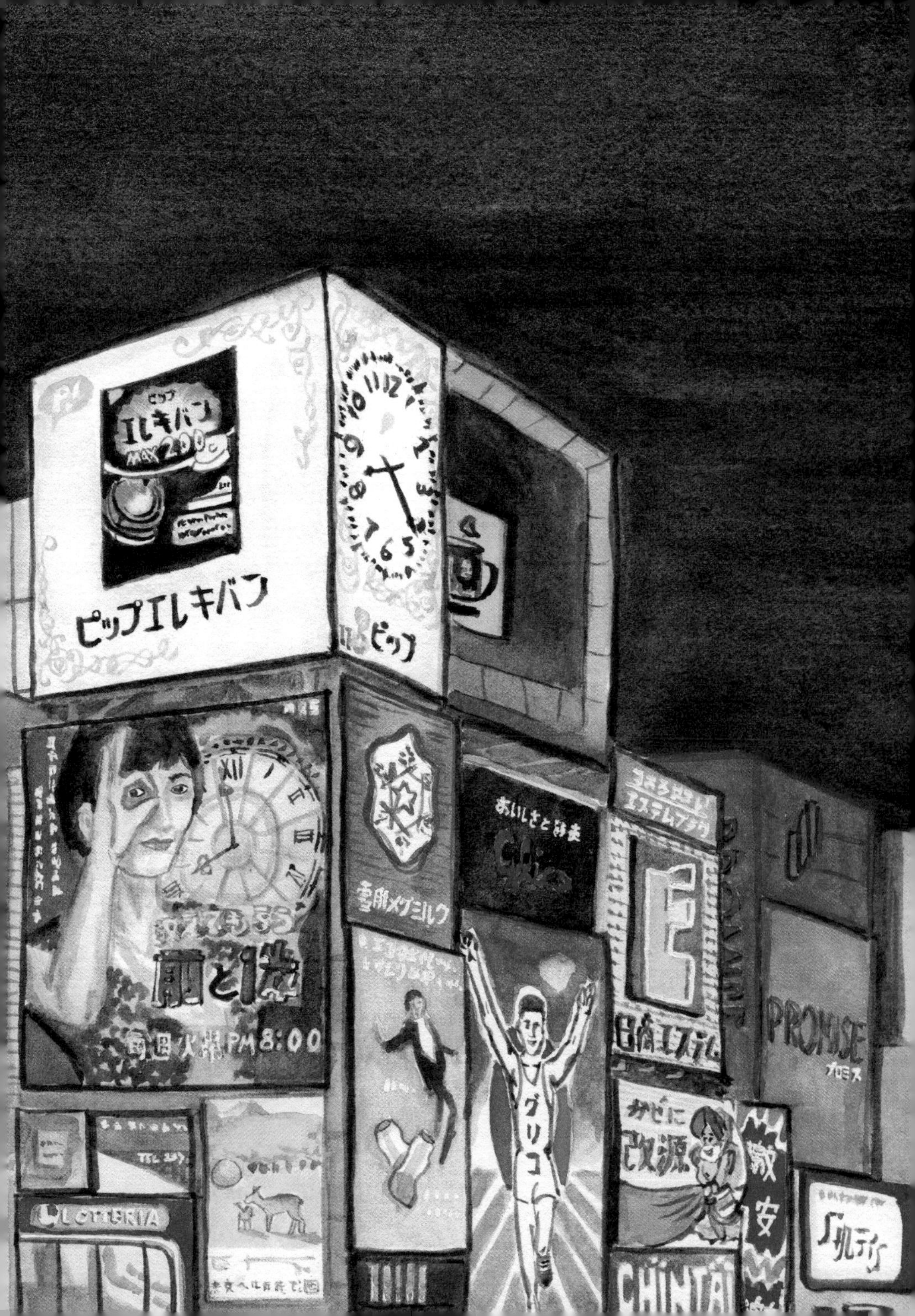

ピップエレキバン
MAX200
ピップ
毎週火曜PM 8:00
雪印メグミルク
おいしさと健康
グリコ
PROMISE
プロミス
改源
激安
LOTTERIA
CHINTAI

We were hungry by the time I finished painting, so we walked to the nearby Dotonbori street for dinner. There are many iconic signs there. My favorite was the one for Zuboraya, a famous restaurant serving puffer fish (fugu).

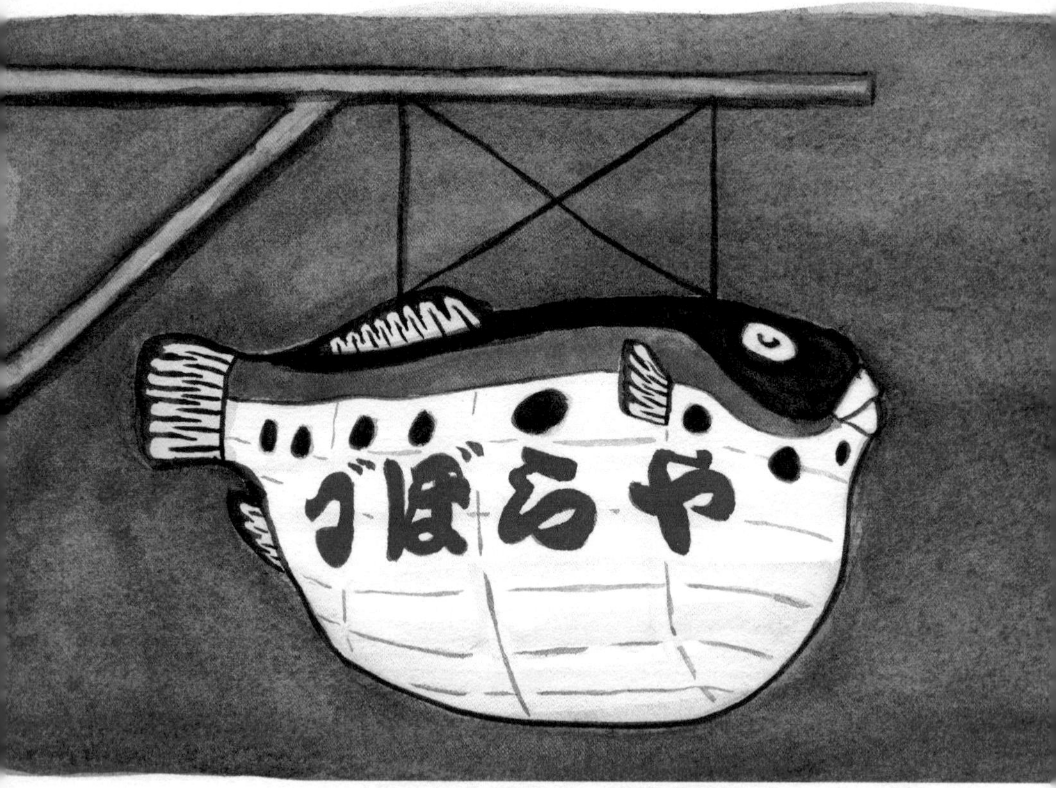
ずぼらや

After dinner we faced the Osaka train-ticket machines again.

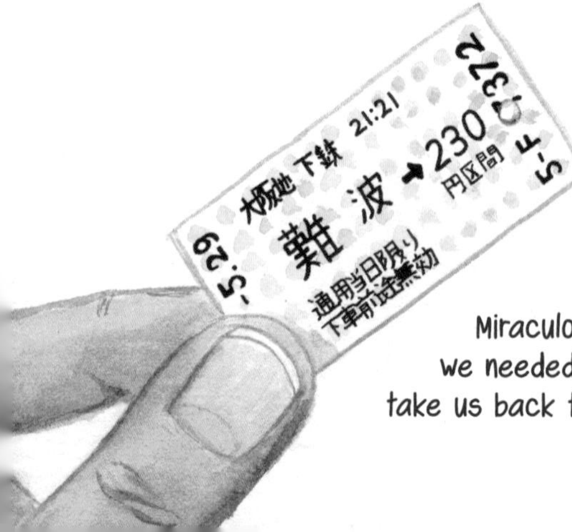
5.-29
大阪地下鉄 21:21
難波 ➔ 230
円区間
通用当日限り
下車前途無効
5-F C372

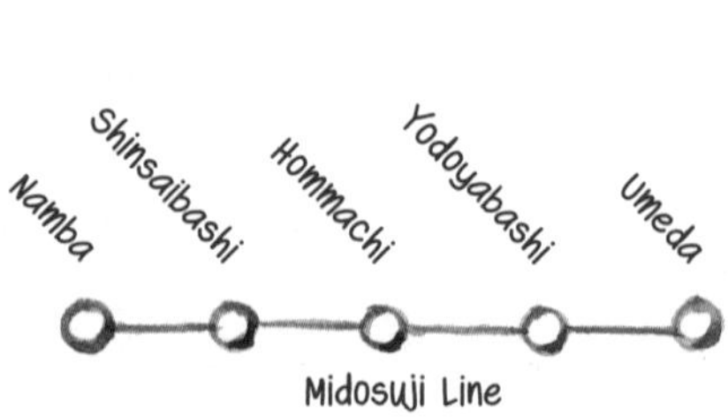
Namba
Shinsaibashi
Hommachi
Yodoyabashi
Umeda
Midosuji Line

Miraculously, I was able to determine which train we needed and how to buy the correct tickets to take us back to the place where we were staying.

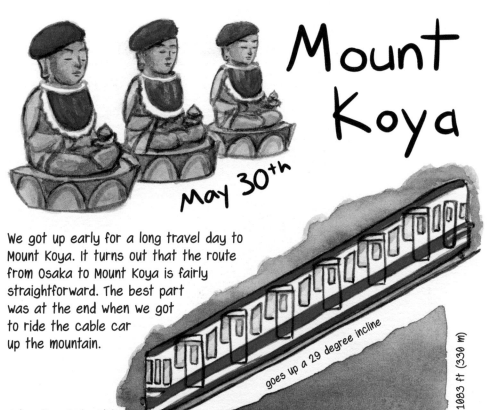

# Mount Koya

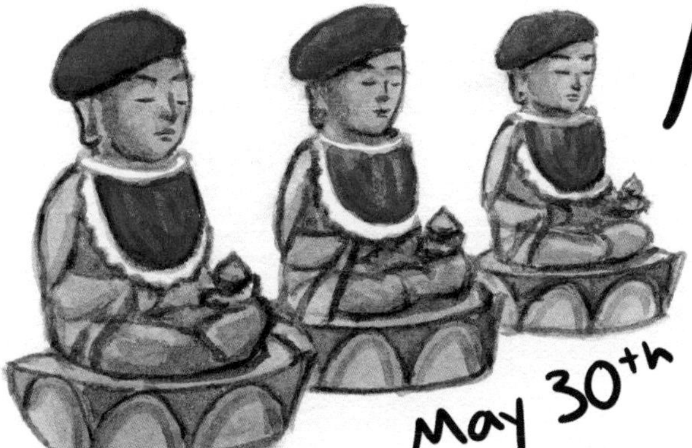

May 30th

We got up early for a long travel day to Mount Koya. It turns out that the route from Osaka to Mount Koya is fairly straightforward. The best part was at the end when we got to ride the cable car up the mountain.

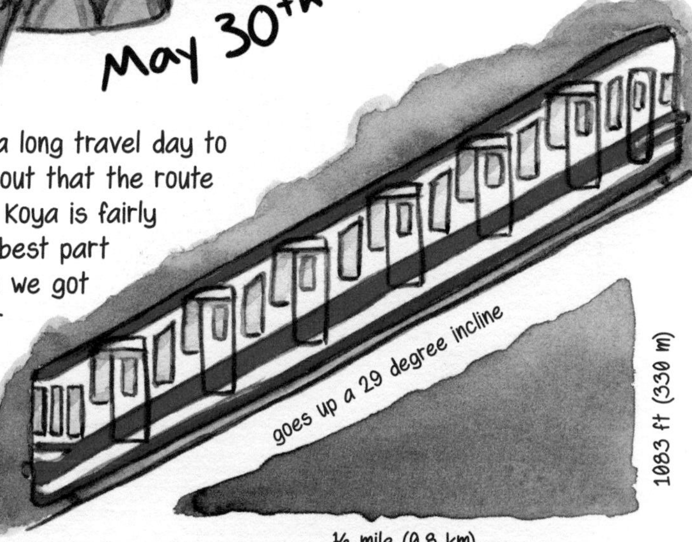
goes up a 29 degree incline
1083 ft (330 m)
Only a five minute ride!
½ mile (0.8 km)

Once we arrived I spotted the visitor information building. They had stamps! It was only later that I realized I had no idea what the stamps were for.

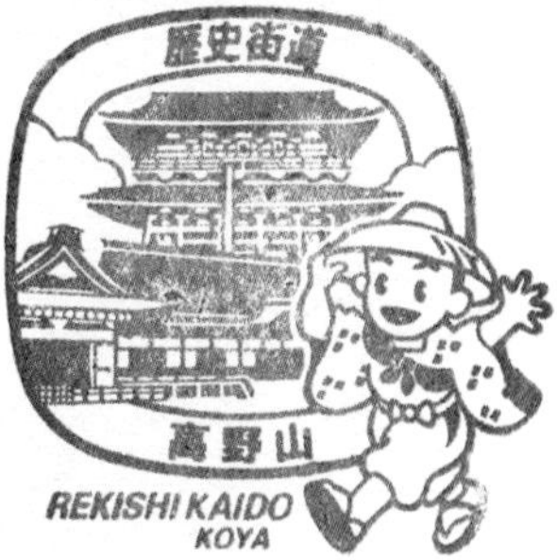
歴史街道
高野山
REKISHI KAIDO
KOYA

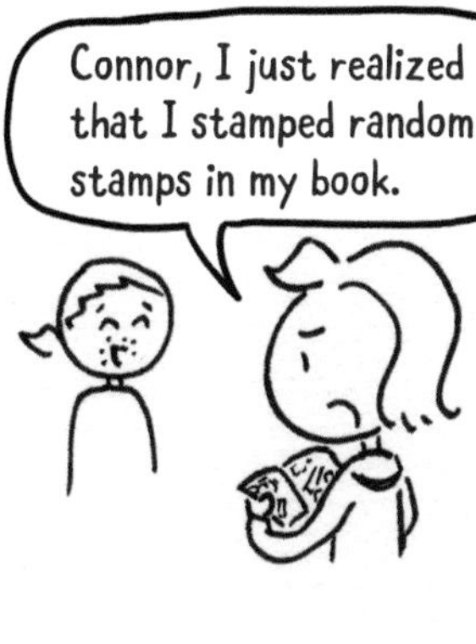
Connor, I just realized that I stamped random stamps in my book.

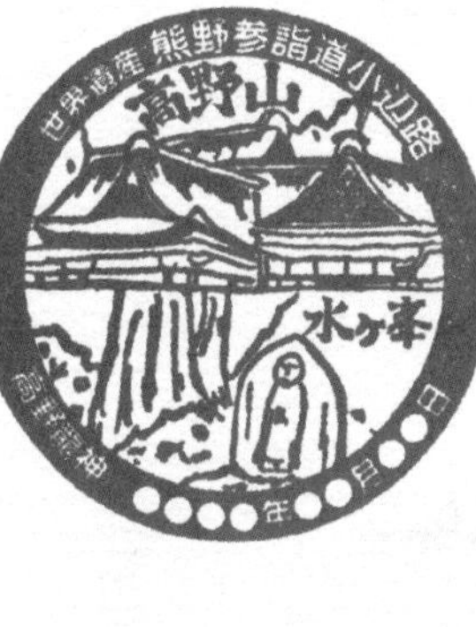
熊野参詣道小辺路
高野山
水ヶ峯

Later we learned that Rekishi Kaido is a cultural project that highlights different parts of Japanese heritage and history. 高野山 means Mount Koya.

We dropped off our bags at our ryokan (inn) and then walked to Okunoin Cemetery to see it before it got dark. With over 200,000 graves, Okunoin is the largest cemetery in Japan. Okunoin is full of fascinating history, traditions, and superstitions. There are many points of interest throughout the grounds.

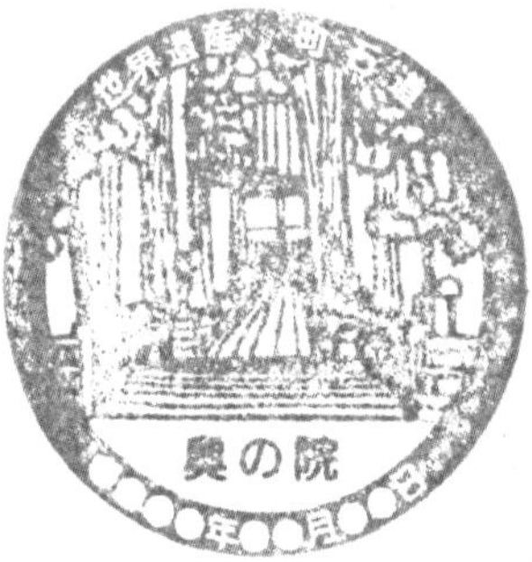
奥の院

Okunoin stamp

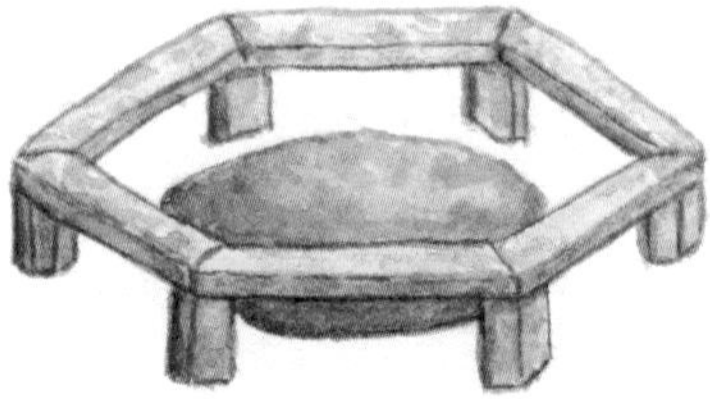

1. Koshikake-ishi: A stone that monk Kobo Daishi possibly sat upon to rest.

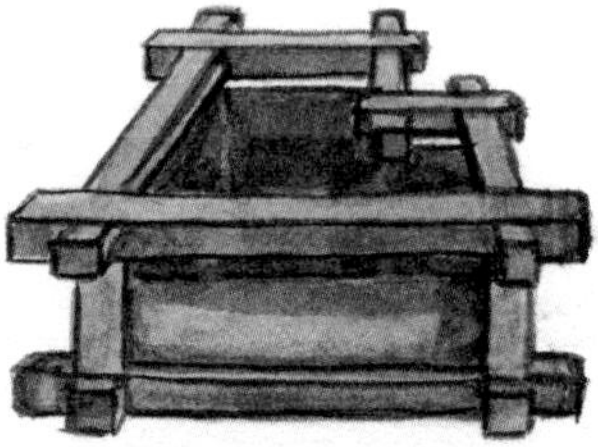

2. Sugatami-no-ido: Well of Reflections. Not seeing your reflection in the water predicts how long you have left to live.

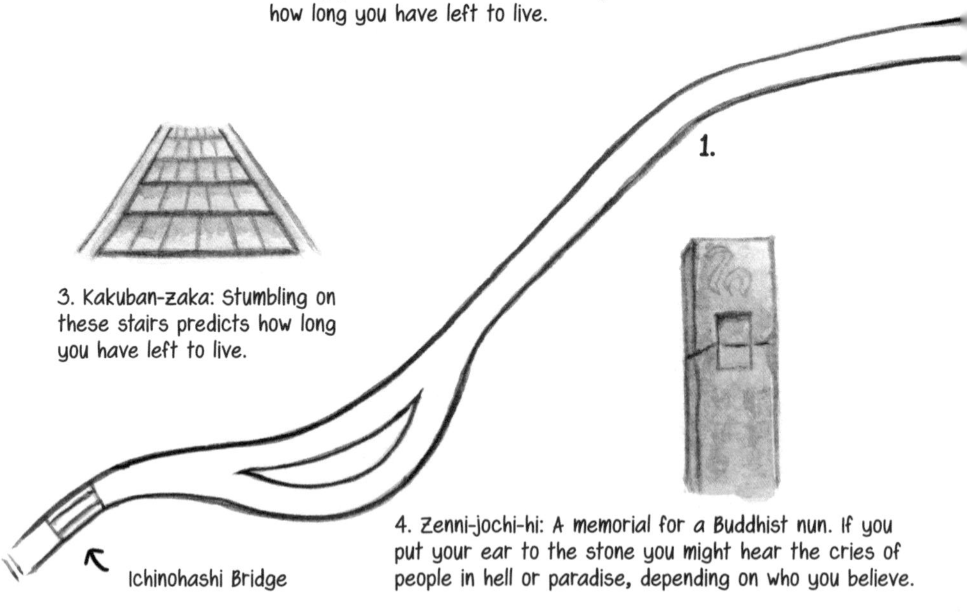
1.
Ichinohashi Bridge

3. Kakuban-zaka: Stumbling on these stairs predicts how long you have left to live.

4. Zenni-jochi-hi: A memorial for a Buddhist nun. If you put your ear to the stone you might hear the cries of people in hell or paradise, depending on who you believe.

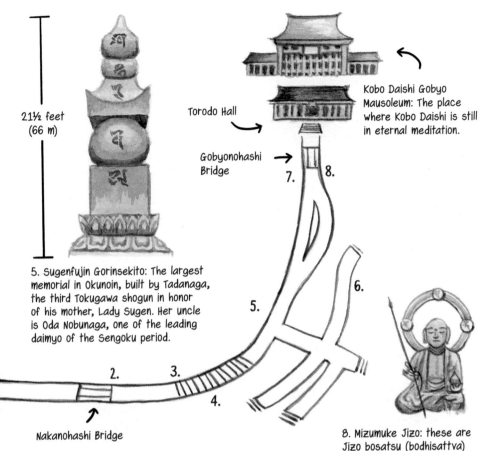

21½ feet (66 m)

Torodo Hall

Gobyonohashi Bridge

Kobo Daishi Gobyo Mausoleum: The place where Kobo Daishi is still in eternal meditation.

7.

8.

6.

5.

2.

3.

4.

Nakanohashi Bridge

5. Sugenfujin Gorinsekito: The largest memorial in Okunoin, built by Tadanaga, the third Tokugawa shogun in honor of his mother, Lady Sugen. Her uncle is Oda Nobunaga, one of the leading daimyo of the Sengoku period.

8. Mizumuke Jizo: these are Jizo bosatsu (bodhisattva) statues you pour water over, to represent self-purification.

6. Muenzuka: A pyramid of Jizo Jizo bosatsu (bodhisattva) statues dedicated to the nameless.

7. Oda Nobunaga: A sixteenth-century warlord who gained control over most of Honshu in a quest to unify Japan. His niece is Lady Sugen.

After dinner at our ryokan, we went to Ekoin Temple for a night tour of the Okunoin cemetery. Our guide was Yuta, a Buddhist monk. As our group walked to the cemetery entrance, we learned about how Kobo Daishi founded Mount Koya as a base for Shingon Buddhism. Yuta also showed us the proper etiquette to follow while in Okunoin.

Before we cross the first bridge and enter the cemetery, we must bow.

We saw lots of graves with the same odd shape. Yuta shared that each shape represents an element.

Consciousness is an implied element, but isn't given a shape.

void

air

fire

water

earth

Yuta was a wealth of information.

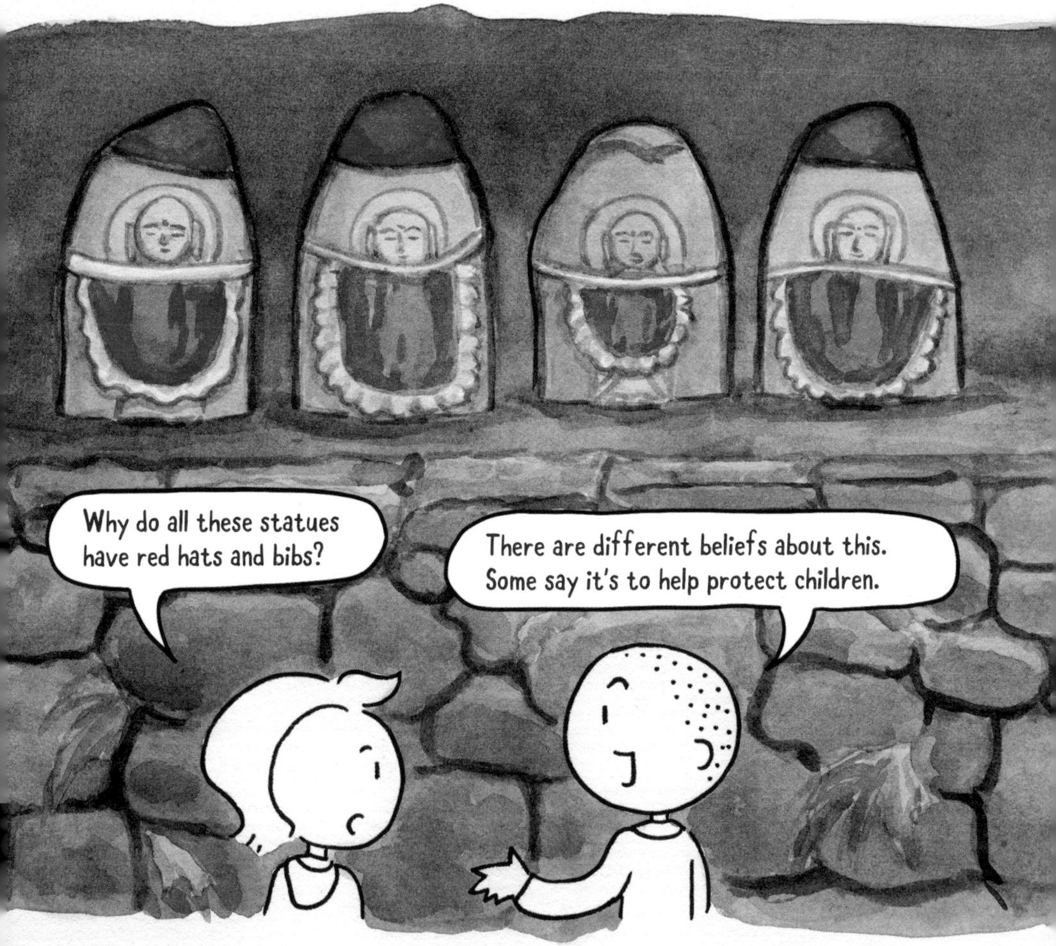

Why do all these statues have red hats and bibs?
There are different beliefs about this. Some say it's to help protect children.


It turned out that he also had a great sense of humor.

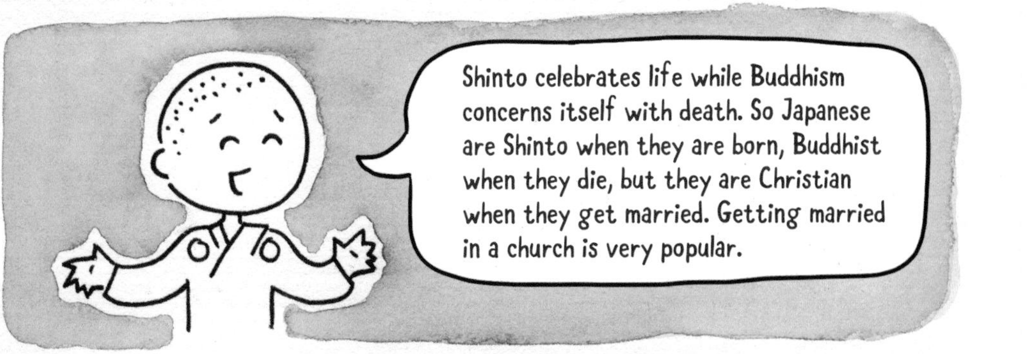

Shinto celebrates life while Buddhism concerns itself with death. So Japanese are Shinto when they are born, Buddhist when they die, but they are Christian when they get married. Getting married in a church is very popular.

Yuta's humor continued to show as he shared some superstitions.

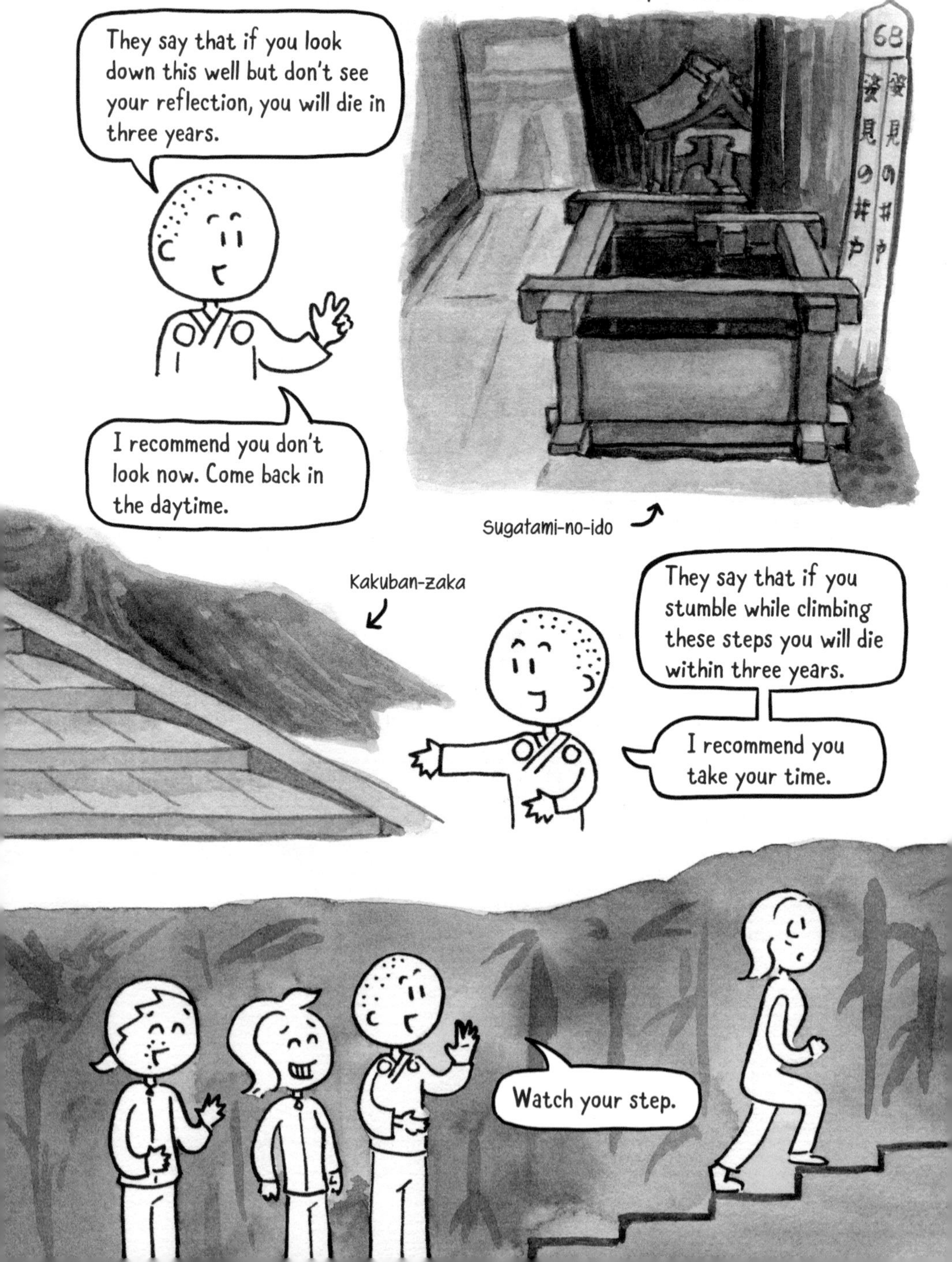
They say that if you look down this well but don't see your reflection, you will die in three years.
I recommend you don't look now. Come back in the daytime.
68
姿見の井戸
Sugatami-no-ido
Kakuban-zaka
They say that if you stumble while climbing these steps you will die within three years.
I recommend you take your time.
Watch your step.

Along the main walkway of Okunoin cemetery are hundreds of stone lanterns, each with a different phase of the moon.

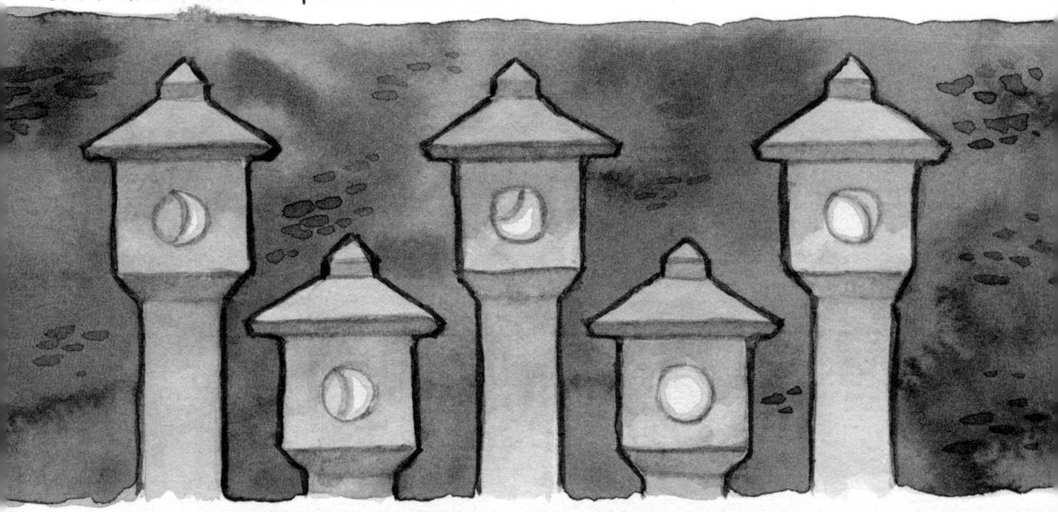

We learned that the moon imagery wasn't just an artistic choice.

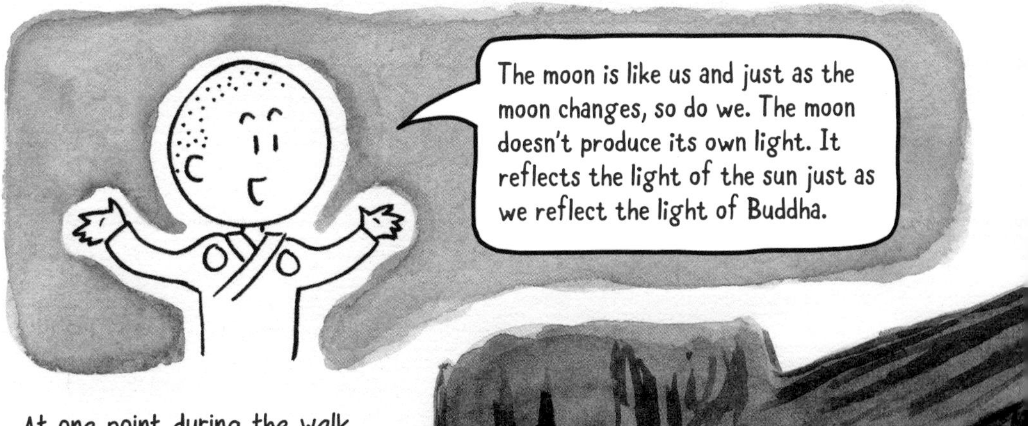
The moon is like us and just as the moon changes, so do we. The moon doesn't produce its own light. It reflects the light of the sun just as we reflect the light of Buddha.

At one point during the walk we stopped because Yuta heard a flying squirrel. We weren't lucky enough catch sight of one that night. Yuta told us that July was the best time to see them.

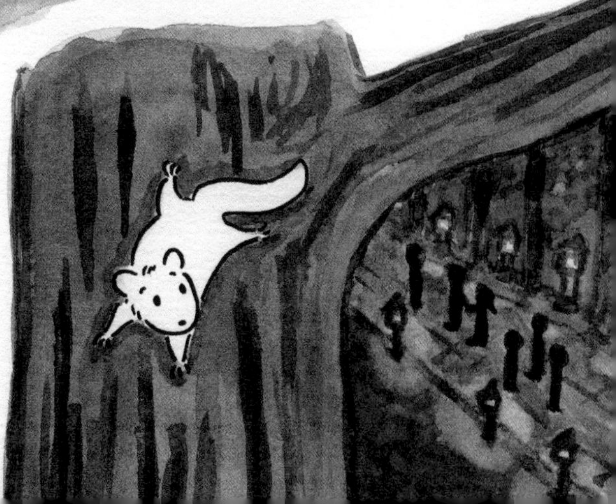

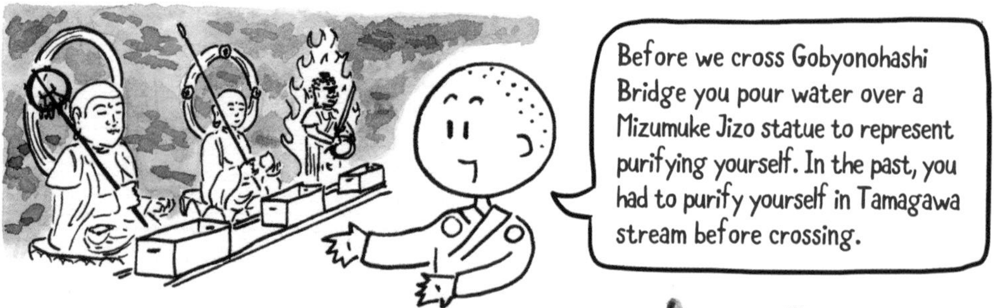
Before we cross Gobyonohashi Bridge you pour water over a Mizumuke Jizo statue to represent purifying yourself. In the past, you had to purify yourself in Tamagawa stream before crossing.

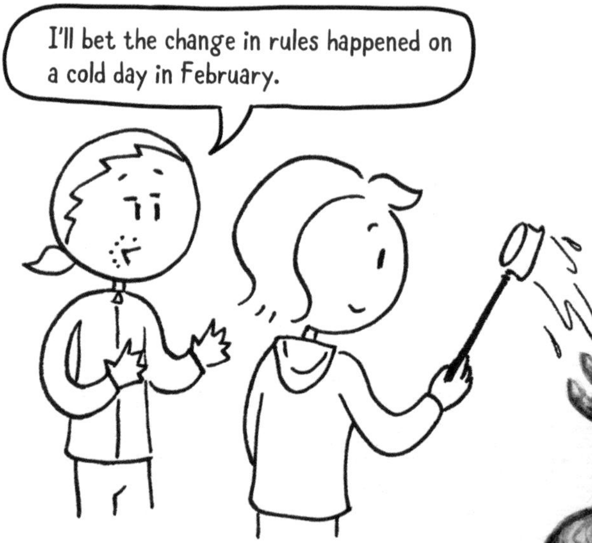
I'll bet the change in rules happened on a cold day in February.

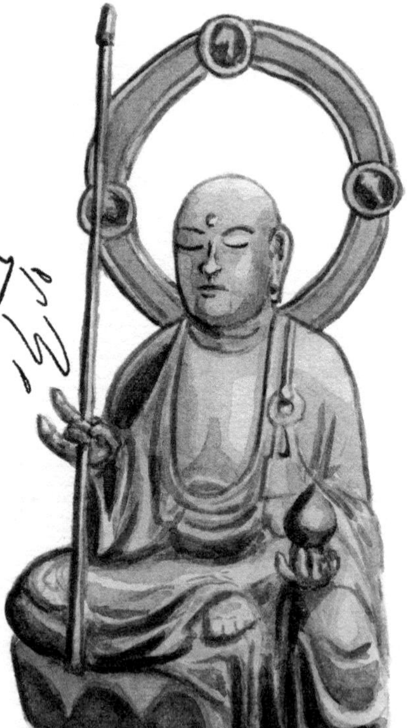

Across the bridge is the mausoleum where Kobo Daishi still is in eternal meditation.

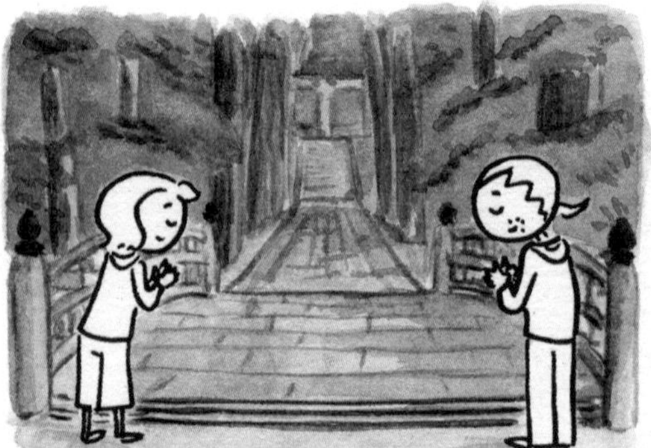

Before crossing the bridge, you bow and greet Kobo Daishi in your mind. When you're ready to leave, you cross back over the bridge, then turn and bow while saying a silent goodbye to Kobo Daishi.

# To Nara and Kyoto

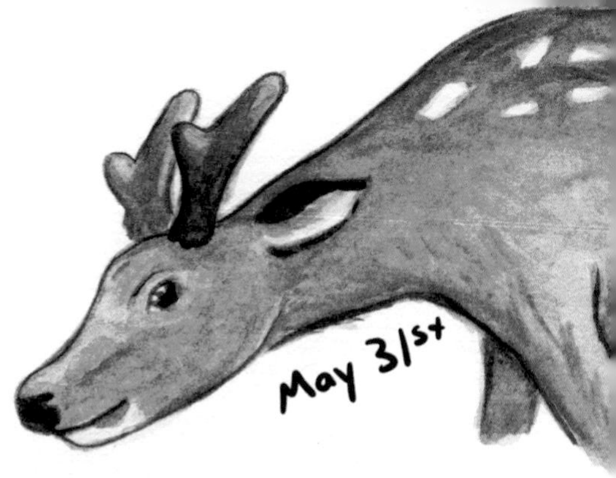

May 31st

We left our ryokan by 5:30 AM so we could watch the procession of monks bring Kobo Daishi breakfast. They do this ritual twice a day. After bringing the breakfast offering to Torodo Hall, the monks chanted for over an hour. It was amazing to listen to them.

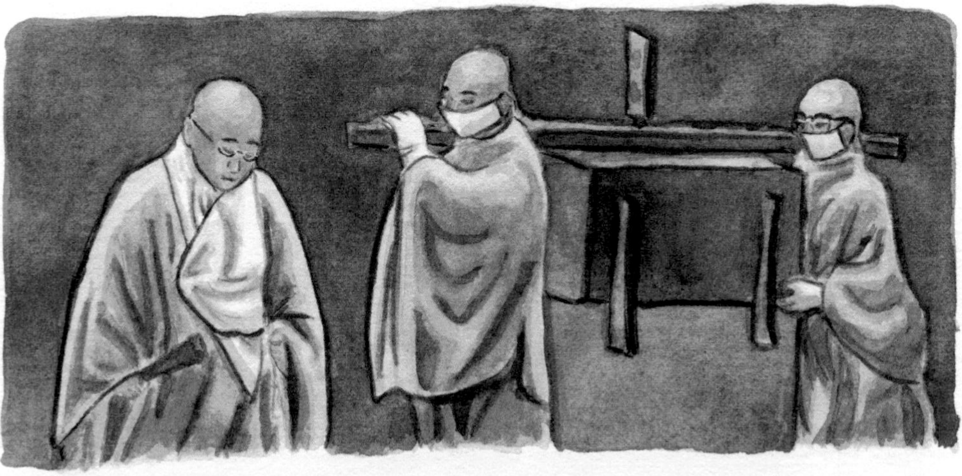

As we left Okunoin cemetery, we passed several pilgrims going down the path.

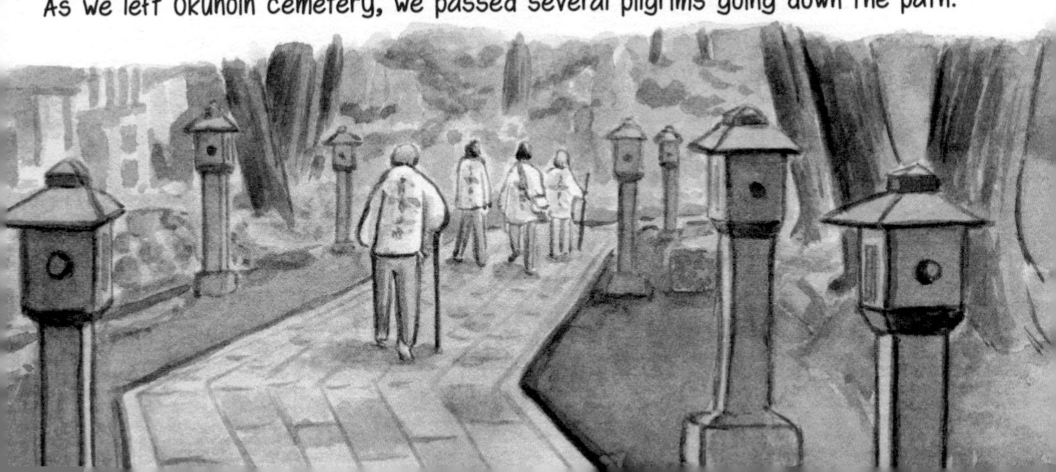

After leaving Mount Koya, Connor and I took the train to Nara to see the deer at Nara Park. We decided to eat lunch first and found a place that served kamameshi, a rice dish traditionally cooked in a kama (iron pot).

served with a wooden lid

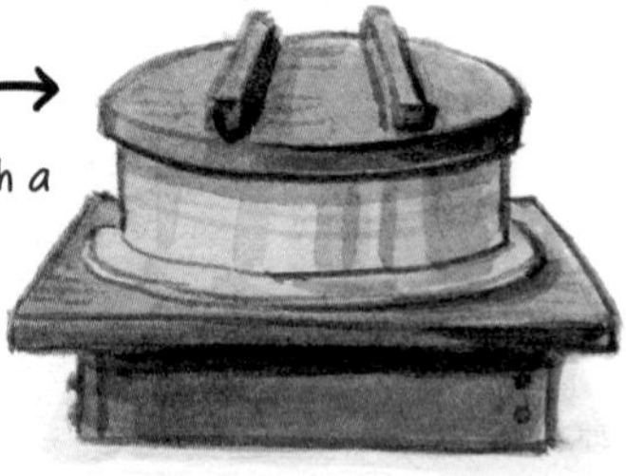

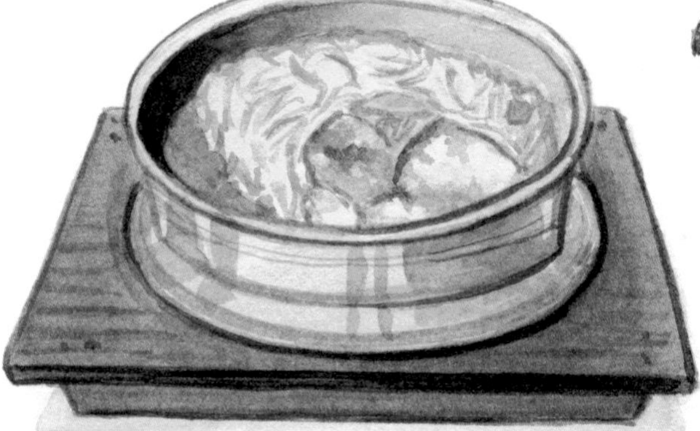

dessert was a deer cake

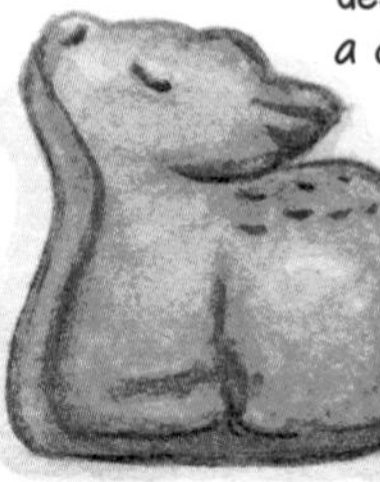

I had read that the deer in Nara will bow in exchange for crackers and I was excited to see this for myself. There are cracker stands all over Nara Park.

all the stands seemed to be run by older ladies

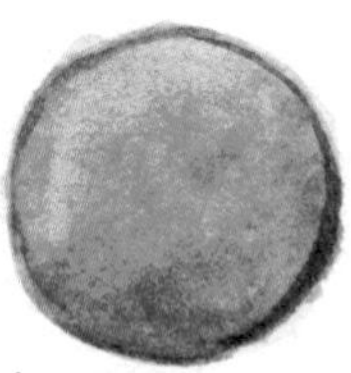

shika senbei (deer cracker)

sold in stacks of ten

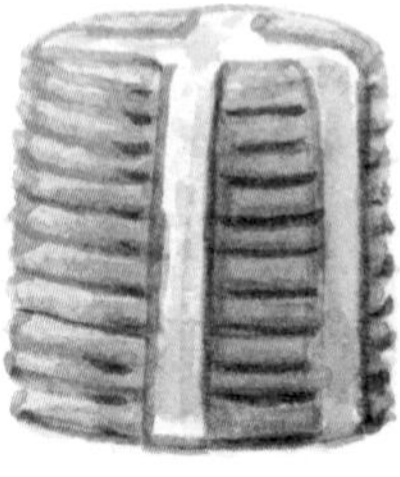

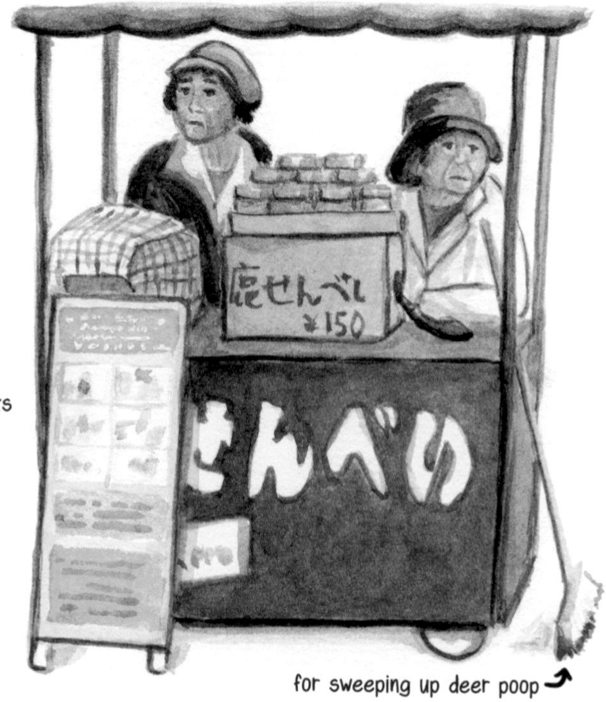
鹿せんべい
¥150

for sweeping up deer poop

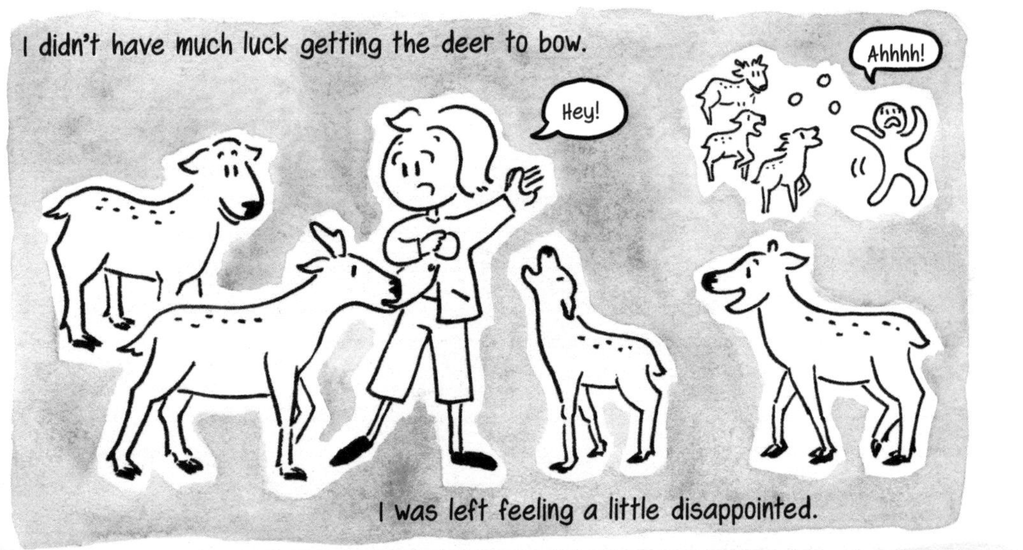
I didn't have much luck getting the deer to bow.
Hey!
Ahhhh!
I was left feeling a little disappointed.

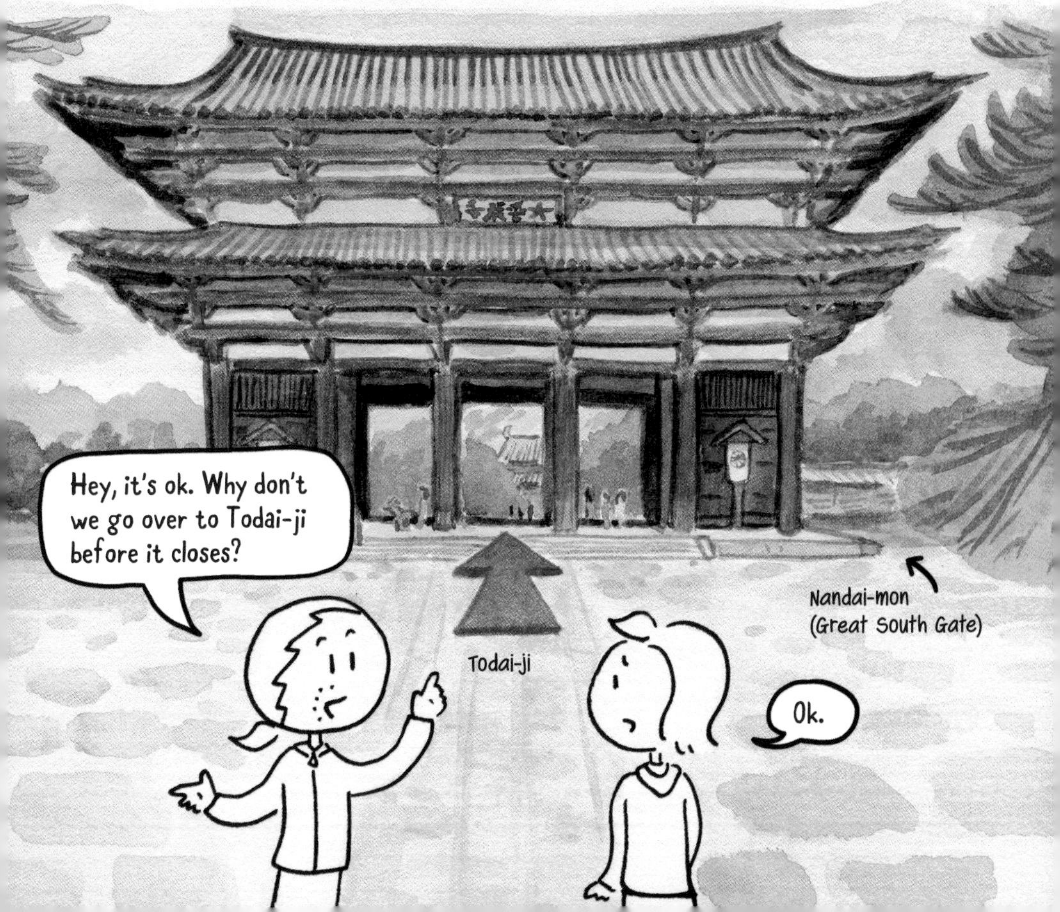
Hey, it's ok. Why don't we go over to Todai-ji before it closes?
Todai-ji
Nandai-mon (Great South Gate)
Ok.

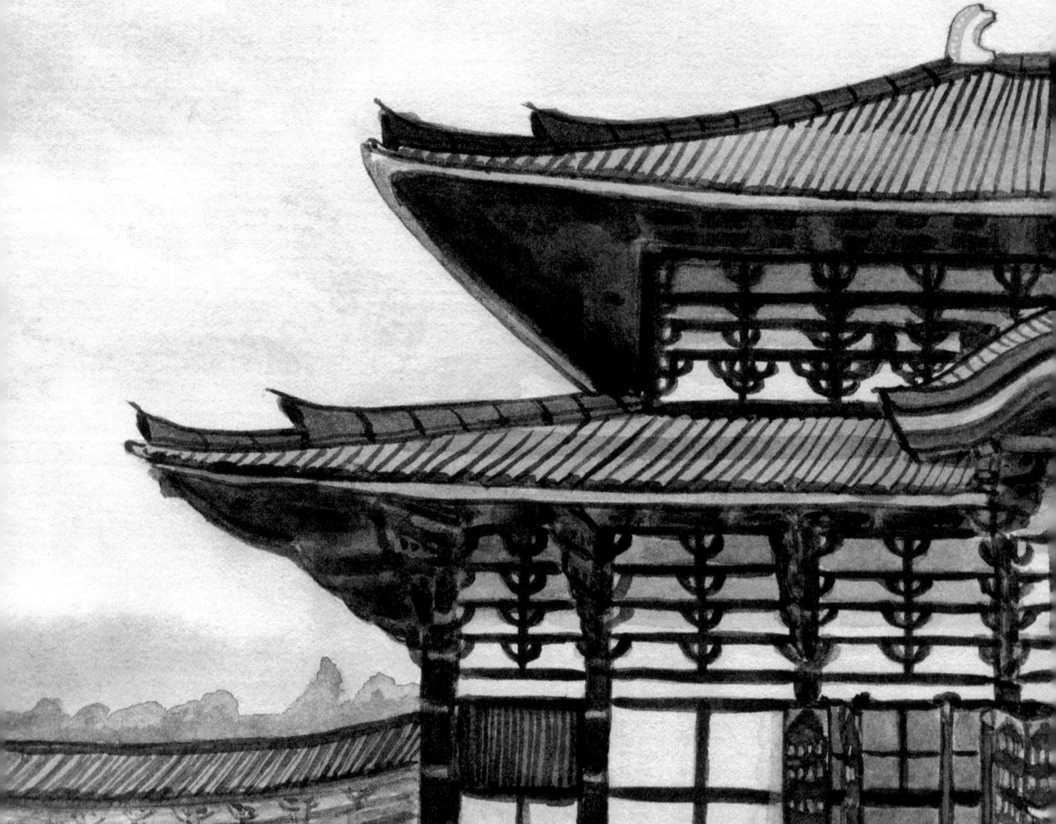

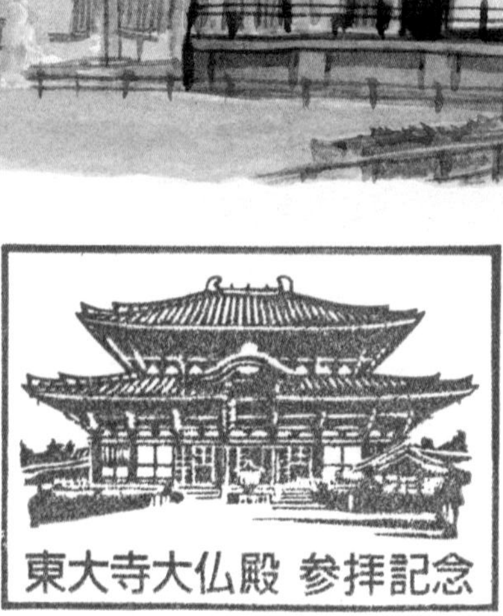
東大寺大仏殿 参拝記念

Todai-ji (Great Eastern Temple) was completed in 752. The Daibutsuden (Great Buddha Hall) was the world's largest wooden building until it was surpassed in 1998.

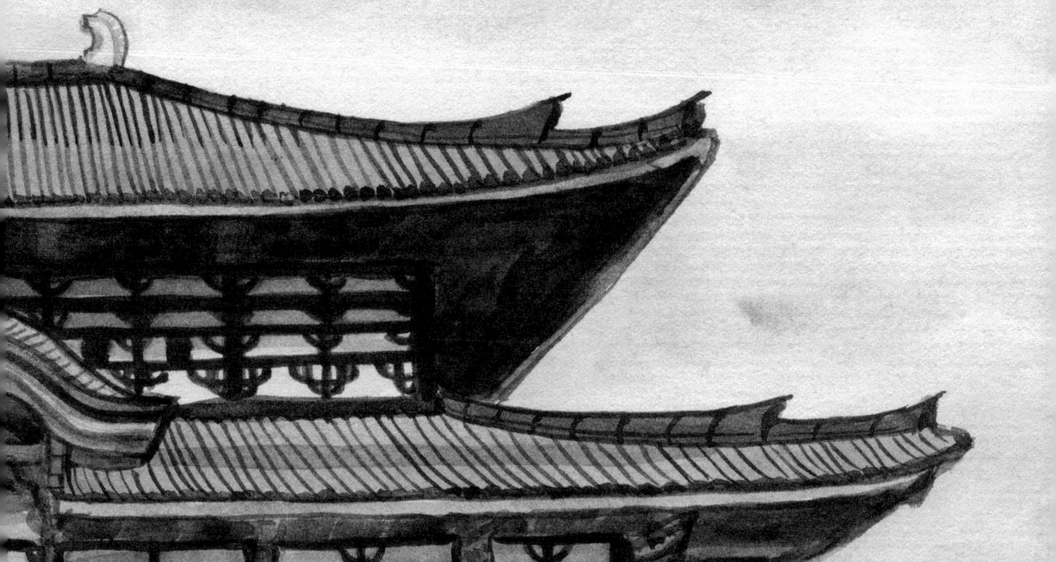

We found another Rekishi Kaido stamp like the ones we spotted in Himeji and Mount Koya. This one had been stamped so many times the image was almost gone.

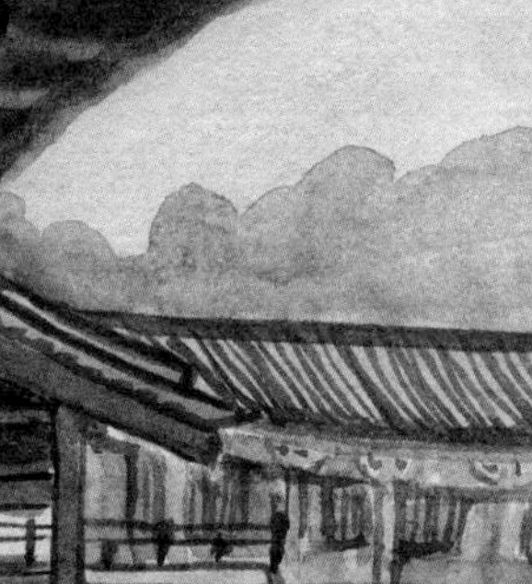
歴史街道
REKISHI KAIDO

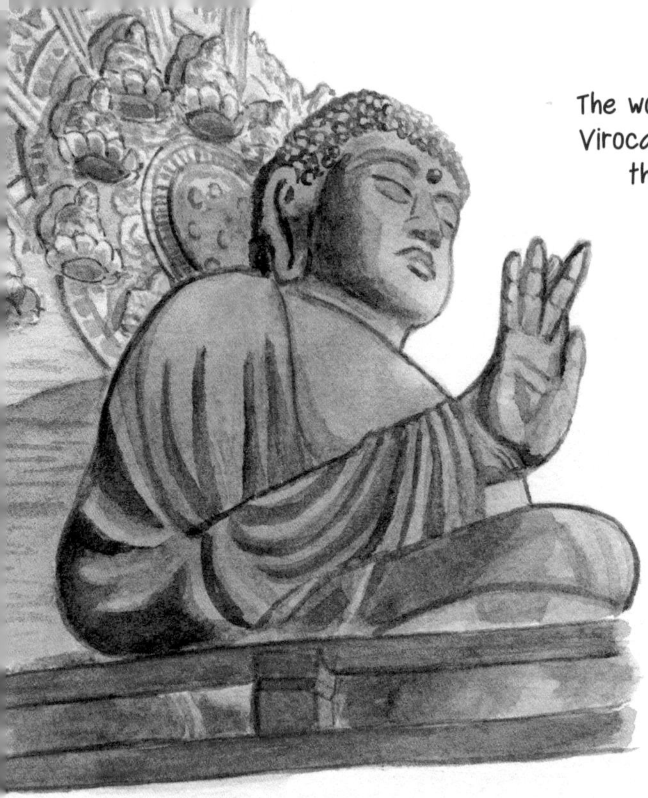

The world's largest bronze Virocana Buddha can be found inside the Daibutsuden at Todai-ji. It was completed in 752 and cost so much to construct that it nearly bankrupted Japan.

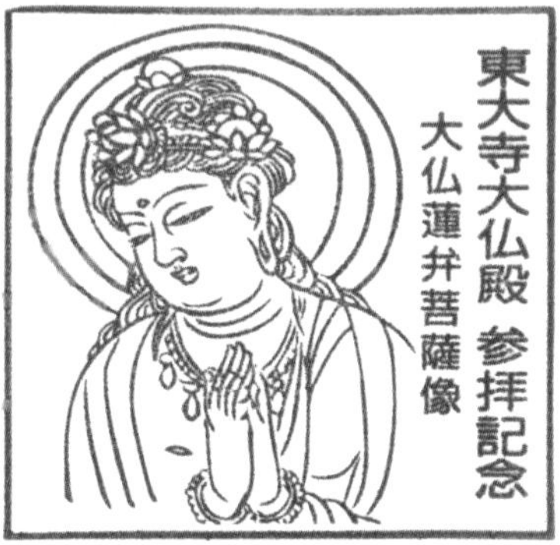
東大寺大仏殿 参拝記念
大仏蓮弁菩薩像

Inside the temple, there's a wooden pillar with a hole the size of the big Buddha's nostril. If you can squeeze through, it is said you will gain enlightenment in the next life.

## Tips to Fit through the Nostril of Buddha

1. Enter with both arms up.

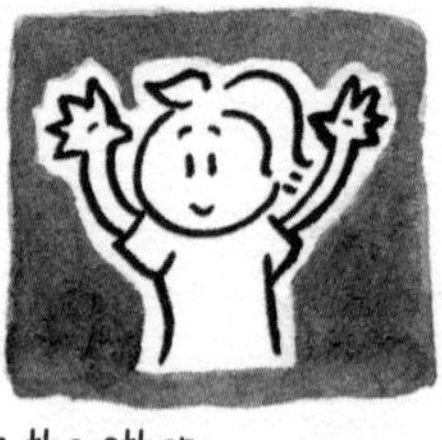

2. Go in sideways. The hole is taller than it is wide.

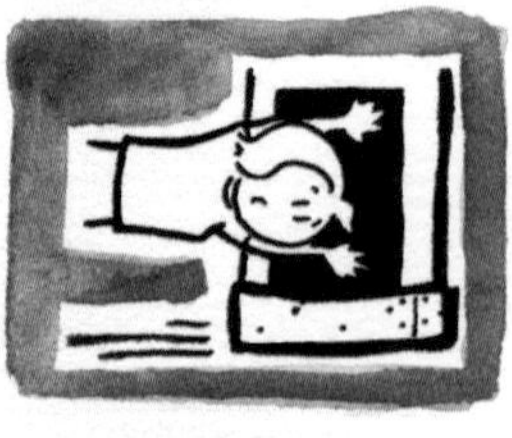

3. Have someone on the other side pull you through.

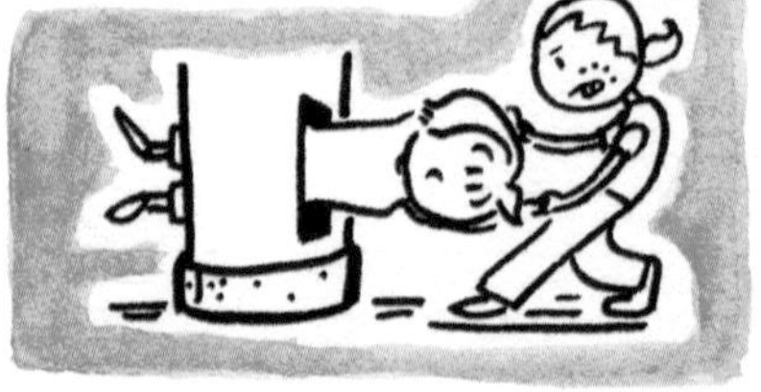

4. Success! Enlightenment will be yours.

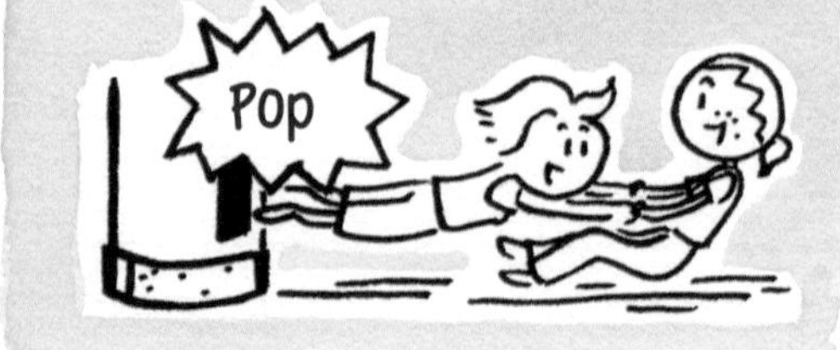
Pop

By the temple exit was a place you could buy a goshuin (temple seal). Each one is hand drawn by a calligrapher before being stamped with red ink.

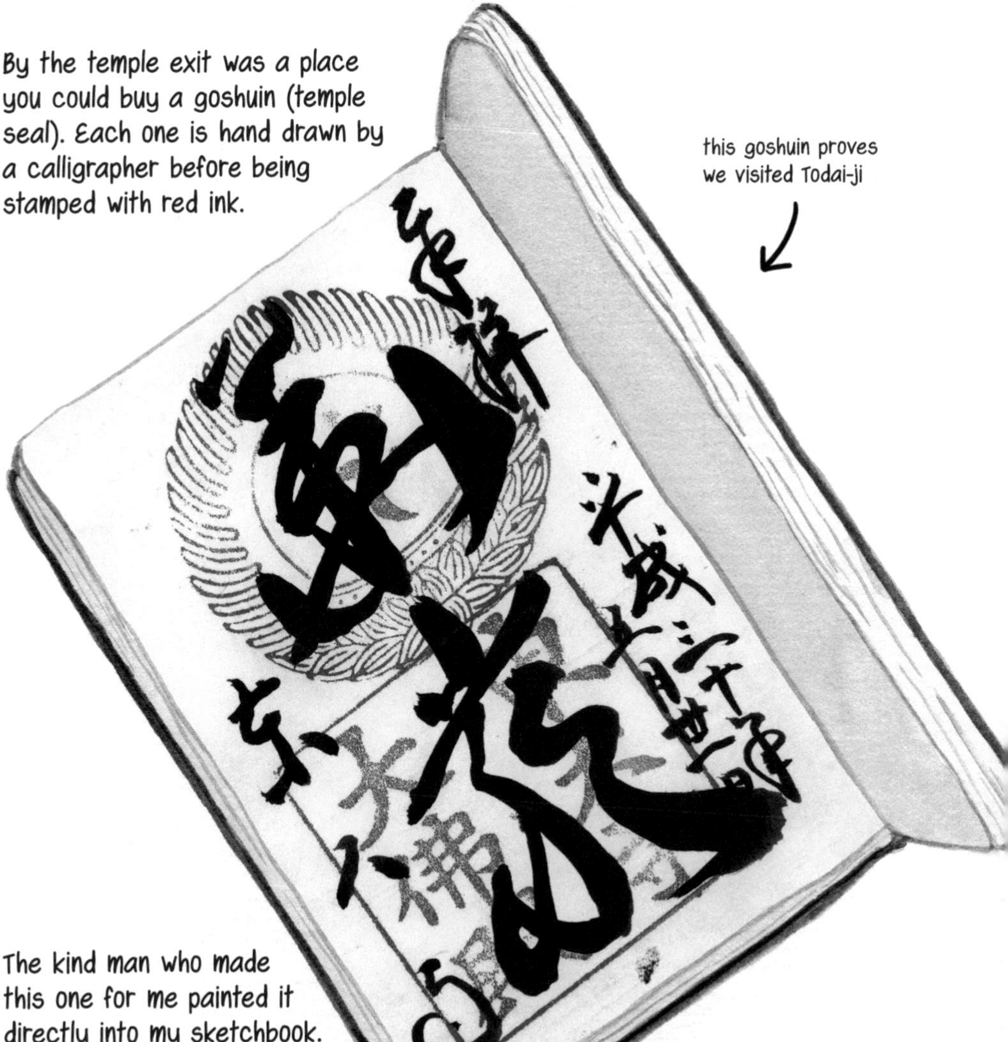
this goshuin proves we visited Todai-ji

The kind man who made this one for me painted it directly into my sketchbook.

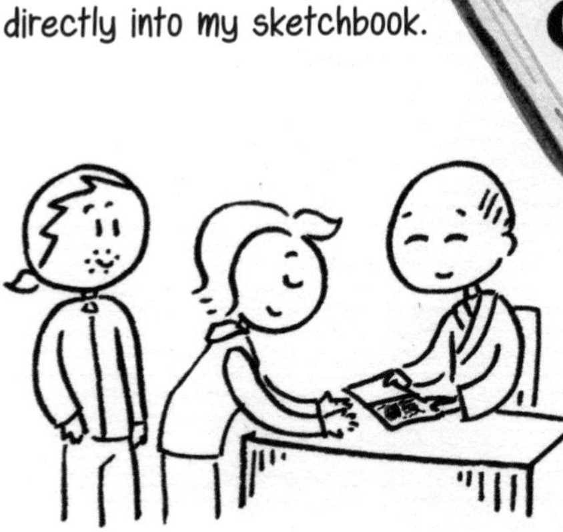

I later learned he had made an exception for me. Most temples are strict about only placing a goshuin in a goshunicho (book of seals). Many, but not all, temples and shrines offer goshunicho for sale.

We had a little more time before we had to leave Nara. I decided to have another attempt at getting the deer to bow to me. This time I studied other tourists to figure out a new strategy.

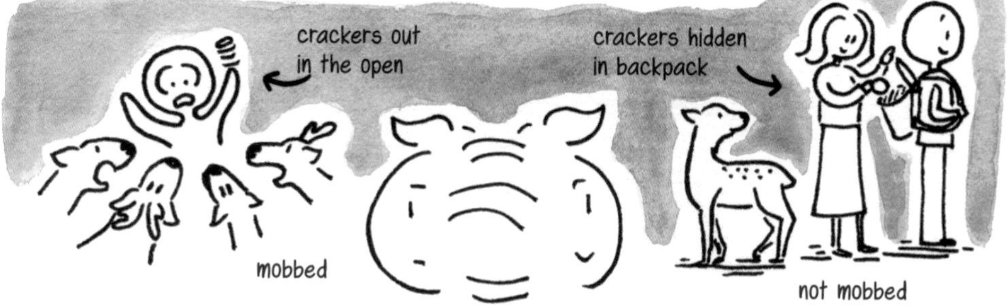
crackers out in the open
crackers hidden in backpack
mobbed
not mobbed

## Tips for Getting the Deer at Nara to Bow for Crackers

1. Hide the crackers as soon as you buy them. The deer swarm when they see the stack of crackers. They want you to drop them all.

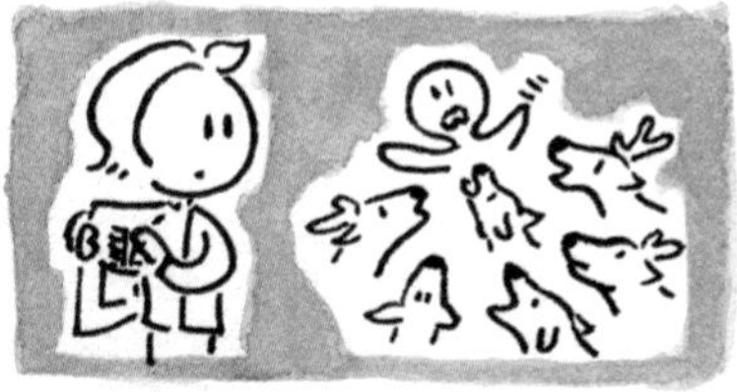

2. Find a deer by itself. Once a cracker is out, any deer in the area who sees it will come over.

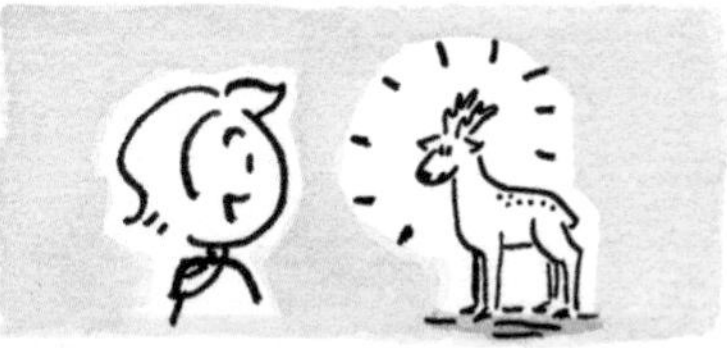

3. With cracker in hand, bow to the deer. If it bows back, give it a large piece of the cracker. Too small a piece makes them less willing to bow.

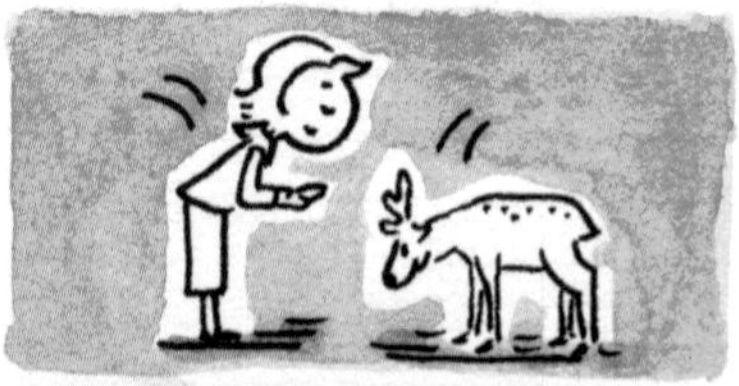

4. Not all the deer bow deeply. The big ones with horns bow the best.

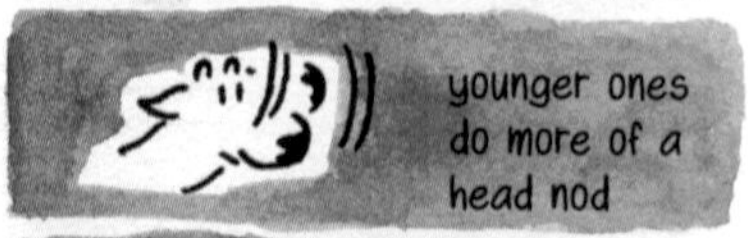
younger ones do more of a head nod

5. If the deer gets pushy, give it the rest of the cracker and leave. You may have to show it your empty hands to end the encounter.

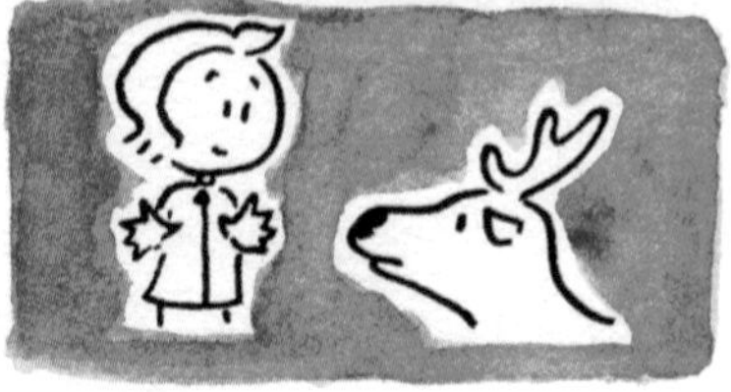

I became so successful getting deer to bow for me that people stopped to take pictures!

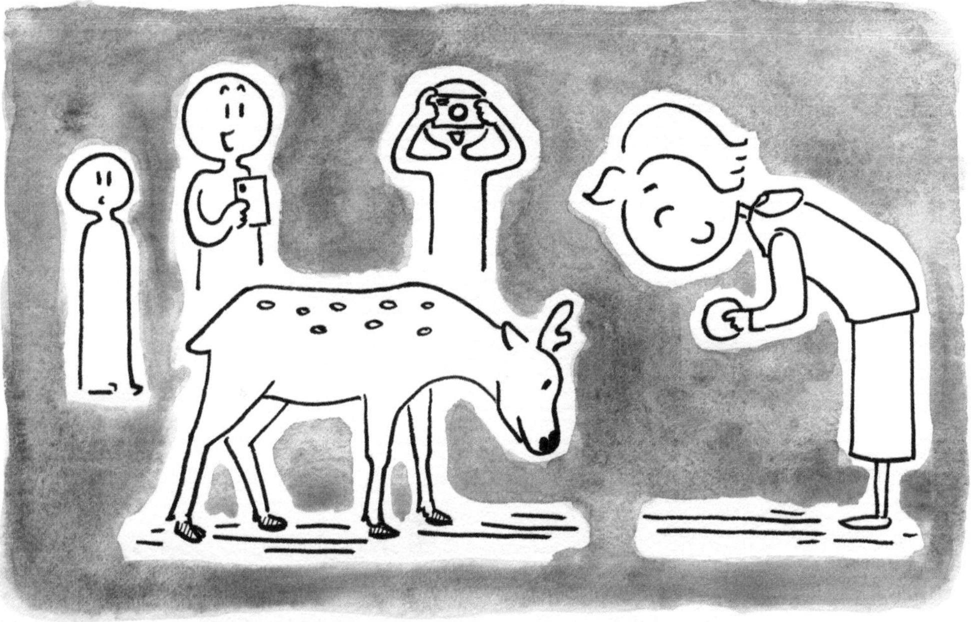

It was getting late so we took the bus back to Nara Station. It was dusk by the time we made it to our final destination of the day: Kyoto.

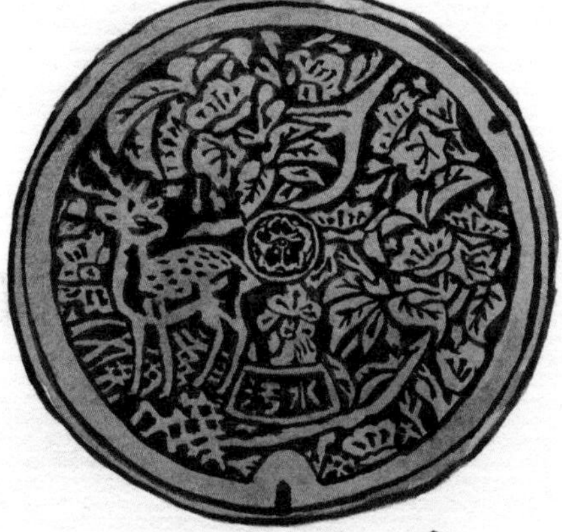

manhole cover while walking to the bus in Nara

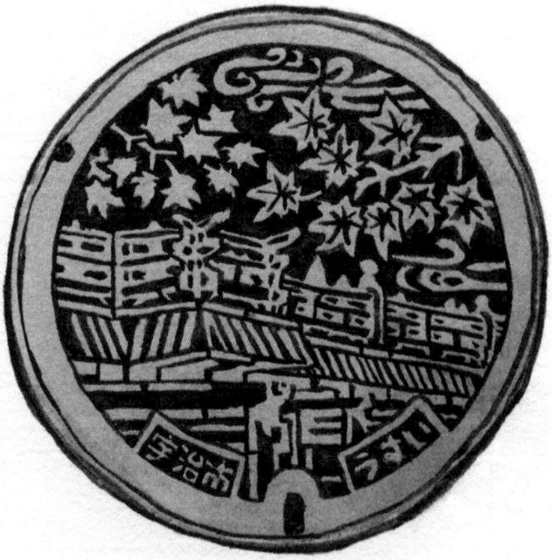

Kyoto manhole cover seen after exiting the train station

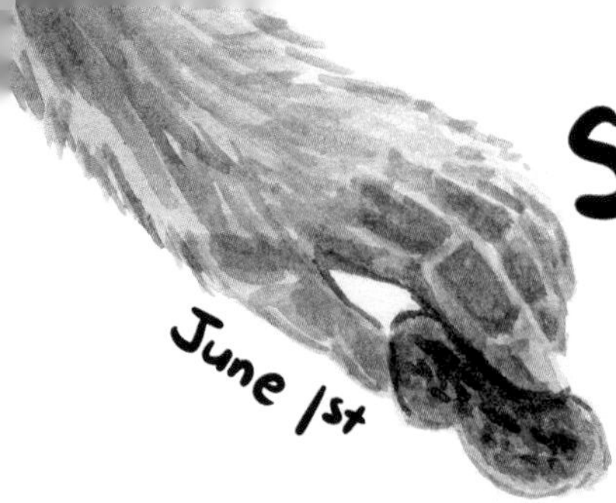

# Seeing the Sights in Kyoto

June 1st

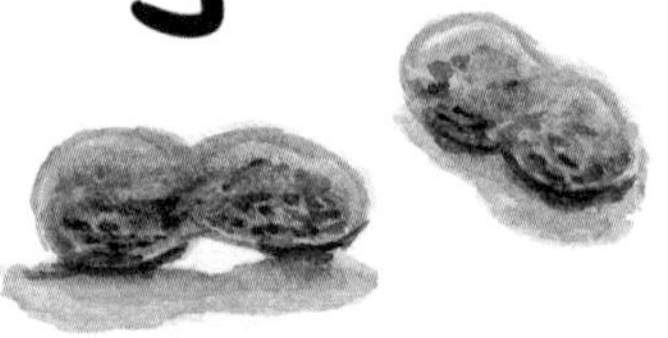

We had a lazy morning in Kyoto before going to Arashiyama Bamboo Forest. Lots of other people had the same idea as us.

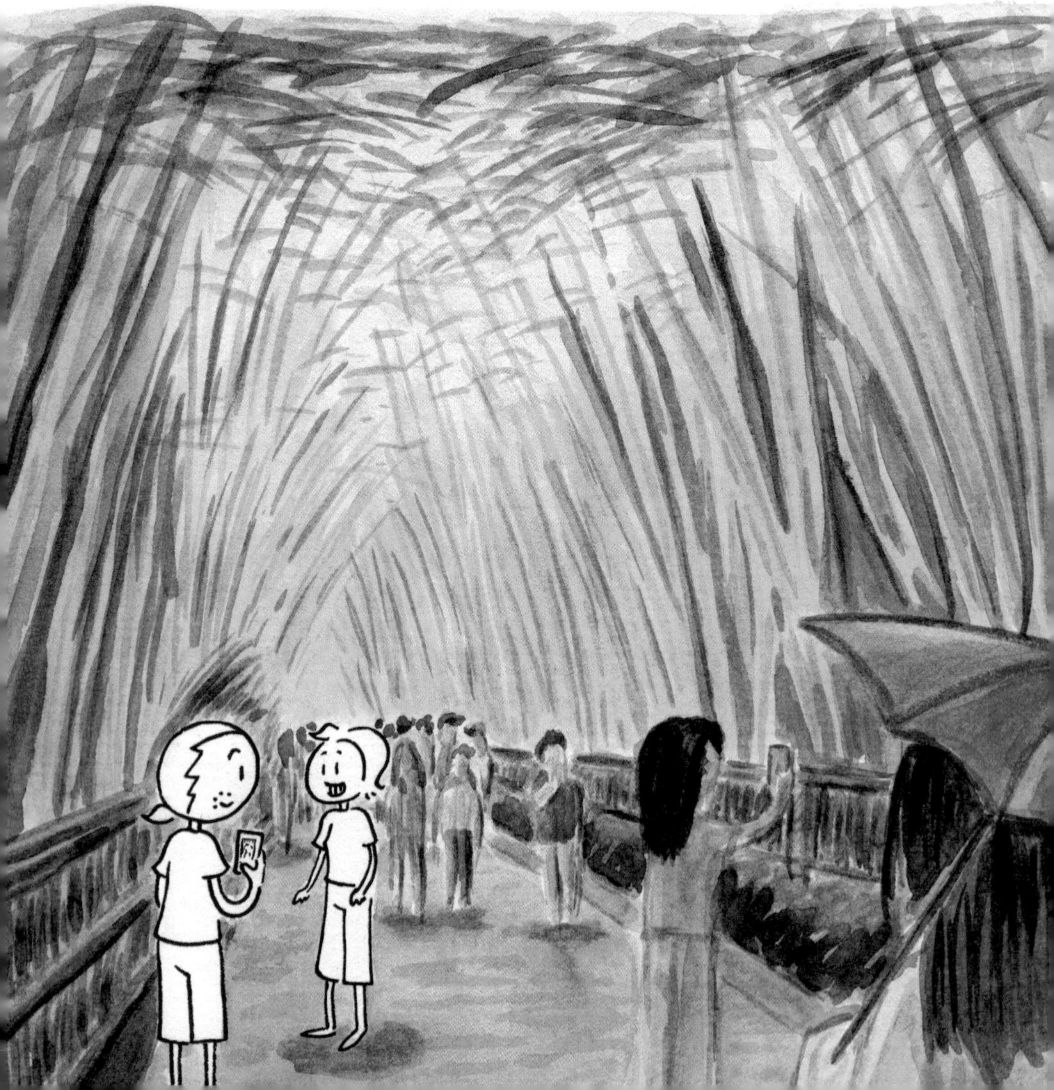

After walking through the bamboo forest we made our way to Saruyama (monkey mountain) to see the monkeys. You can go inside a cage to feed them.

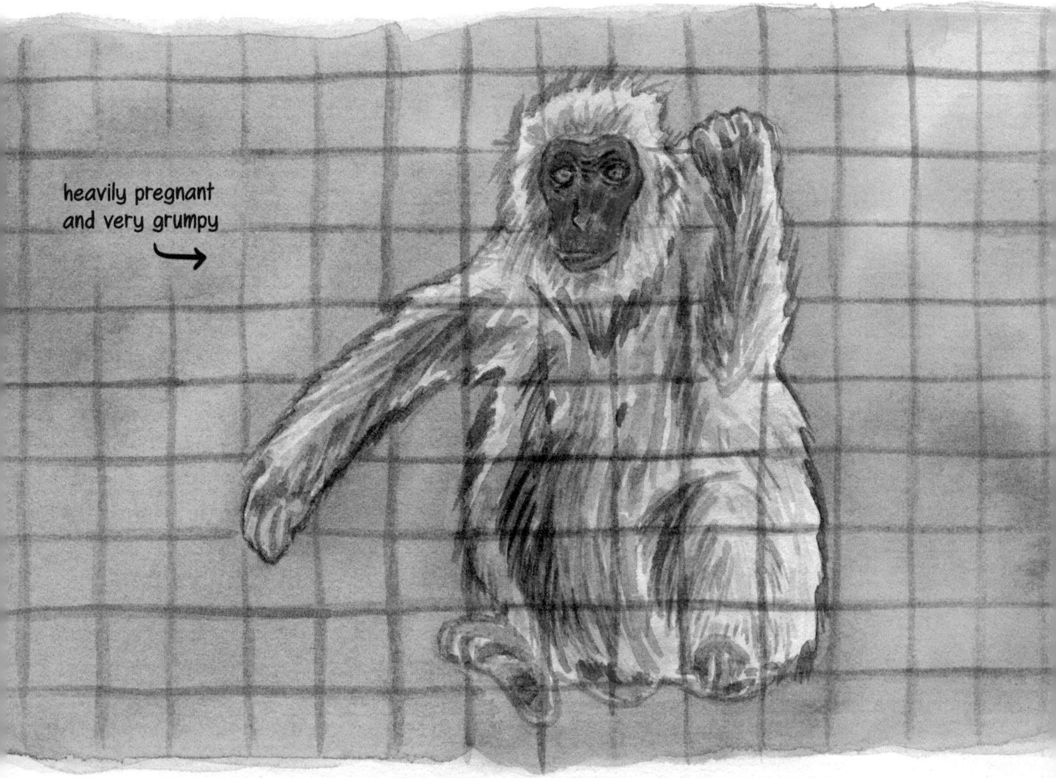
heavily pregnant
and very grumpy

Connor helped me by feeding one of the monkeys while I painted her.

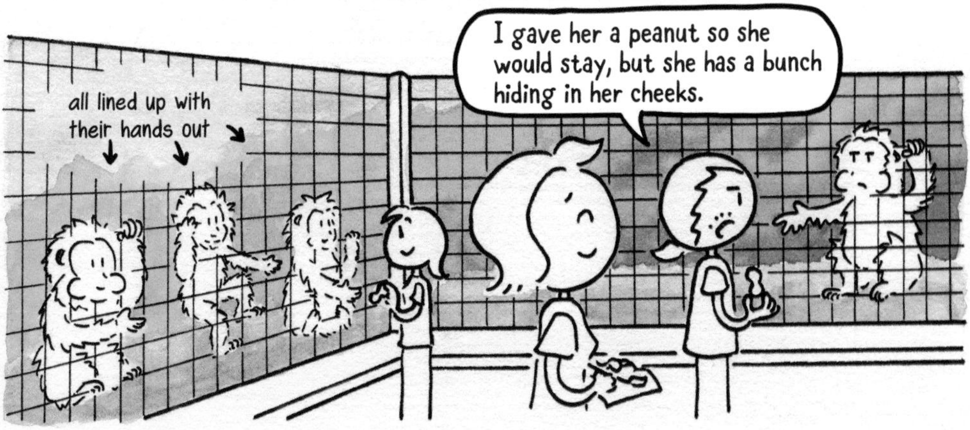
all lined up with
their hands out
I gave her a peanut so she would stay, but she has a bunch hiding in her cheeks.

I was excited to see that several of the monkeys had babies.

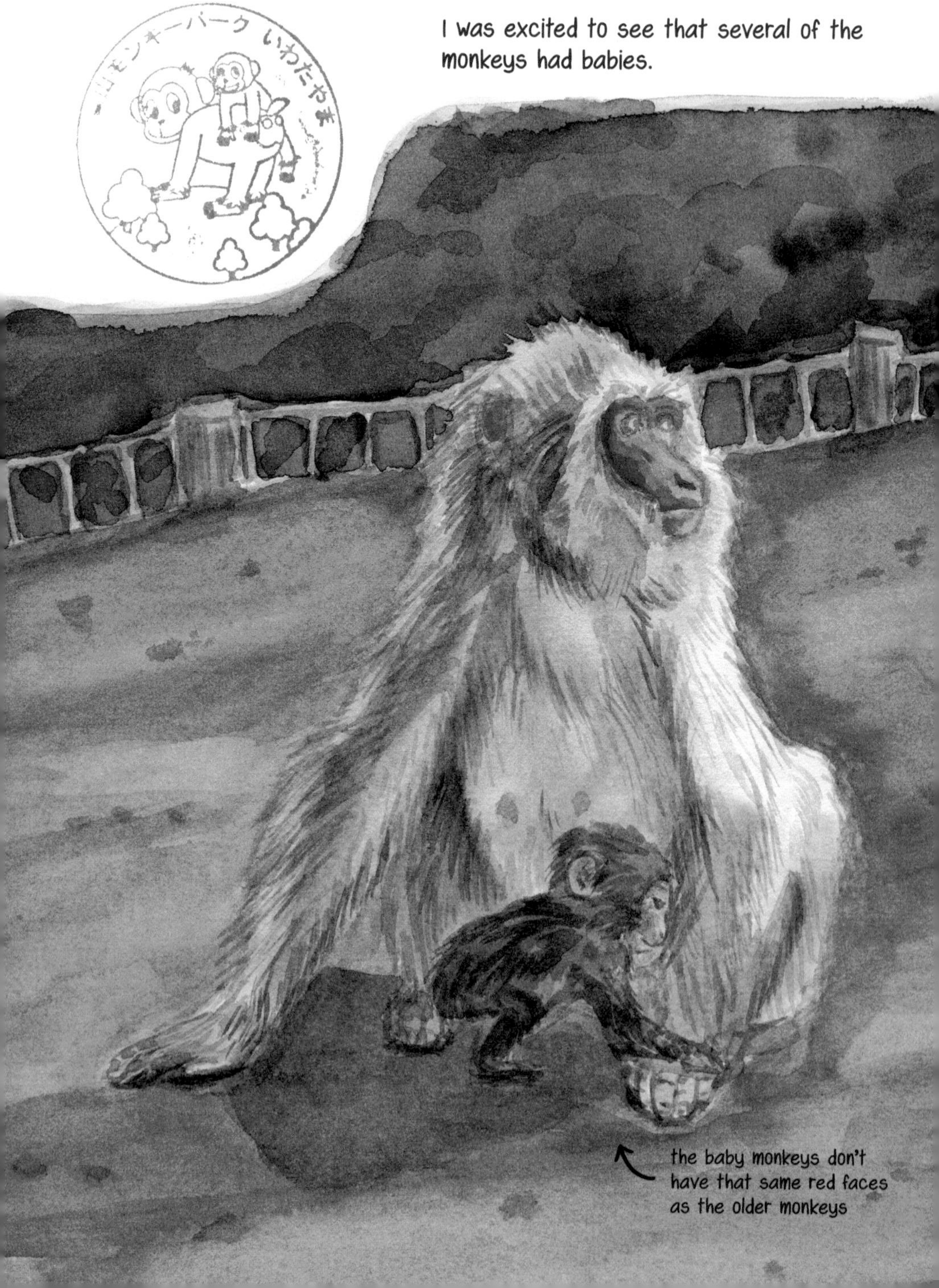
モンキーパーク いわたやま

the baby monkeys don't have that same red faces as the older monkeys

We said goodbye to the monkeys and hiked back down the mountain. After getting some shumai (dumplings), we waited for the bus so we could visit Kinkaku-ji (Golden Pavilion).

← very hungry

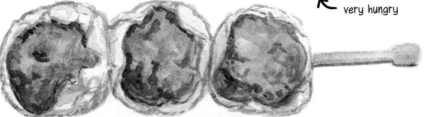

In Japan, the buses aren't nearly as efficient as the trains. Realizing that we wouldn't make it to Kinkaku-ji before closing, we opted to take a taxi instead.

Fushimi Inari. #1 place!

Hai! (Yes!) We're going ashita (tomorrow).

Our taxi driver was quiet until Connor spoke some Japanese.

When we reached the temple, our driver dropped us off by the gate and wished us well.

Kinkaku-ji was originally the retirement villa of the third Ashikaga Shogun, Yoshimitsu. After his death it was converted into a Rinzai Zen Buddhist temple. Although the estate was originally known as Rokuon-ji, today it's more popularly referred to as Kinkaku-ji (kin means gold) for the gold leaf-covered building on the grounds.

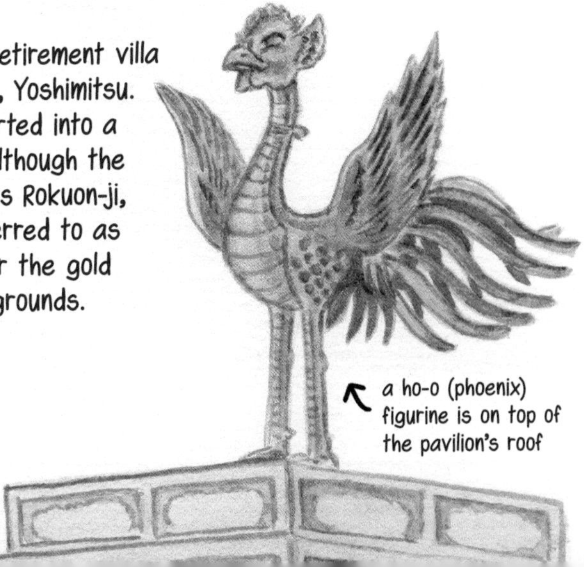

← a ho-o (phoenix) figurine is on top of the pavilion's roof

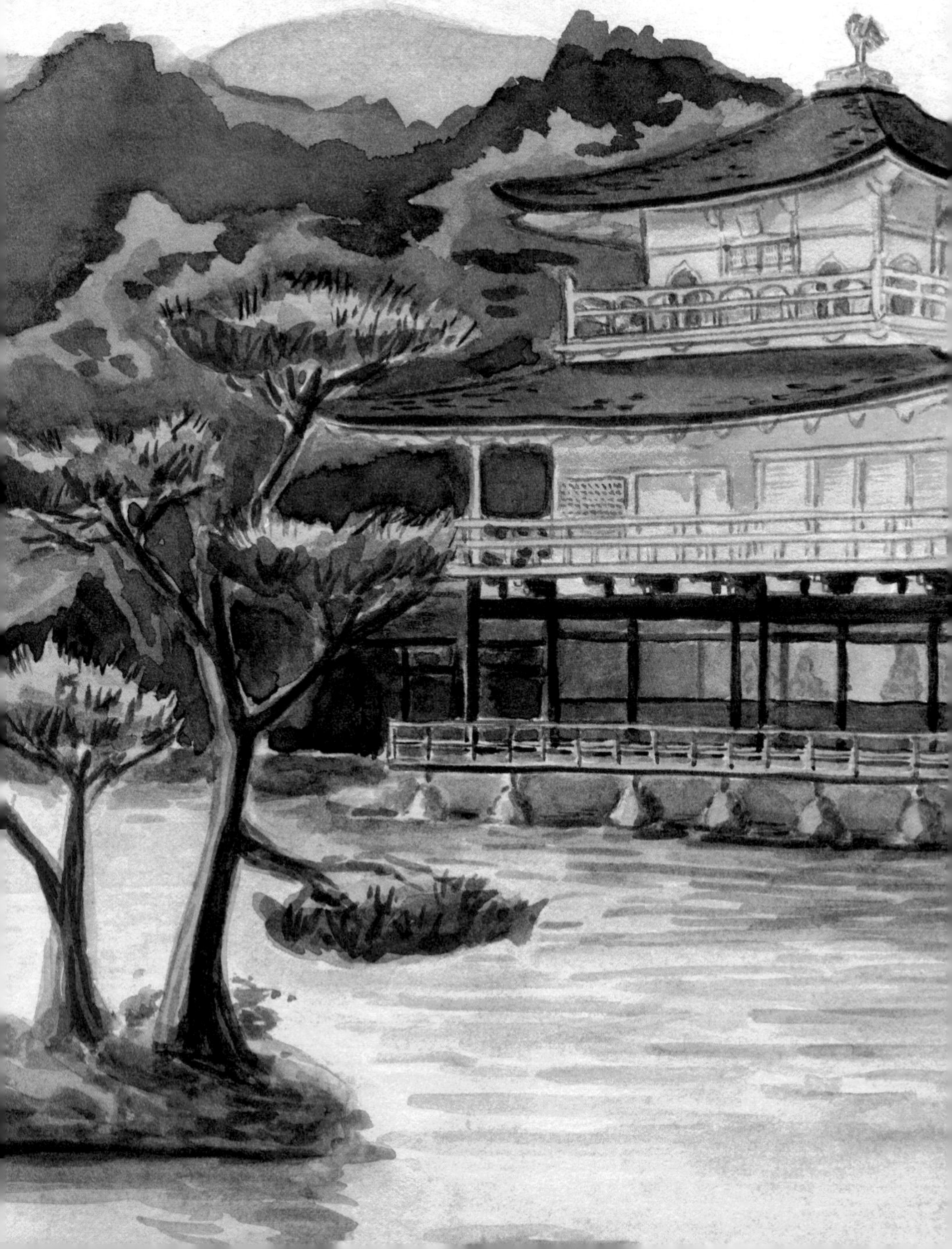

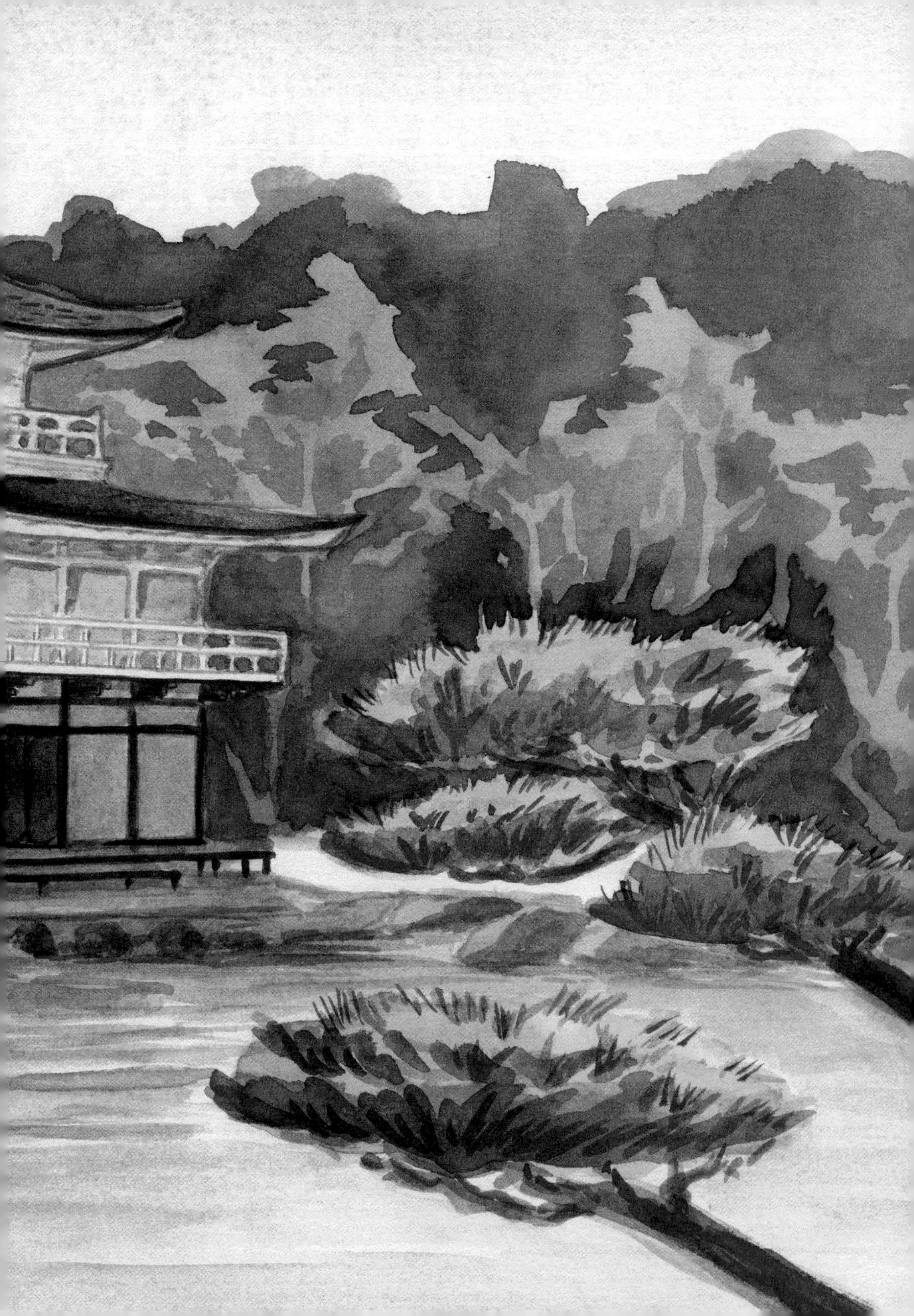

We walked around Kinkaku-ji until a bell was rung, letting us know it was closing time. On our way to catch a bus, we saw a bottle of Pocari Sweat in a drinks vending machine.

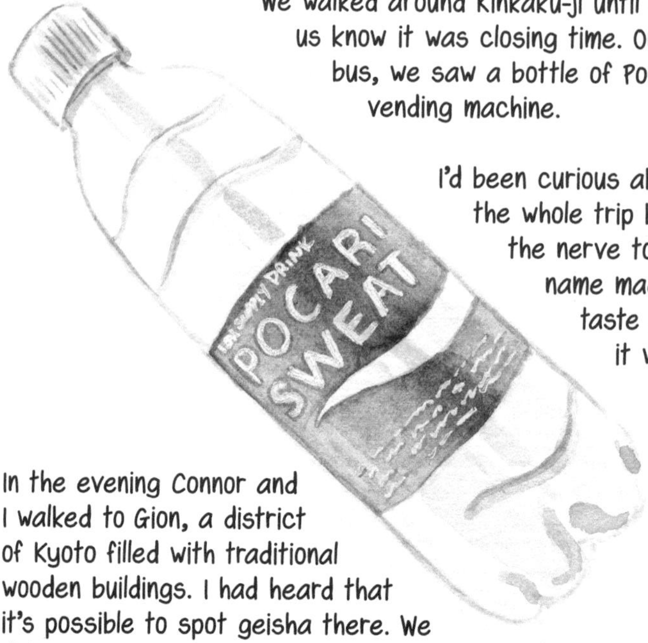
POCARI
SWEAT

I'd been curious about Pocari Sweat for the whole trip but hadn't worked up the nerve to try it until now. The name made me think it would taste salty like sweat, but it was sweet like a sports drink.

In the evening Connor and I walked to Gion, a district of Kyoto filled with traditional wooden buildings. I had heard that it's possible to spot geisha there. We didn't manage to see any, but we did see fireflies along Shirakawa Canal. While we strolled along the streets we treated ourselves to dango, a sweet rice-flour treat on a stick

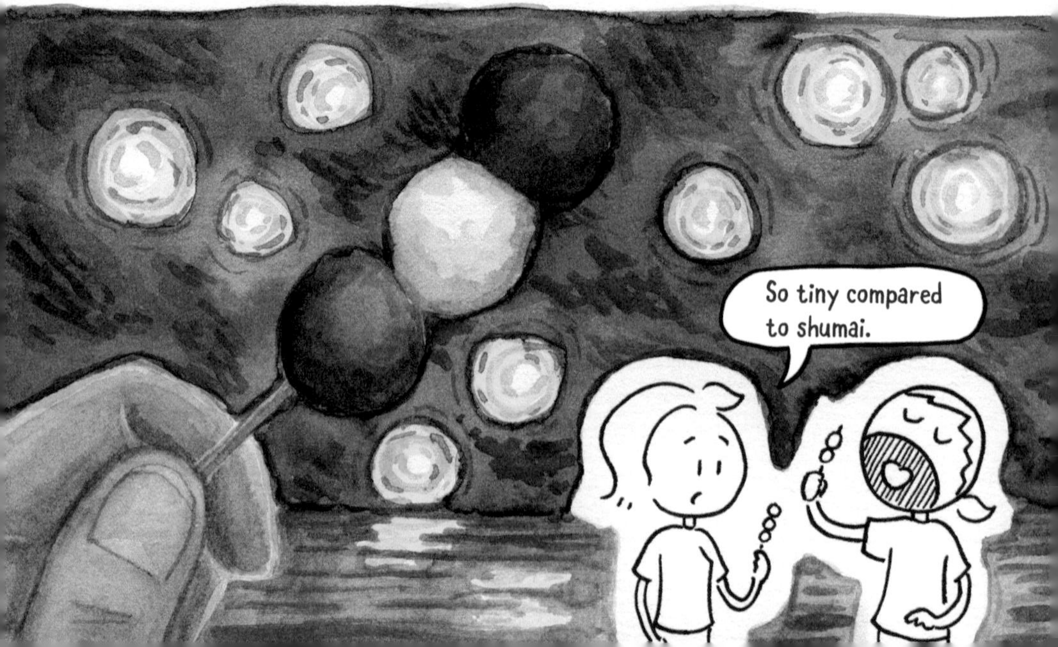
So tiny compared to shumai.

# Kyoto
## Shrines and Temples
### June 2nd

We started our day by taking the train to the main shrine in Japan for the Shinto rice god Inari: Fushimi Inari. Thousands of torii gates cover the mountain.

Crowds were thick while walking through the Senbon Torii (one thousand torii gates).

I had read that it was less crowded higher up the mountain, so we opted to hike the full loop around Mount Inari.

During our hike we saw many different sized torii gates. The biggest ones straddled the trail while smaller ones were placed off to the side. Part way through the walk we saw a curious sign.

| 5 | 175,000 |
| 6 | 383,000 |
| 7 | 482,000 |
| 8 | 708,000 |
| 9 | 826,000 |
| 10 | 1,302,000 |

What do you think all those numbers mean?

I think the small number is the height of the gate and the big number is how much you have to donate to install the gate.

91

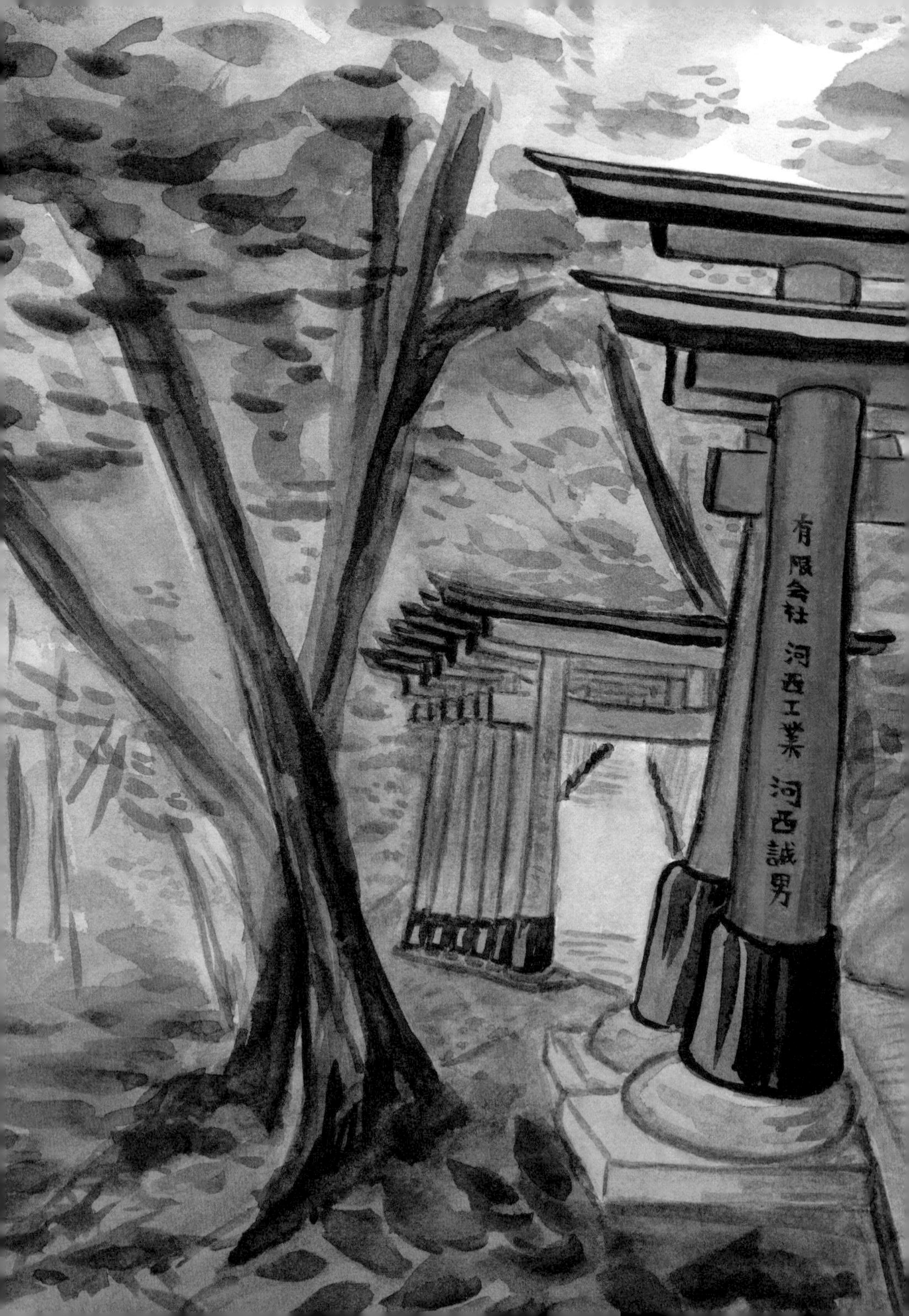
有限会社 河西工業 河西誠男

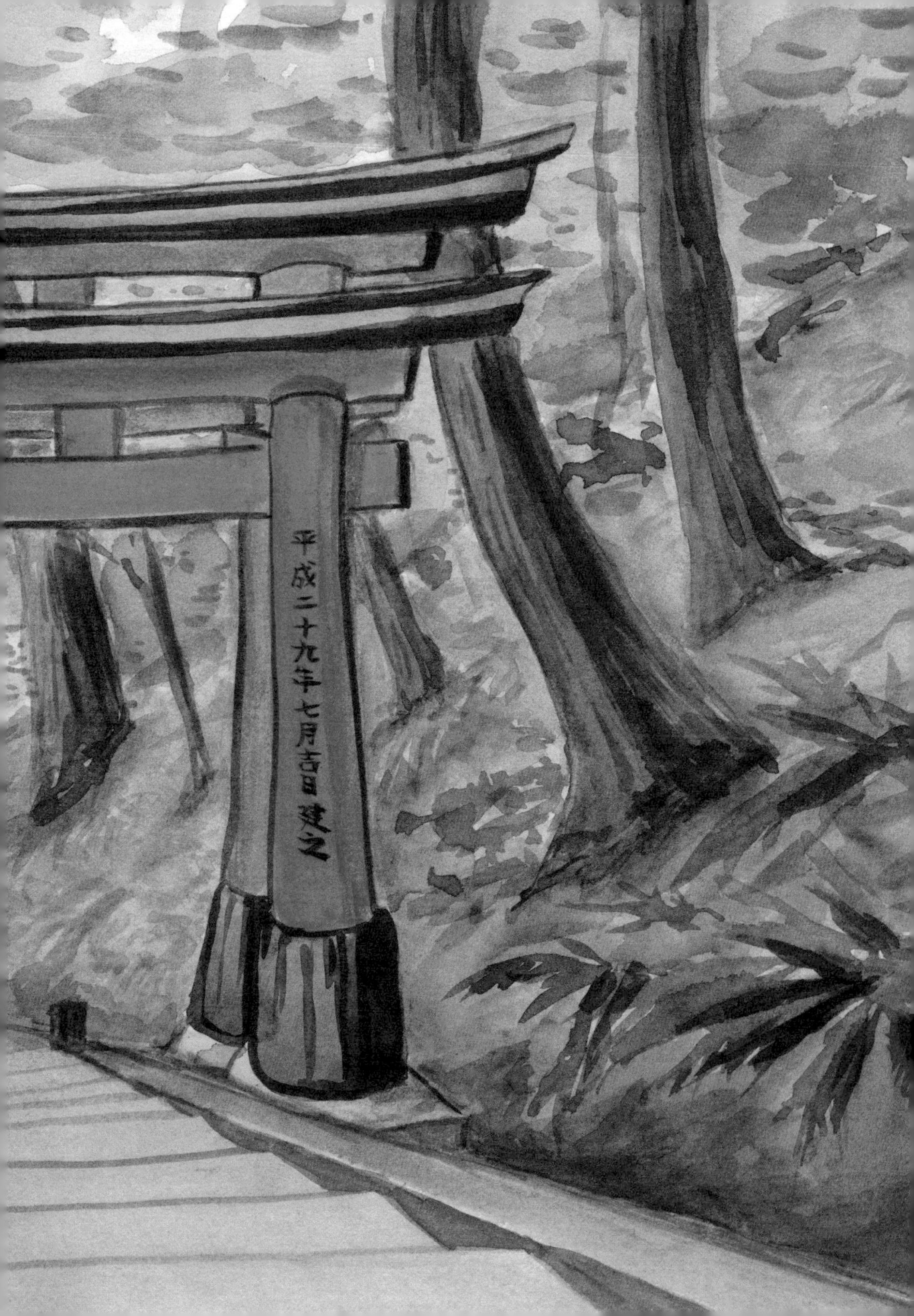
平成二十九年七月吉日建之

In addition to the torii gates there were many statues of the kitsune (fox), messengers of the rice god, Inari. Frequently we saw the statues appear as a pair on either side of the path.

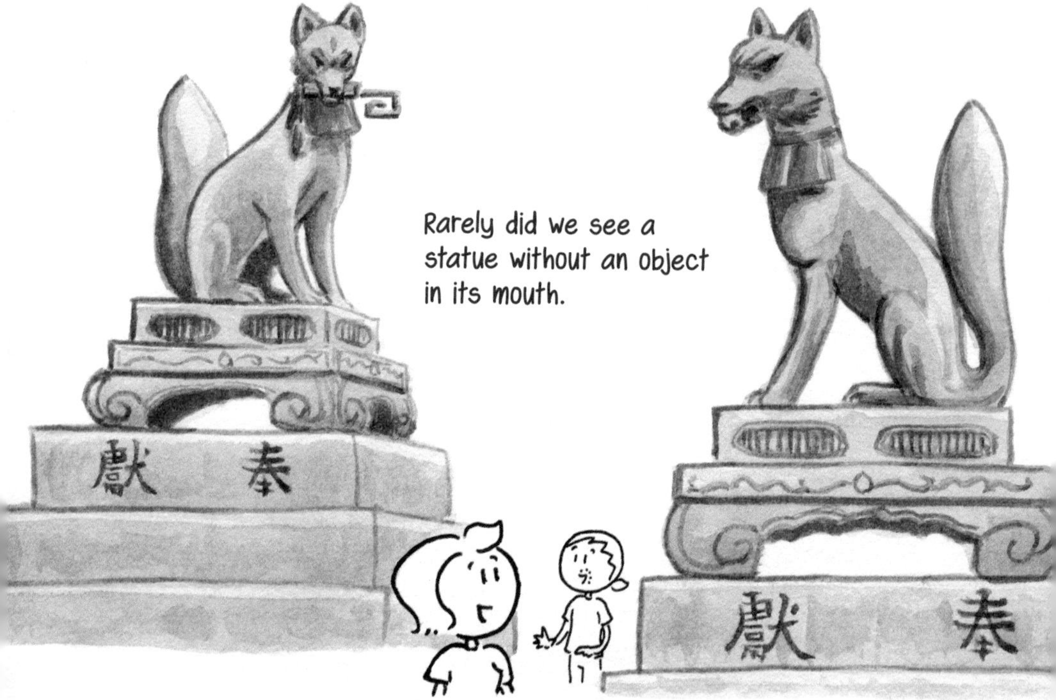
Rarely did we see a statue without an object in its mouth.
奉獻
奉獻

Common symbols seen in the mouths of the kitsune statues:

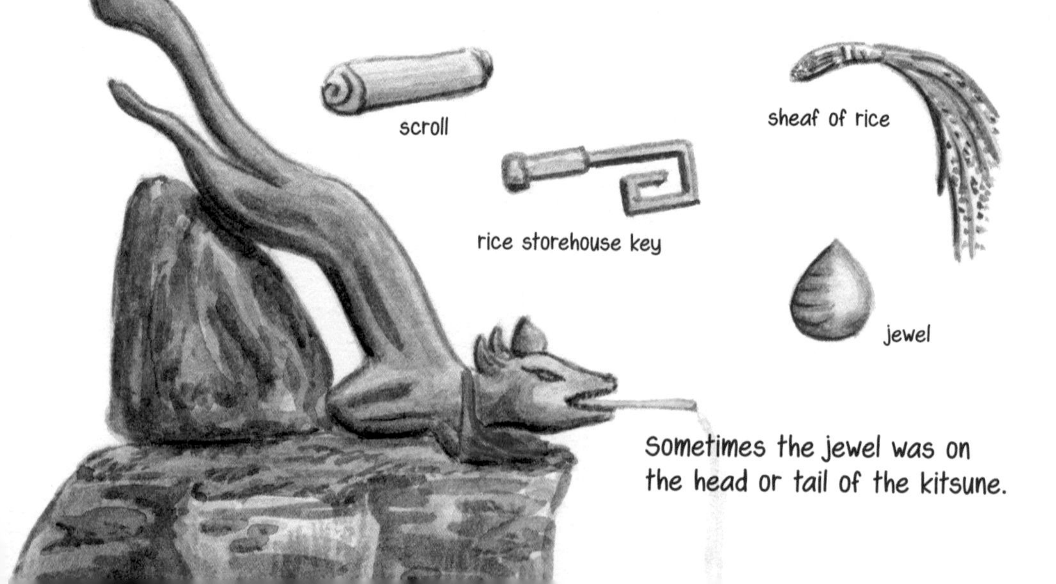
scroll
sheaf of rice
rice storehouse key
jewel
Sometimes the jewel was on the head or tail of the kitsune.

From Fushimi Inari we took a long walk to Sannenzaka, a famous slope covered with historical buildings. We were famished once we reached our destination, so we ducked into the first teahouse we saw.

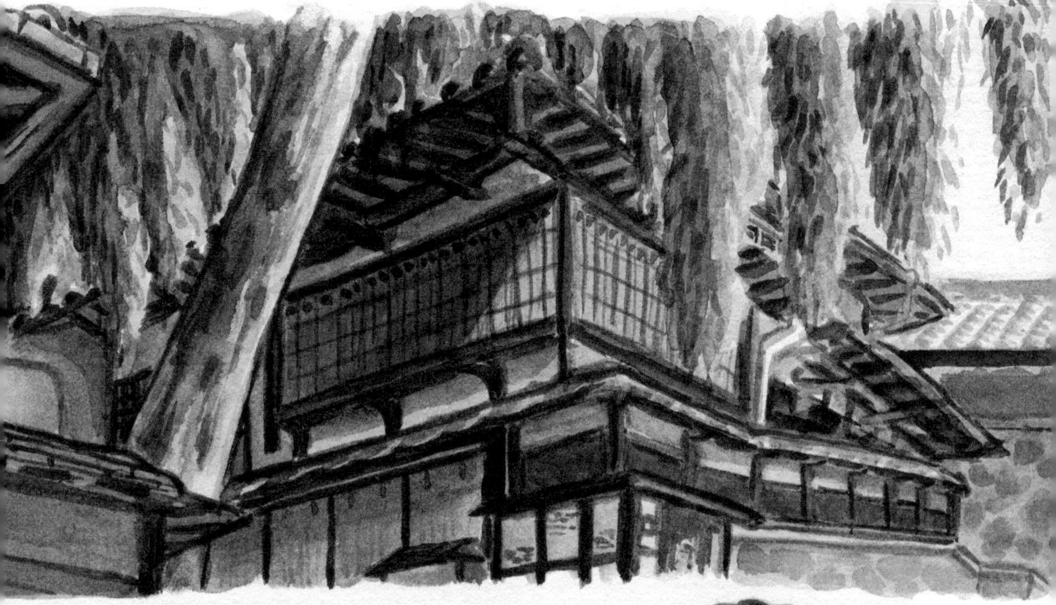

When we left we noticed a sign out front.

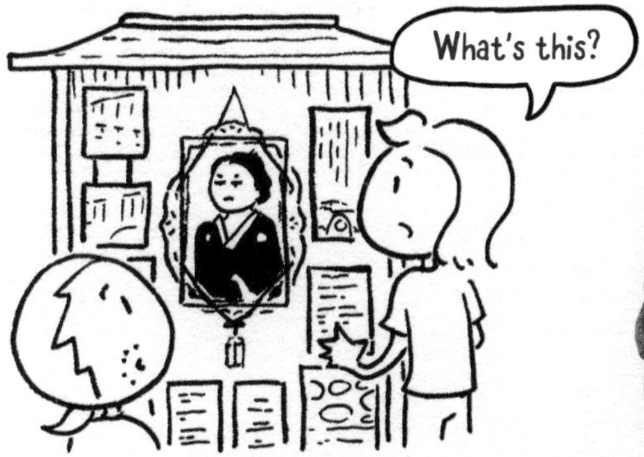
What's this?

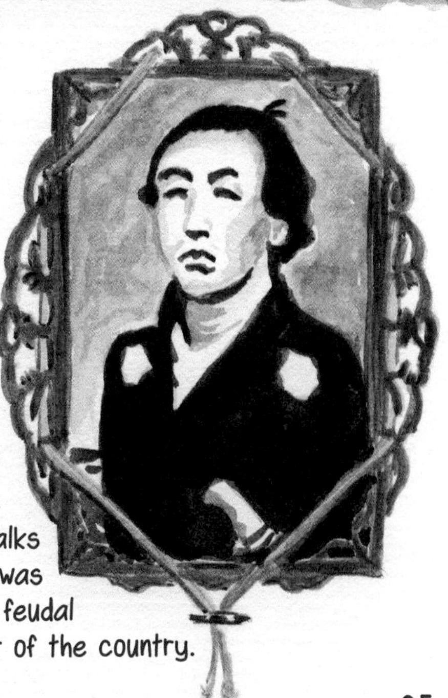

It turns out that we ate at Akebono-tei, or the Rising Sun Inn. It was here that Ryoma Sakamoto, a famous samurai, had secret talks about overthrowing the Edo shogunate. He was key in the Meiji Restoration, which removed feudal lords and reinstalled the emperor as leader of the country.

We walked to Ninenzaka, another famous slope, before heading over to Yasaka Koshindo, a temple for the Koshin faith.

The hear-no-evil, say-no-evil, see-no-evil monkeys are the most widely known Koshin symbols.

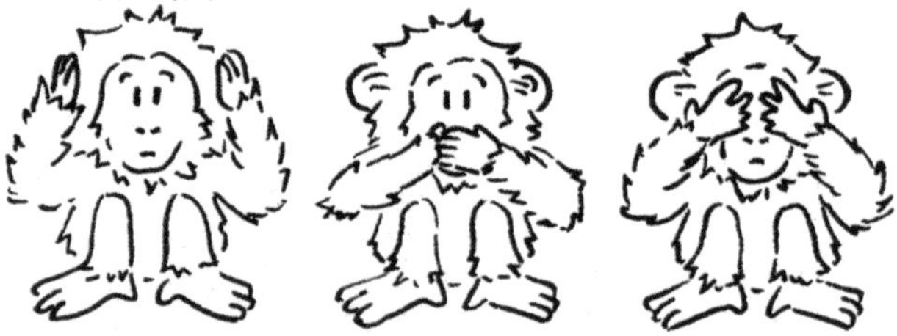

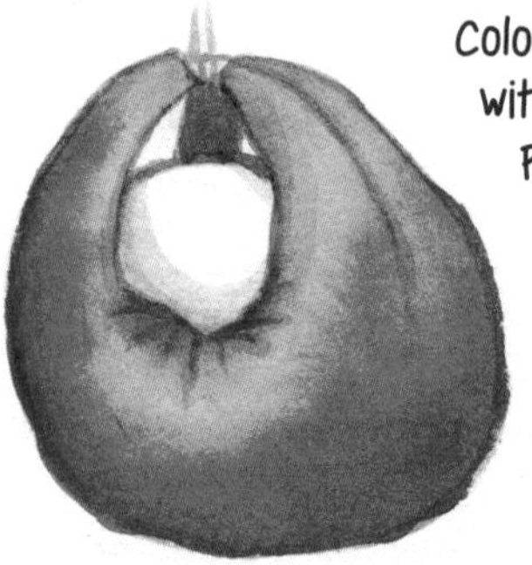

Colorful Kukurizaru (cloth representations of a monkey with its feet bound) are hung all over the temple. People buy them and write their wishes on them before they hang them up. Supposedly, in order to get your wish, you have to give up a desire because desires are what prevent dreams from coming true.

While we were there we saw a lot of people in yukata (a casual summer kimono) around the temple. Renting and wearing a yukata seemed to be a popular thing to do in this part of town.

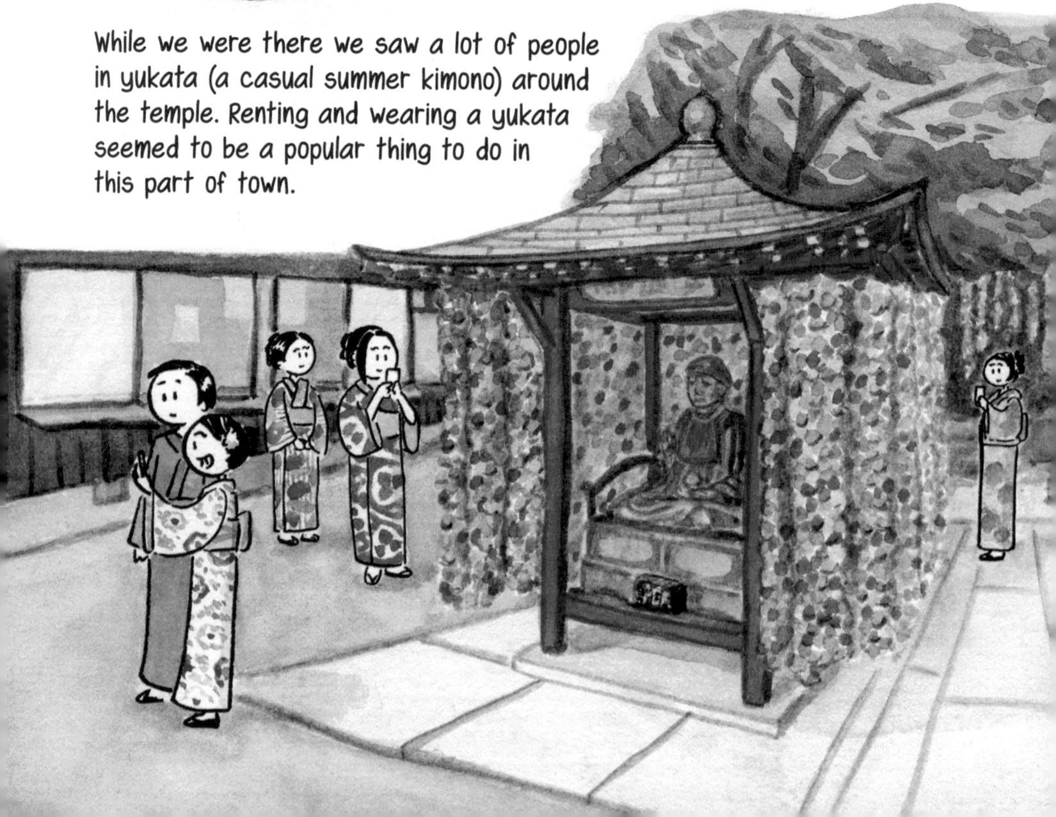

From Yasaka Koshindo we strolled over to Maiko Antiques, which was full of interesting bits of Japanese history.

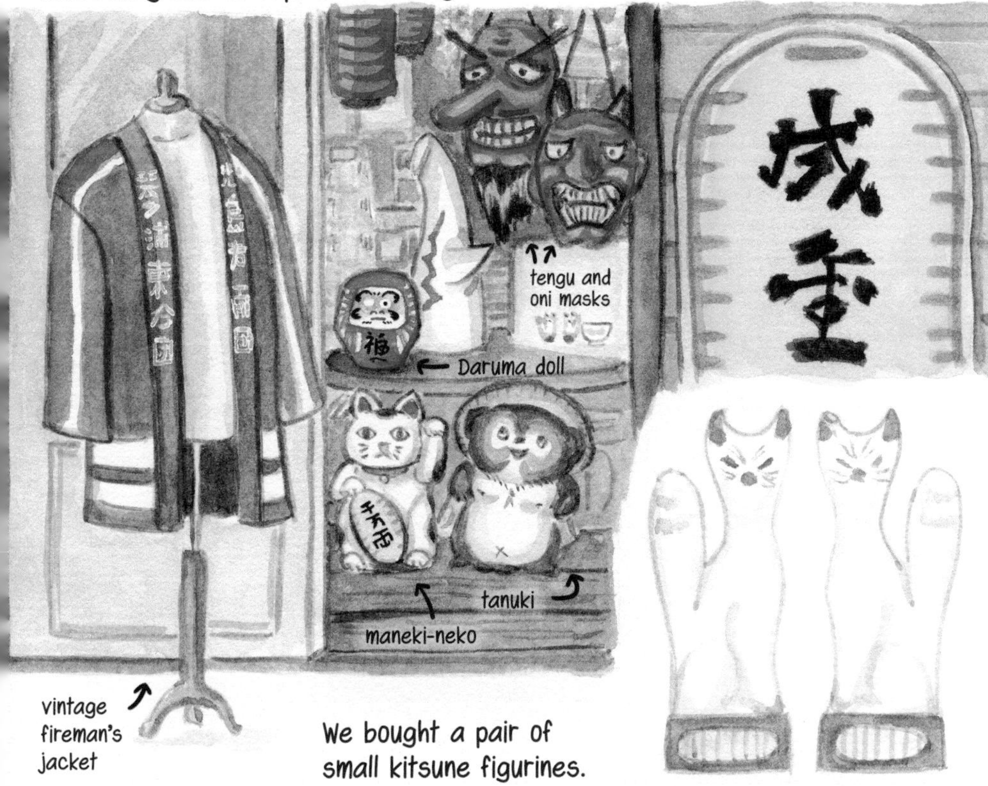

tengu and oni masks
Daruma doll
tanuki
maneki-neko
vintage fireman's jacket


We bought a pair of small kitsune figurines.

On the way back to our lodging I was pleased to spot a familiar piece of art—a pumpkin sculpture by Yayoi Kusama in front of the Forever Museum of Contemporary Art.

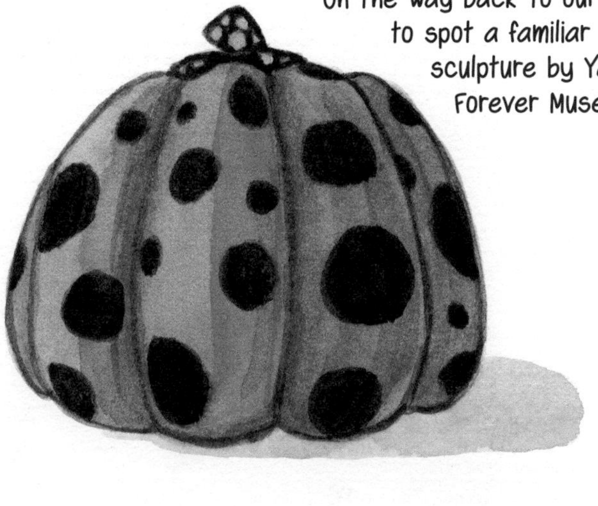

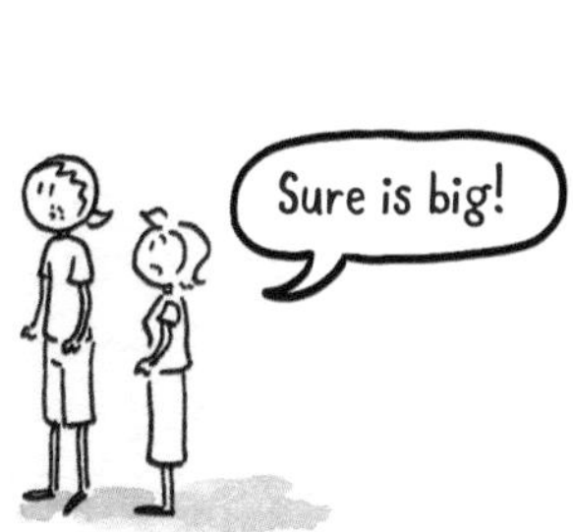

Sure is big!

The path by the pumpkin sculpture was filled with people wearing yukata. Suddenly we were stopped by an older man who pointed down an alley and exclaimed . . .

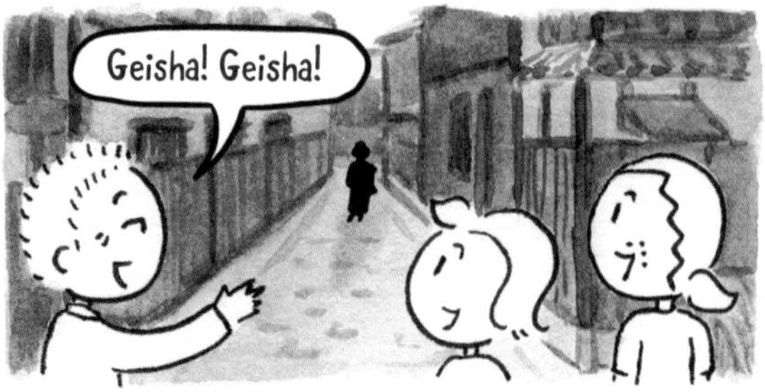
Geisha! Geisha!

And there she was. She disappeared moments later. With so many people wearing yukata, it seemed like the three of us were the only ones who realized a real geisha had just gone by.

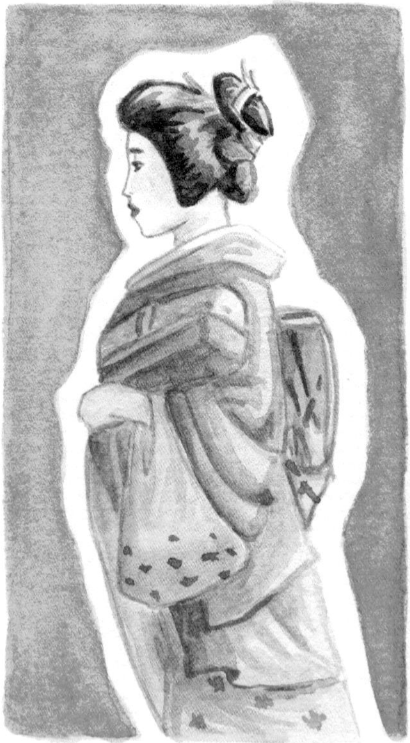

I had heard that geisha are more likely to be seen walking down the narrow alleys in the older parts of town. We walked down the same alley we'd seen the geisha come from, hoping to spot another one of these beautiful ladies. Luck was on our side. A second geisha quickly went past.

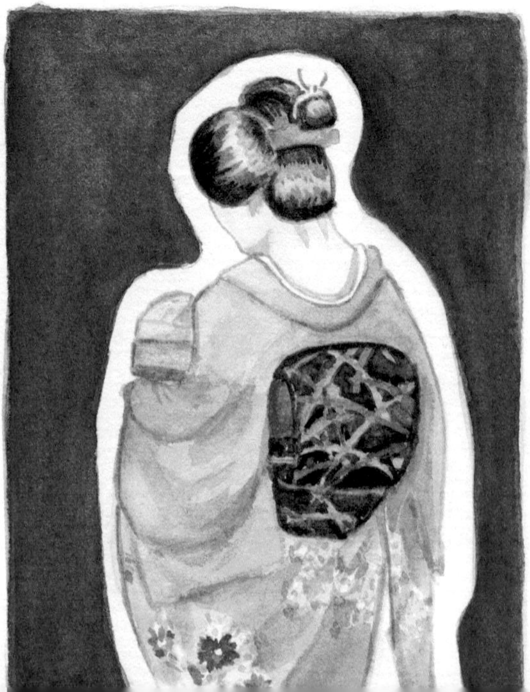

Maiko (geisha-in-training) are a rare sight, but it's even more rare to see a geisha. It's nearly unheard of to see two geisha in one evening.

# Tips to Tell the Difference between
## Geisha and Maiko

simple kanzashi (ornamentation) is styled into a wig

fancy kanzashi (ornamentation) is styled into the wearer's natural hair

collar is lined in pure white

collar is lined with red or a combination of red and white

obi (sash) is tied in a taiko knot which looks like a neat square on the back

obi (sash) is tied in a darari knot which allows the ends to nearly touch the ground

low sandals called zori

high sandals called okobo

Iro-tomesode kimono has short sleeves and features one main color other than black with patterning below the waist.

Furisode kimono has long sleeves and features bright colors with patterning all over.

Fun fact: Geisha in Kyoto are called geiko.

Just before going to our room, we stopped to get some ice cream.

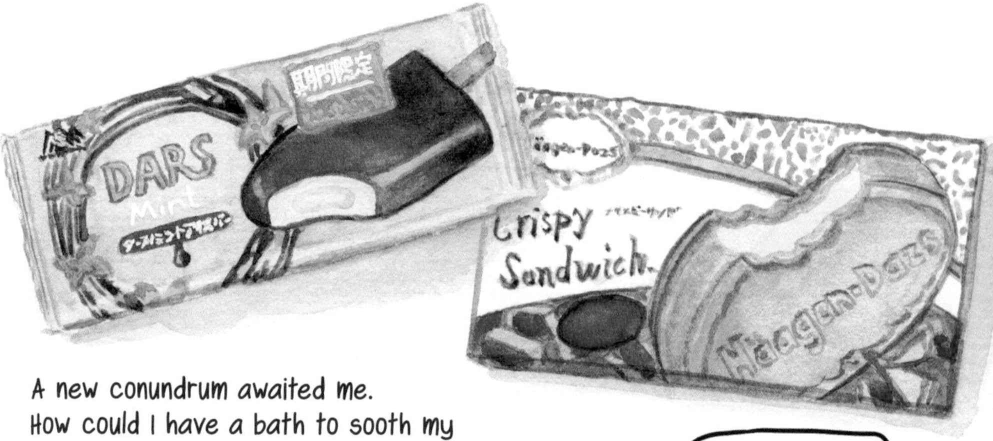
DARS
Mint
Crispy
Sandwich
Häagen-Dazs

A new conundrum awaited me.
How could I have a bath to sooth my sore feet and also eat ice cream at the same time?

A plastic bowl found in the kitchen provided the ideal solution.

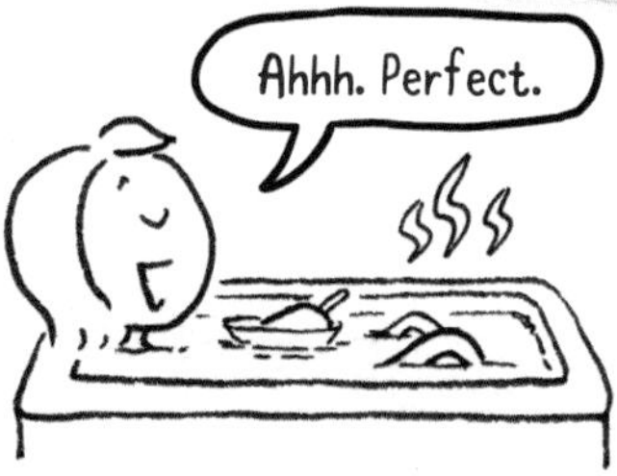
Ahhh. Perfect.

As darkness fell we strolled over to Tetsugaku-no-michi (The Philosopher's Path), named for the twentieth century philosophers who walked there.

While watching local families enjoy the fireflies, I realized that the fireflies in Japan behaved much differently than the ones I had seen while visiting Kentucky. In Japan, all the fireflies hovered over the water, but in Kentucky they all avoided the water.

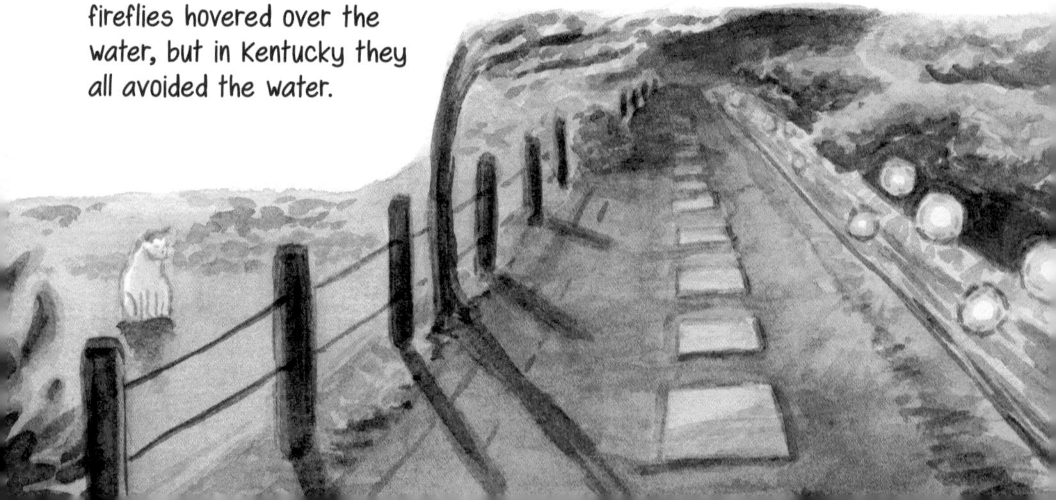

We walked the entire path before turning back to find dinner. There is phenomenal food in Kyoto. Despite the many options, we ate at Ramen Miyako all three nights. Connor tried different bowls of ramen each night while I chose the same thing each time: a pork rice bowl.

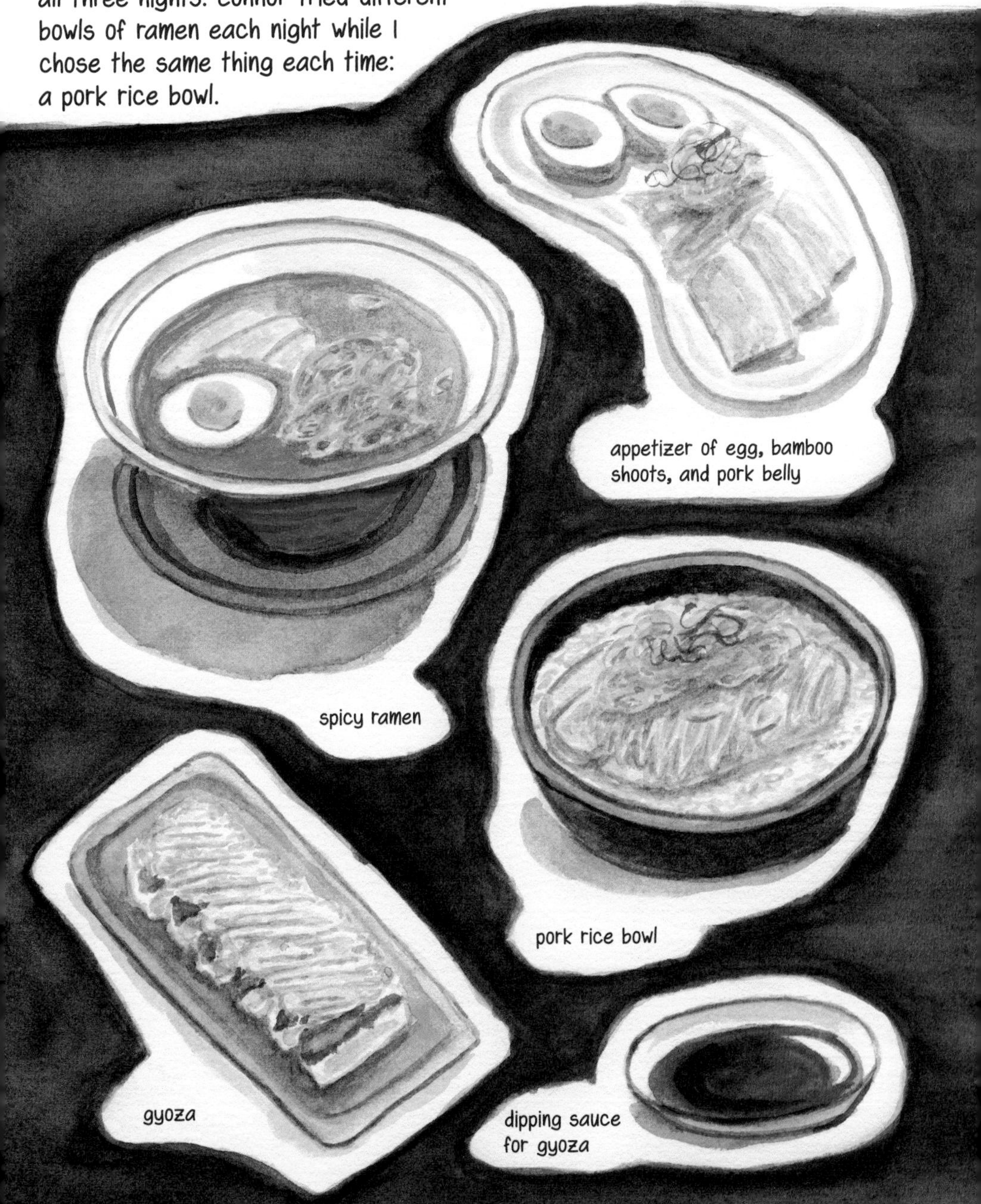
appetizer of egg, bamboo shoots, and pork belly
spicy ramen
pork rice bowl
gyoza
dipping sauce for gyoza

While walking back to our lodging, I was captivated by the glow of all the vending machines we passed by. Many of the machines dispensed both hot and cold drinks.

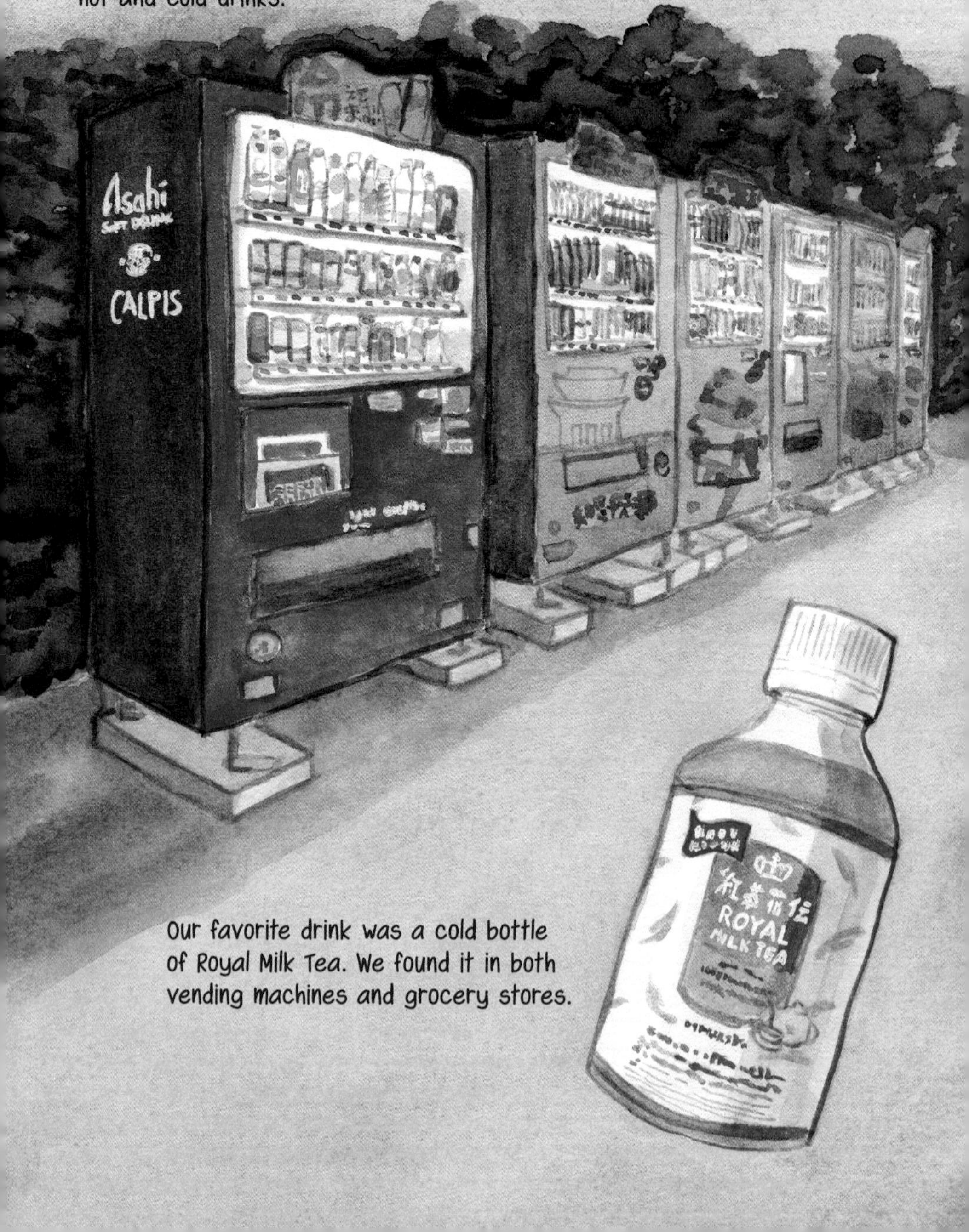
Asahi
CALPIS
ROYAL
MILK TEA

Our favorite drink was a cold bottle of Royal Milk Tea. We found it in both vending machines and grocery stores.

# Arriving in Tokyo

June 3rd

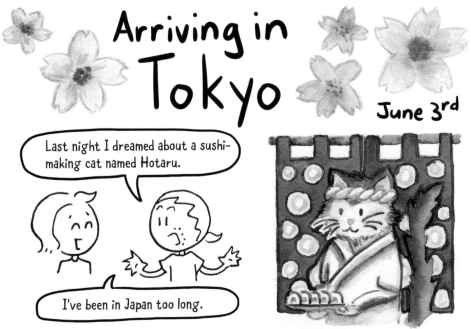

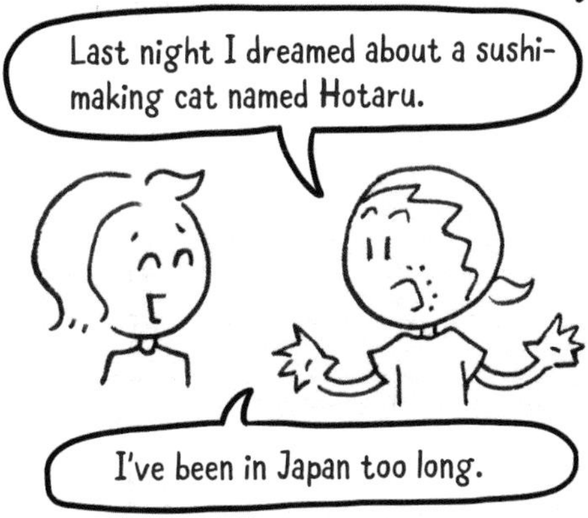
Last night I dreamed about a sushi-making cat named Hotaru.
I've been in Japan too long.

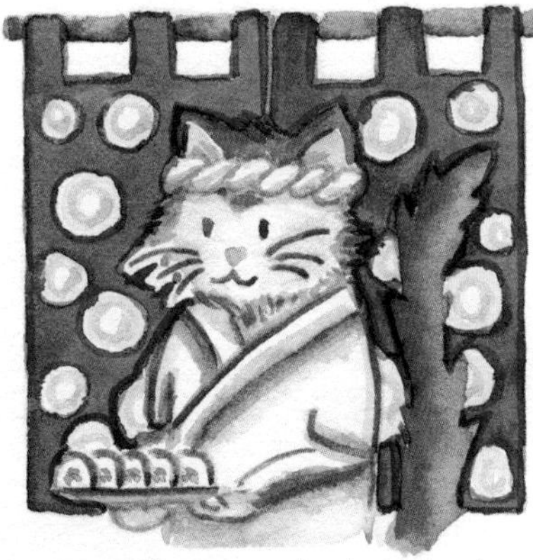

By late morning we left Kyoto for Tokyo. Our Japan Rail passes had expired, so we had to figure out how to buy Shinkansen tickets. We waited in three different tourist-information lines before we found the one that could help us.

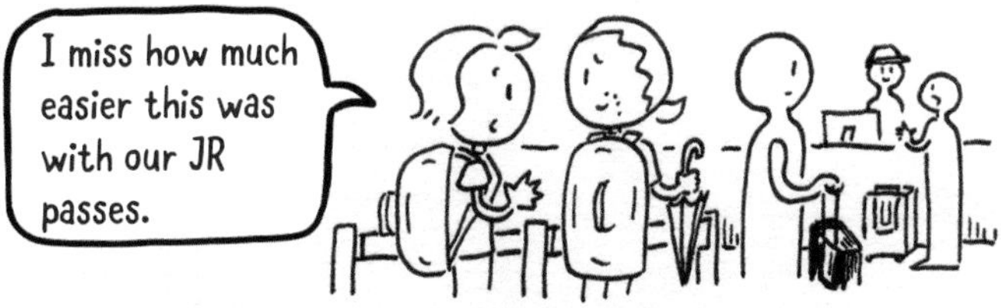
I miss how much easier this was with our JR passes.

Our first stop in Tokyo was at Shinagawa Station. Here we discovered that the 77 stations around Tokyo provide special paper to collect each stamp.

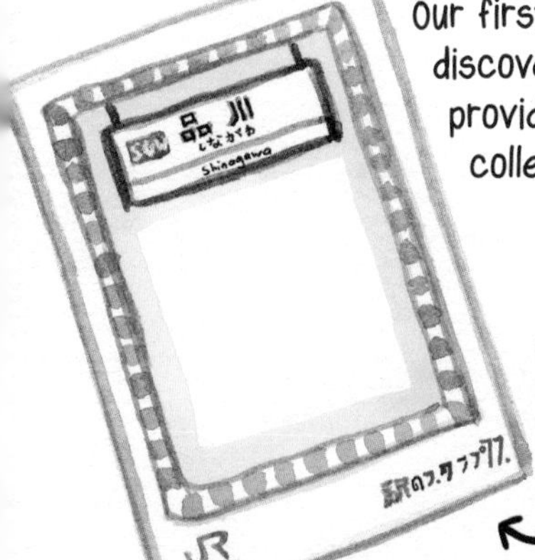
品川

Shinagawa Station stamp paper

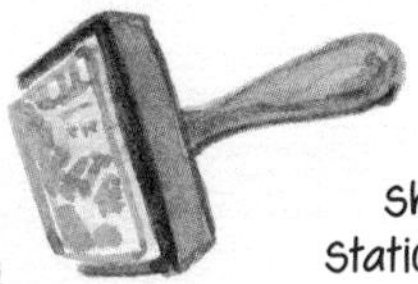

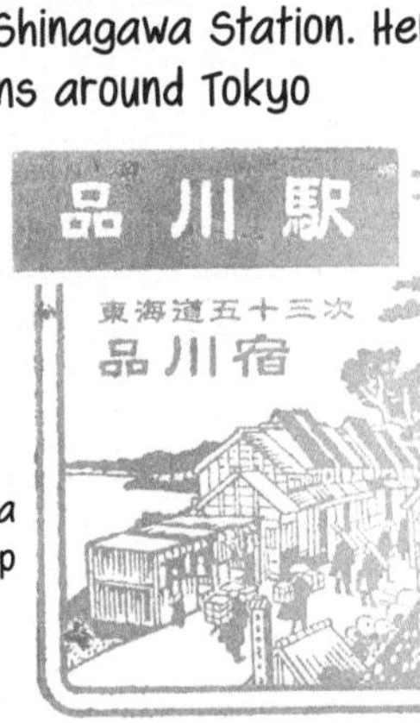
品川駅
東海道五十三次
品川宿

Shinagawa Station stamp

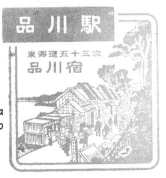

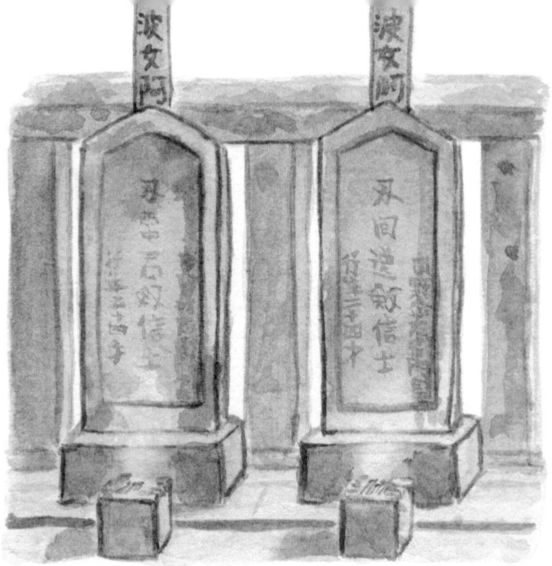

From Shinagawa Station we walked to Sengaku-ji to visit the temple graveyard where the 47 Ronin (samurai without a master) are buried.

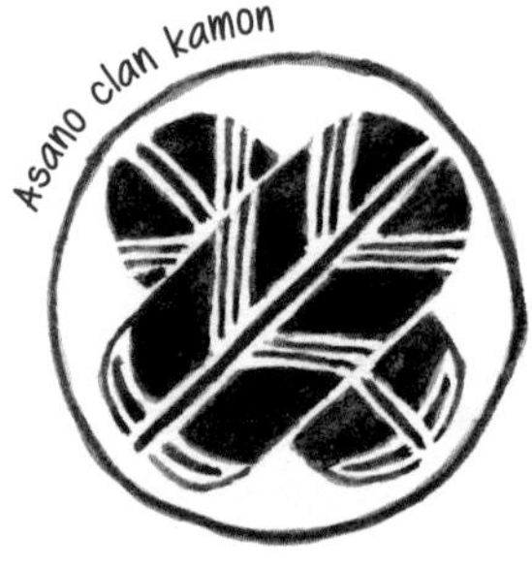
Asano clan kamon

Also referred to as the Ako incident or the Ako Vendetta, the story of the 47 Ronin begins with the fifth Tokugawa Shogun, Tsunayoshi, giving high-ranking court official Kira Yoshinaka the task of teaching lower-ranked official Asano Naganori the correct manner of receiving a representative of the Emperor.

After being subjected to many insults by Kira, Asano felt compelled to defend his honor by attacking Kira while at Edo Castle. This was a grave offense. Asano was sentenced to commit seppuku (ritual suicide) and his household was to be dissolved.

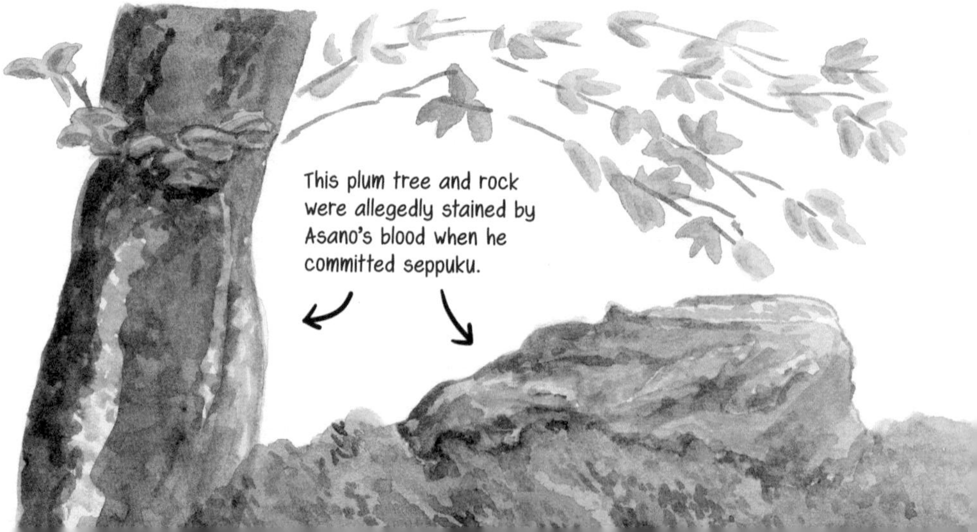
This plum tree and rock were allegedly stained by Asano's blood when he committed seppuku.

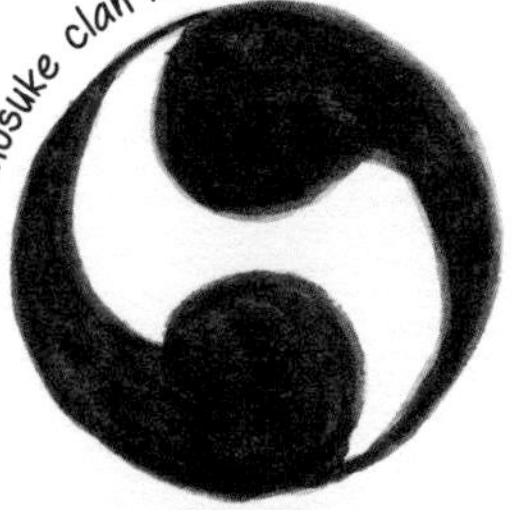

Kuranosuke clan kamon

Kira, conversely, was left unpunished. This angered 47 of Asano's now leaderless samurai, or ronin. Led by Oishi Kuranosuke, Asano's head chamberlain, the 47 Ronin conspired to kill Kira in order to restore their fallen leader's honor.

Knowing that if they succeeded, they all would likely be sentenced to death, the 47 Ronin still chose vengeance and the consequences that came with that choice.

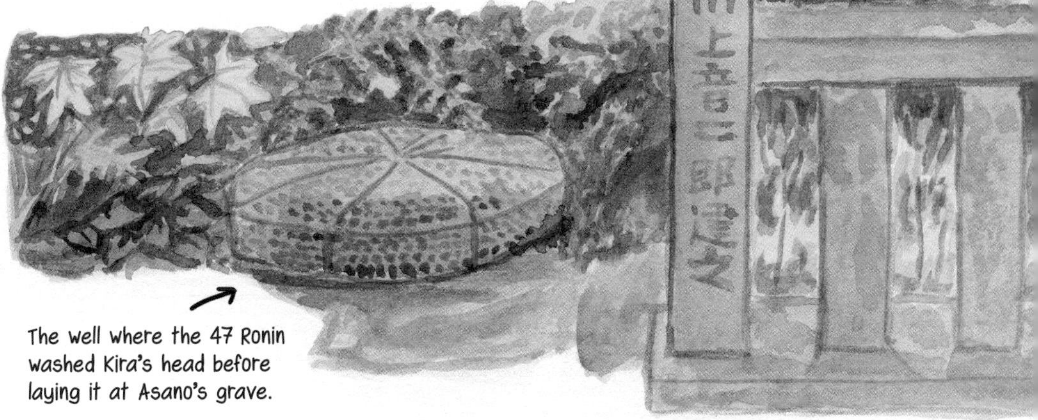
川上音二郎建之

The well where the 47 Ronin washed Kira's head before laying it at Asano's grave.

It took two years, but in the end Asano was avenged. The 47 Ronin were sentenced to commit seppuku, which they accepted, as it was considered an honorable death.

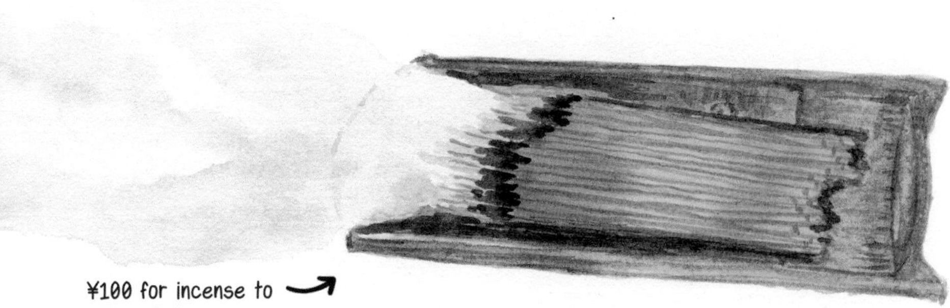

¥100 for incense to offer at the graves

From Sengaku-ji, we took the train to Shibuya. We were delighted to discover that the famous scramble crossing is right outside the station. There are five possible corners to cross to and the traffic lights are synced so that everyone walks at the same time.

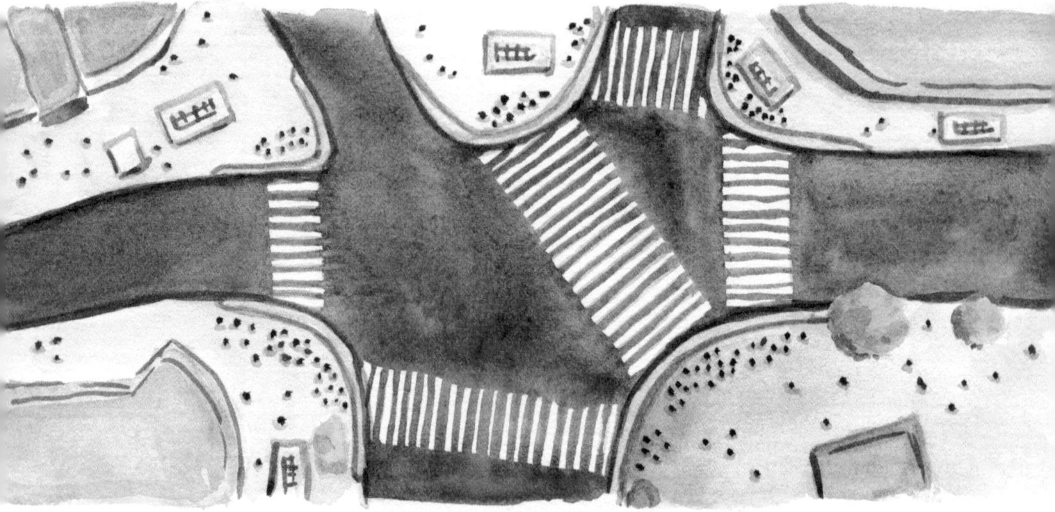

Everyone waits patiently at the corners, but once the walk signal turns on, it becomes organized chaos.

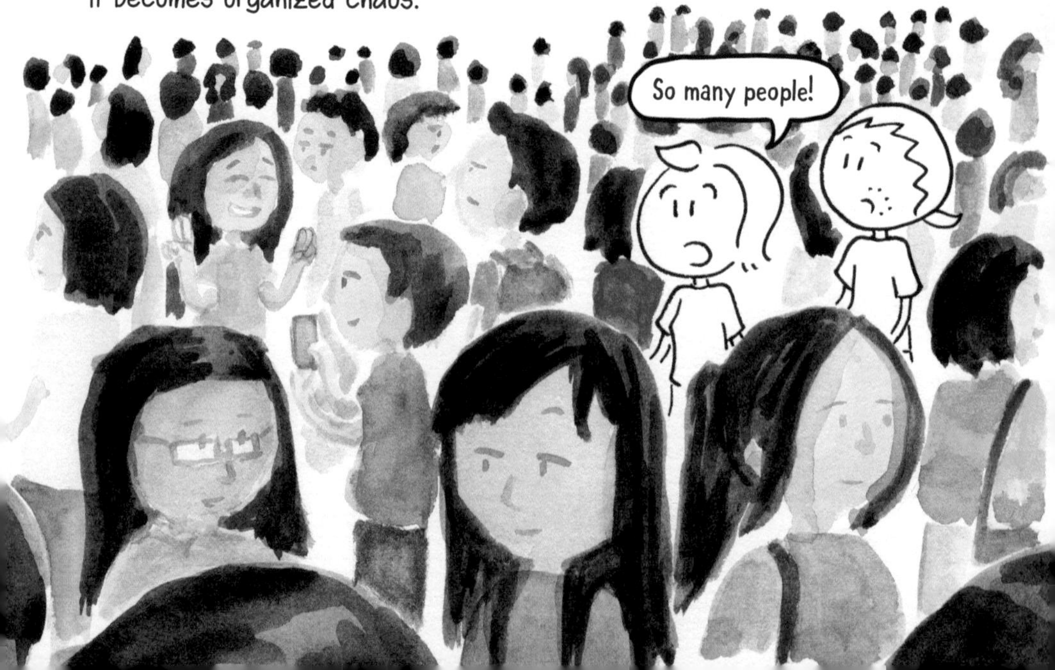
So many people!

A statue dedicated to Hachiko, the dog famous for his loyalty, is within sight of Shibuya crossing. Every workday Hachiko would wait at the station for his owner, Professor Hidesaburo Ueno, to return. One day Professor Ueno passed away while at work. Hachiko continued to come to the train station to wait every day until his own death nine years later.

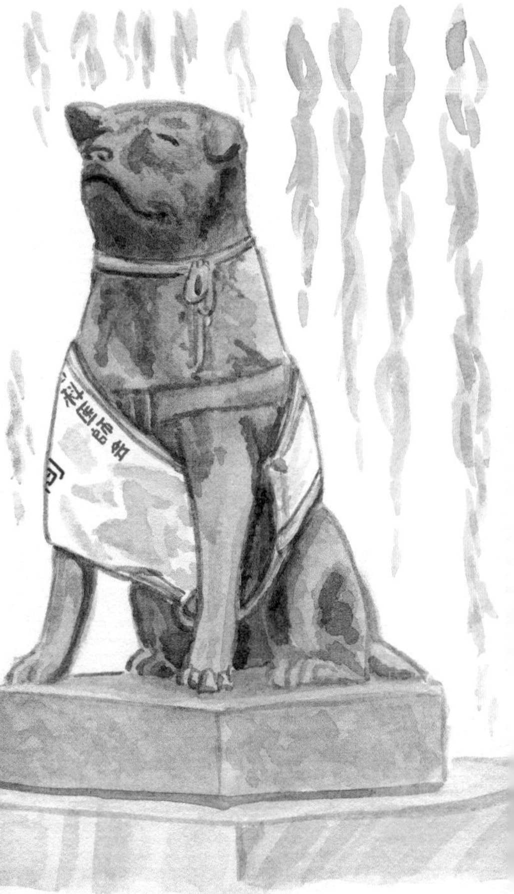

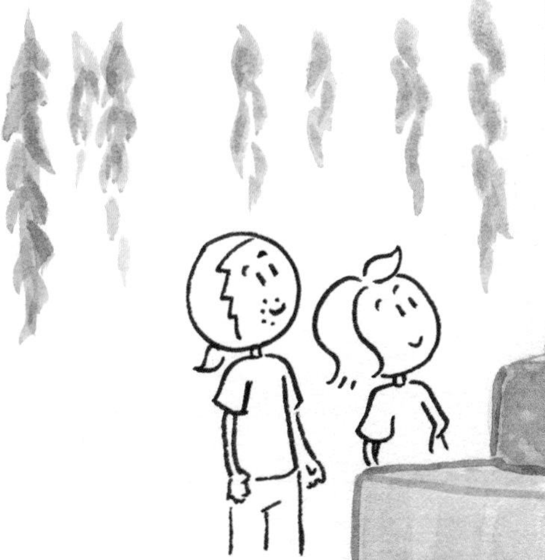

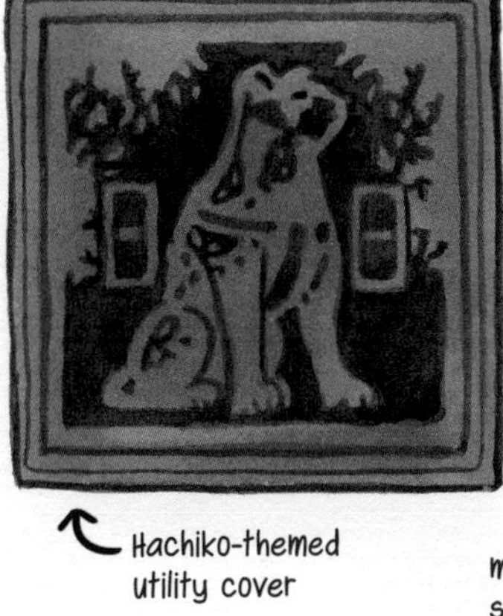

Hachiko-themed utility cover

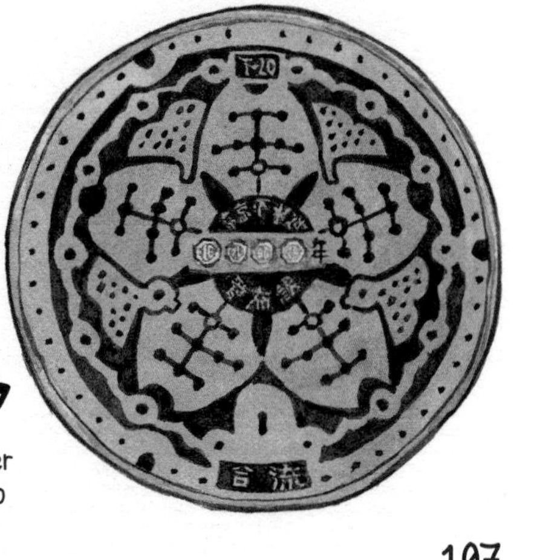

manhole cover seen in Tokyo

We were exhausted, but I wanted to take the train to Ikebukuro to check out some shops. By the time we headed back to Shibuya, it was rush hour.

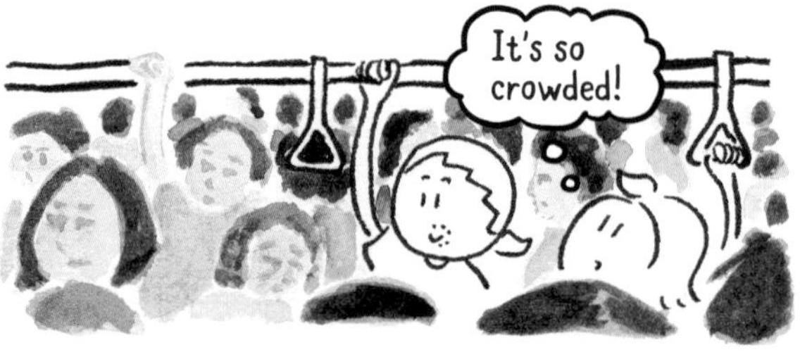
It's so crowded!

The day had been really hot, so there was only one thing to do when we spotted an ice cream vending machine.

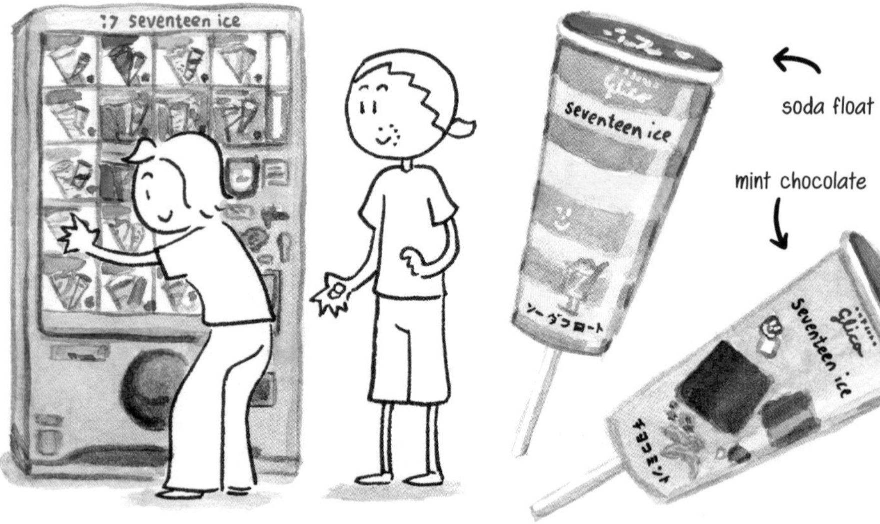
17 seventeen ice
Glico
seventeen ice
ソーダフロート
soda float
mint chocolate
Glico
seventeen ice

We ended our day by taking a bus to Gonpachi, a restaurant where part of Kill Bill Vol. 1 was filmed.

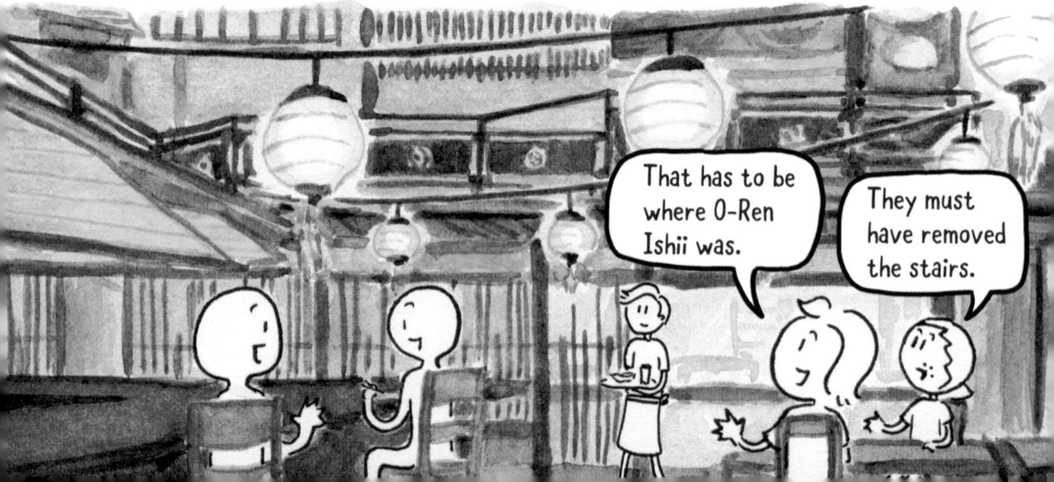
That has to be where O-Ren Ishii was.
They must have removed the stairs.

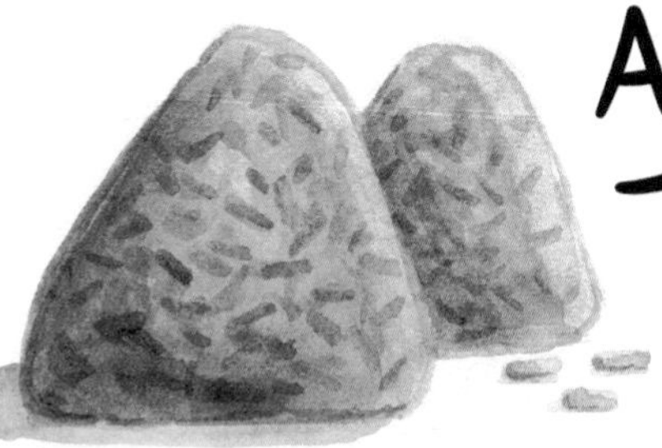

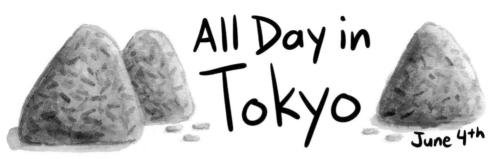

# All Day in Tokyo

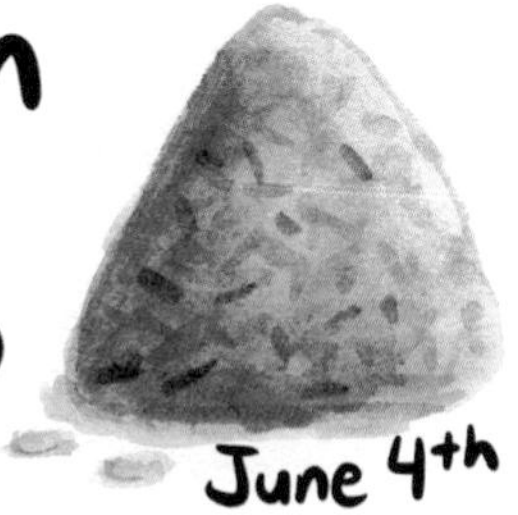

June 4th

We dedicated most of our day to touring the Studio Ghibli Museum which showcases the work of the world-famous Japanese animation studio. It's worth noting that photography is forbidden within the museum. To get there from the train station we had to walk through Inokashira Park.

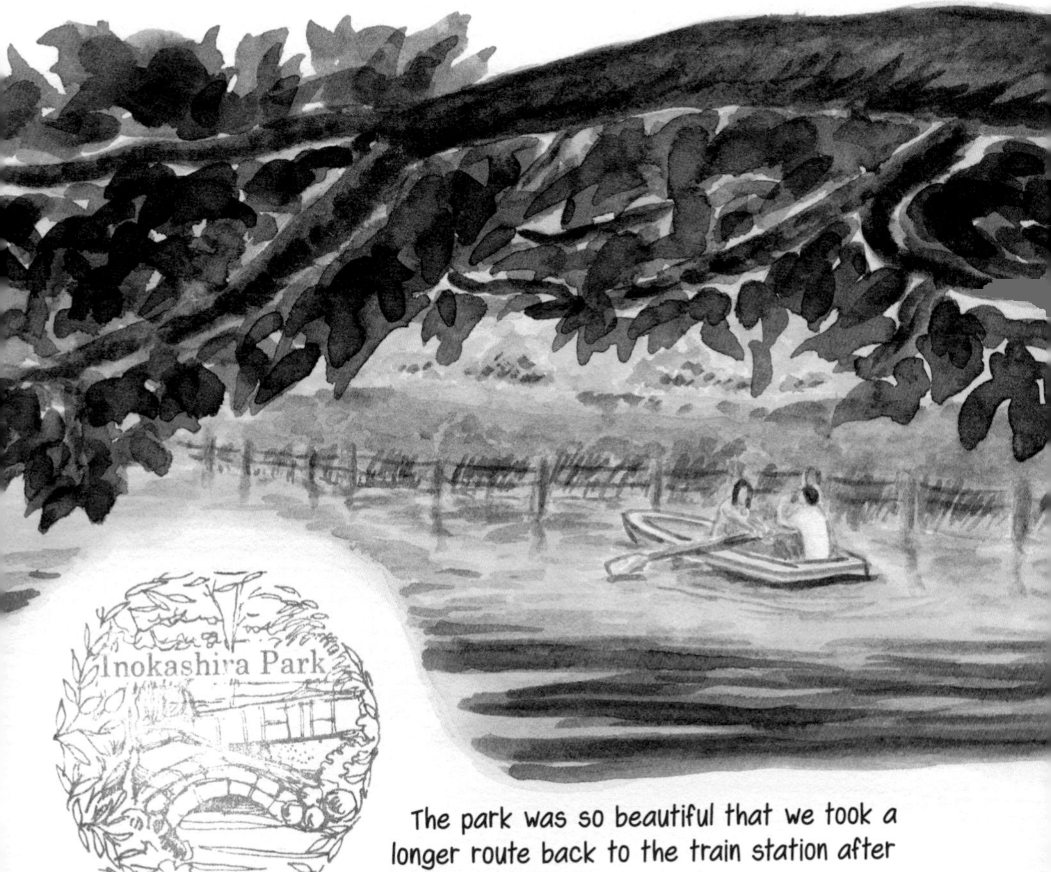
Inokashira Park

The park was so beautiful that we took a longer route back to the train station after visiting the museum.

Our dinner plans took us to Roppongi to meet up with two of Connor's colleagues: Kiyohiro and Bruno. They took us to a Japanese BBQ. The menu was entirely in Japanese, so they kindly ordered for us all.

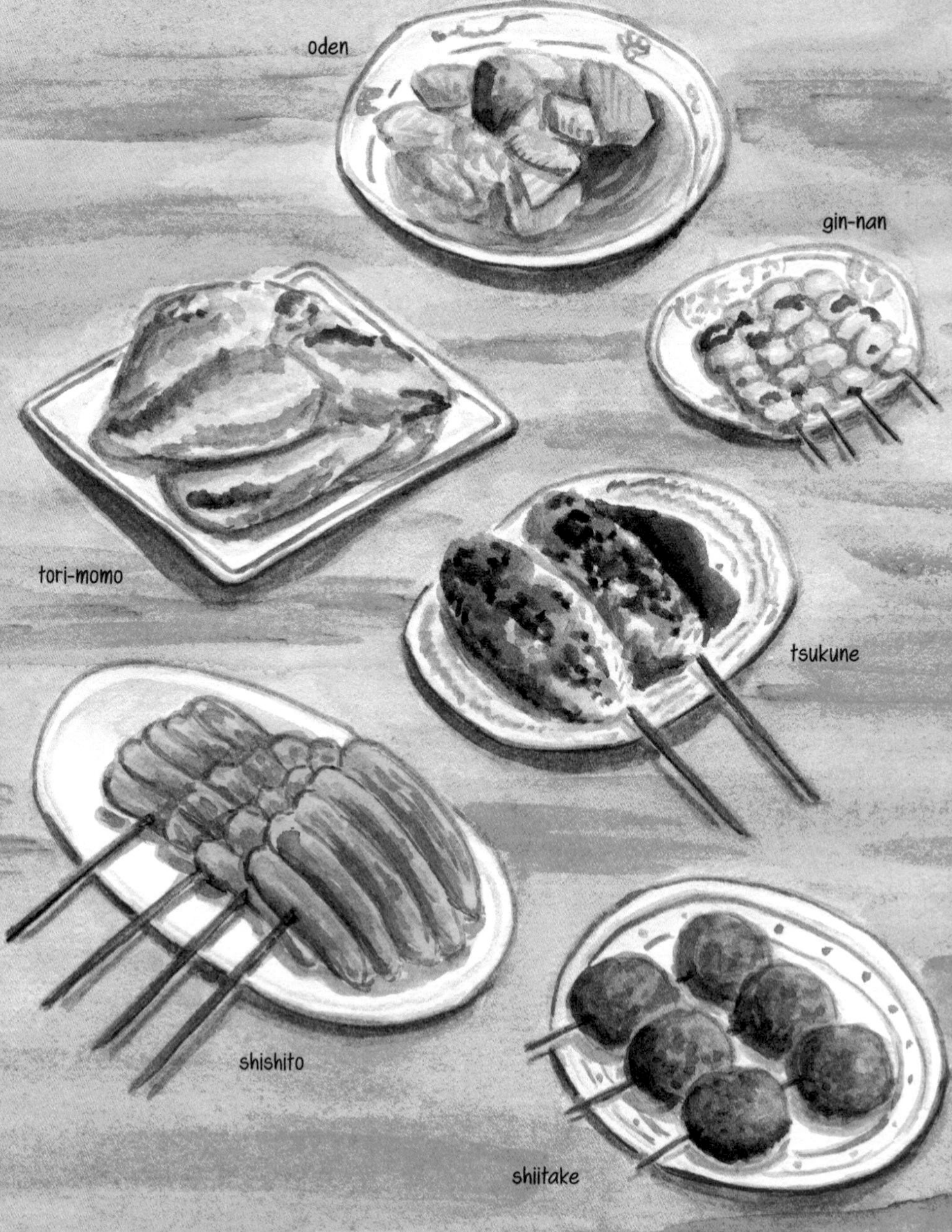
oden
gin-nan
tori-momo
tsukune
shishito
shiitake

We talked about life, business, and politics.

I told Connor he should practice his Japanese by talking to me even if I didn't understand.

Bruno ↓

I tried doing that with my family in English.

They didn't like it.

← Kiyohiro

I learned that Japan's biggest grievance with North Korea is that Japanese citizens were kidnapped and forced to teach North Korean spies how to pass as Japanese. The most famous abductee, Megumi Yokota, was kidnapped in 1977 when she was thirteen years old.

Kiyohiro teared up, so Bruno finished telling us about how North Korea won't give Japan any truthful resolution over whether the remaining kidnapped citizens are alive or dead. I was glad to have been introduced to a part of Japanese history that isn't covered in school back home.

As the evening wound down, Kiyohiro and Bruno introduced me to a dish I'd never seen before: yaki onigiri (BBQ rice ball.)

111

# Going Home

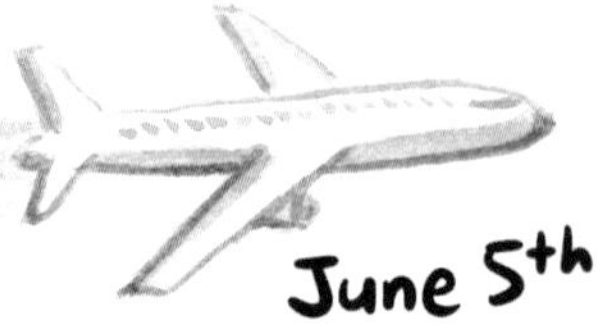

June 5th

We met up with Takuya and Satoko for breakfast.

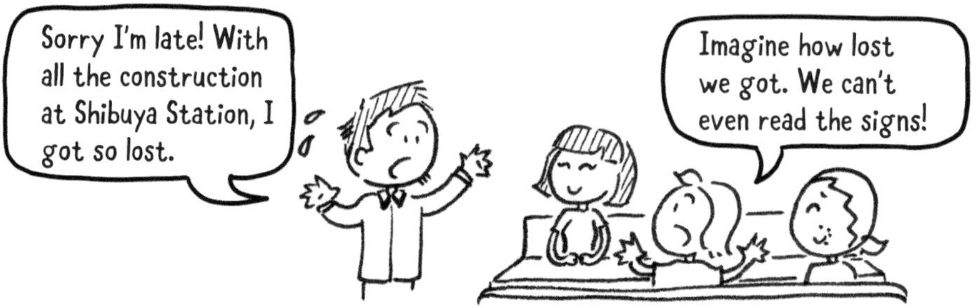
Sorry I'm late! With all the construction at Shibuya Station, I got so lost.
Imagine how lost we got. We can't even read the signs!

After breakfast, our friends helped us catch the train that would take us to Tokyo Station.

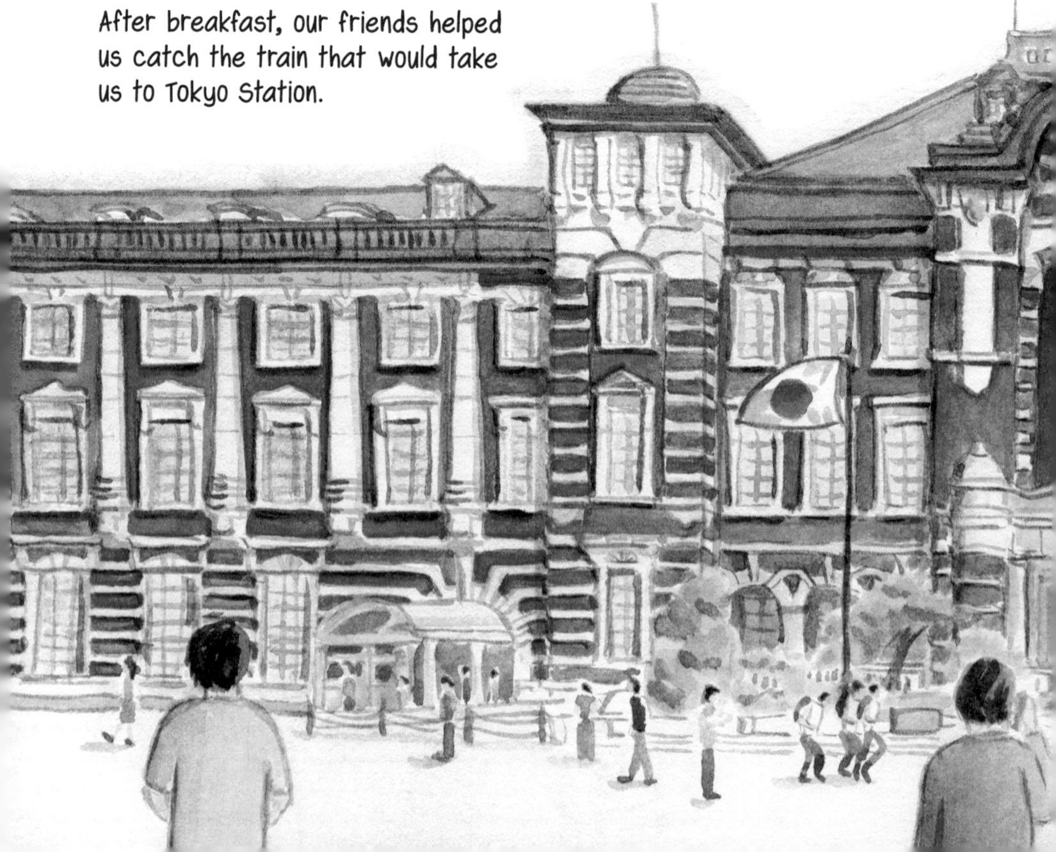

While there, we looked for a Studio Ghibli Nekobasu (Catbus) bath mat I'd seen at the beginning of our trip in Yokohama. I hadn't bought it with the belief that I could find it again at the end of our trip. No luck. I was determined to find the mat before our flight. To speed up our hunt we took a taxi to Donguri, a shop filled with Studio Ghibli merchandise, located at the Tokyo Skytree shopping center. From there we would catch the train to Narita airport. Things did not go according to plan.

Tokyo Station stamp

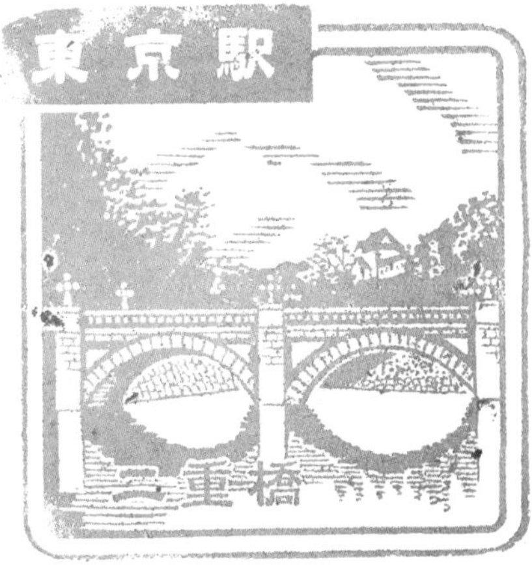
東京駅
二重橋

front of Tokyo Station

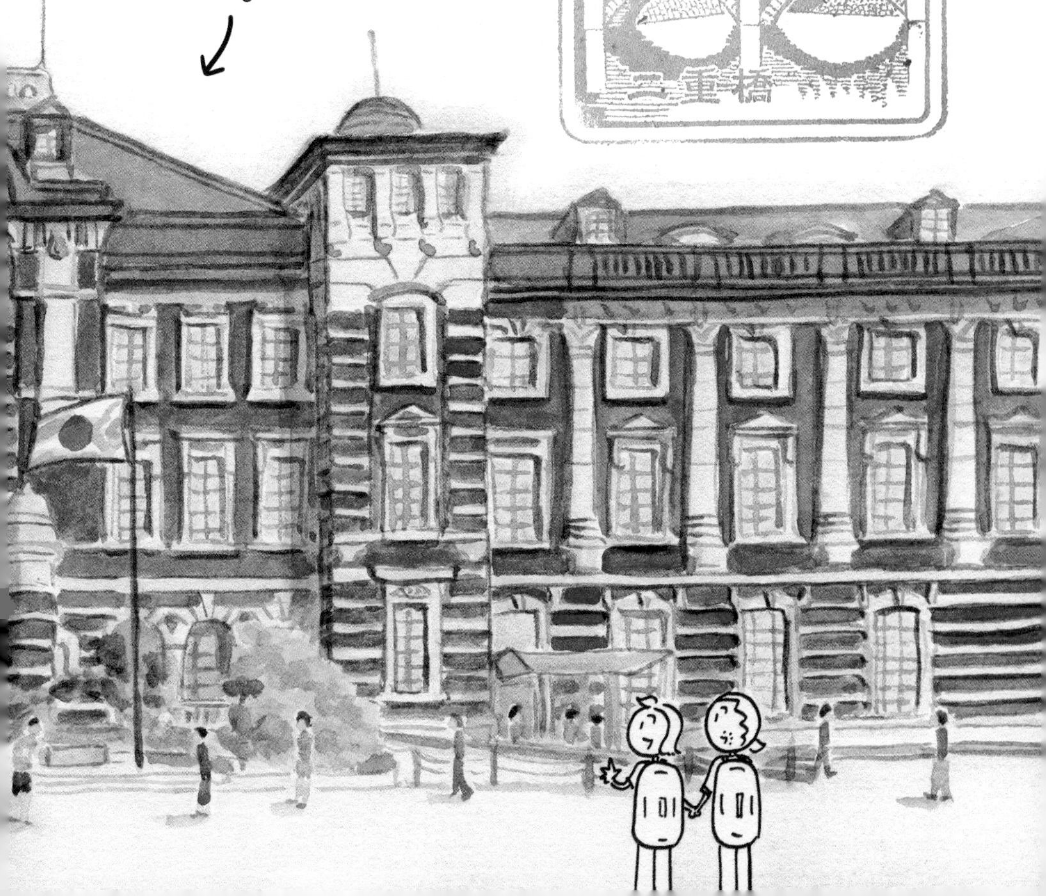

Donguri was a cute shop, but it didn't have the bath mat. Realizing we were short on time, we asked for directions to the nearby train station that would take us to the airport.

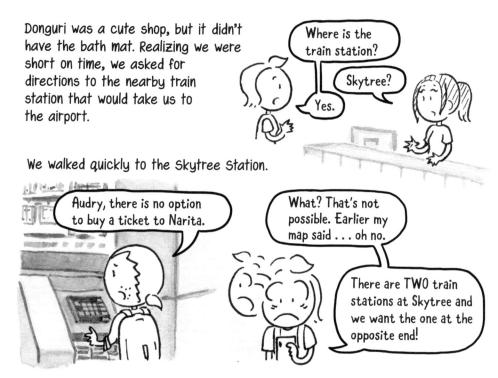

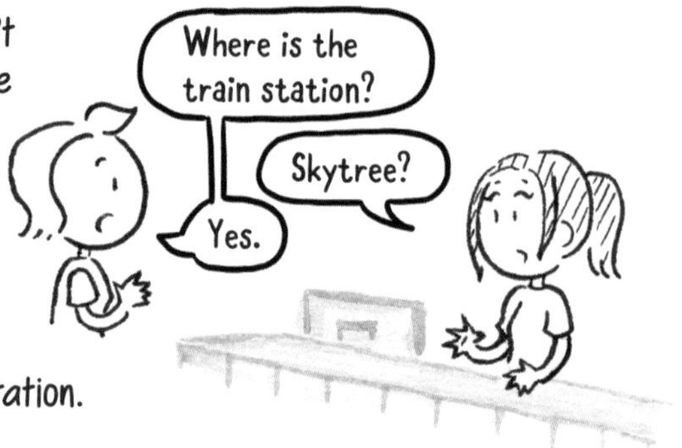
Where is the train station?
Skytree?
Yes.

We walked quickly to the Skytree Station.

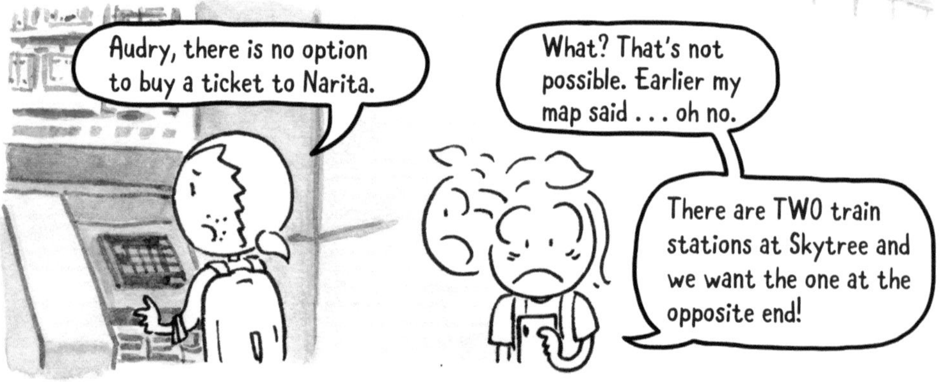
Audry, there is no option to buy a ticket to Narita.
What? That's not possible. Earlier my map said . . . oh no.
There are TWO train stations at Skytree and we want the one at the opposite end!

That day, local shoppers at Tokyo Skytree got to see two very stressed tourists running as fast as they could through the complex.

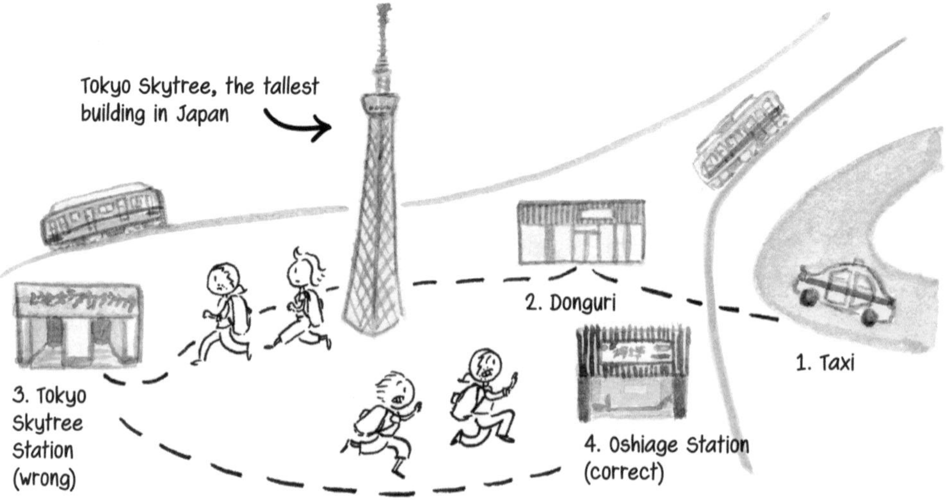
Tokyo Skytree, the tallest building in Japan
2. Donguri
1. Taxi
3. Tokyo Skytree Station (wrong)
4. Oshiage Station (correct)

Despite our best efforts, we narrowly missed our train.

The next train to Narita airport wasn't for another forty minutes which meant missing our flight became a possibility.

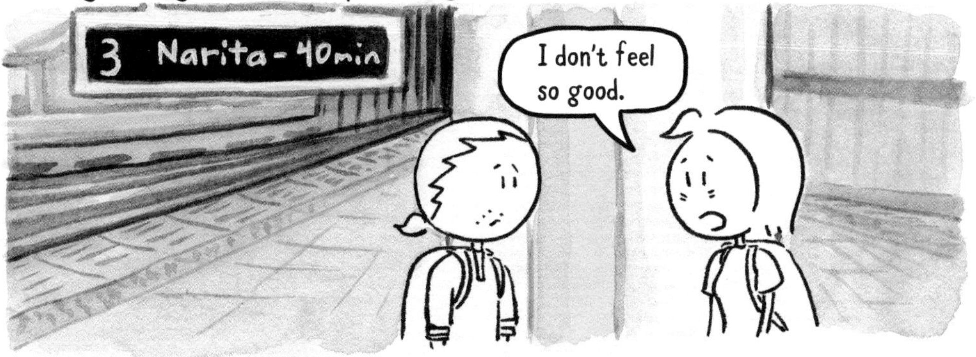
3 Narita - 40min
I don't feel so good.

We caught the next train and when we finally reached the airport, we had to run up several escalators. At the top, a kind ticket agent expedited us through security and we jogged to our gate with only fifteen minutes to spare.

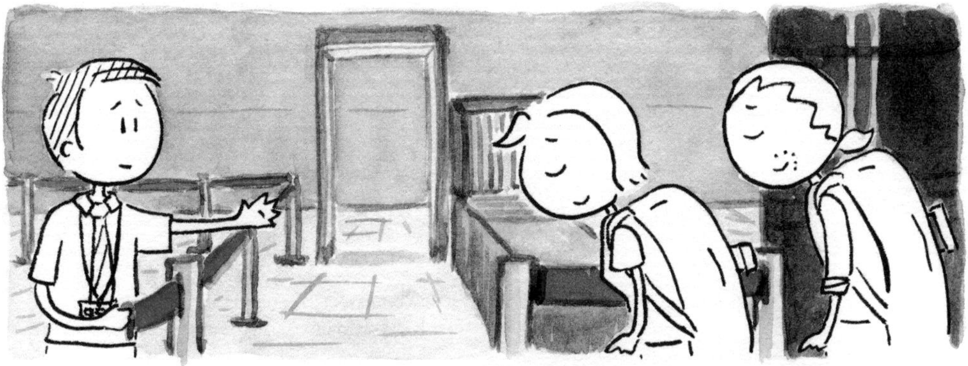

As we sped through the airport, we passed a shop that had something I had spent our whole trip searching for . . .

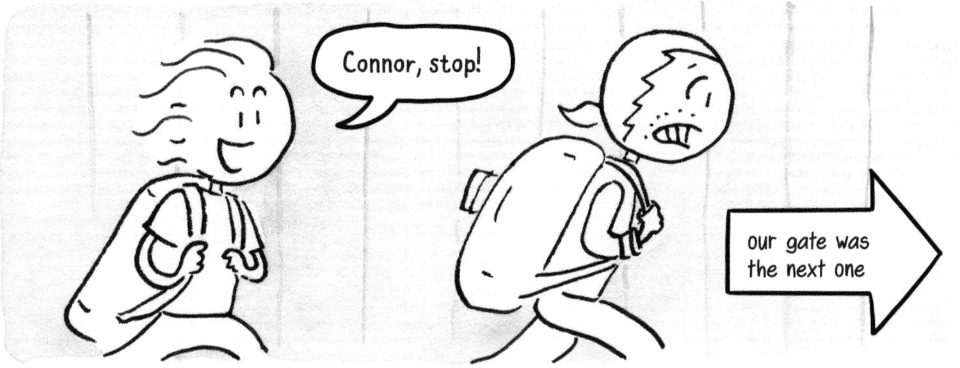
Connor, stop!
our gate was the next one

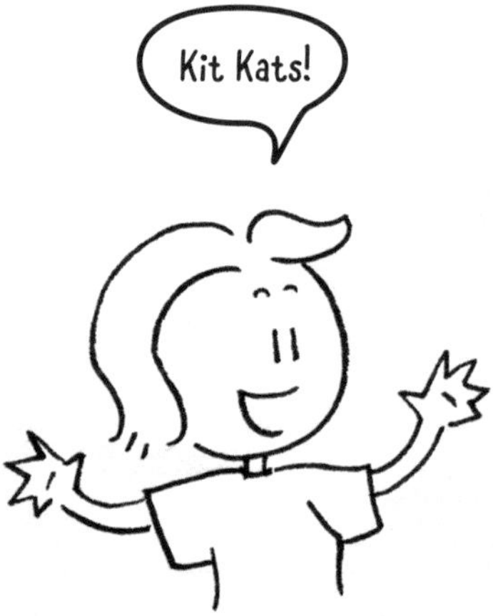
Kit Kats!

I had looked for Kit Kats in all the shops we had visited, but only found two flavors up until now: momiji manju and green tea.

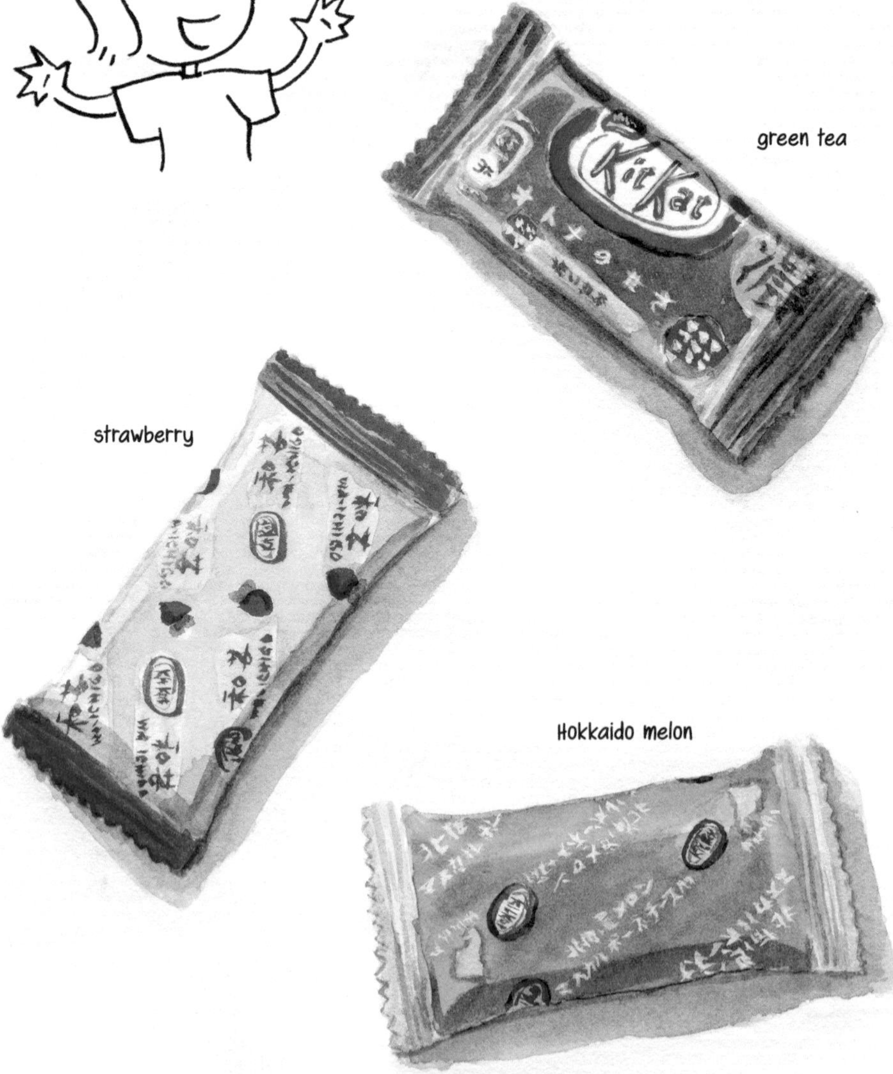
green tea
KitKat
strawberry
Hokkaido melon

There are over a hundred Kit Kat flavors in Japan. Many are regional and some are only seasonal.

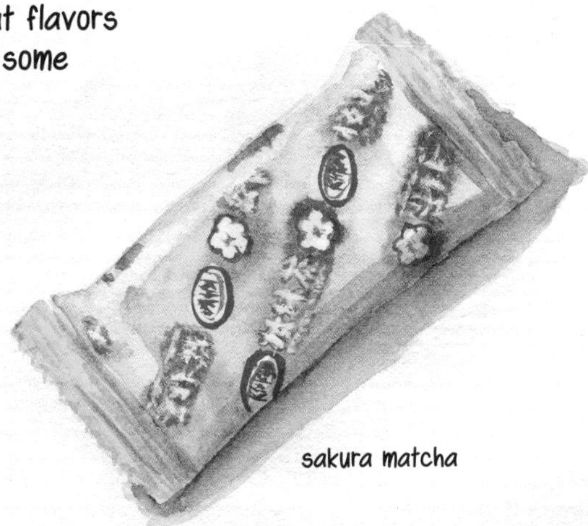

sakura matcha

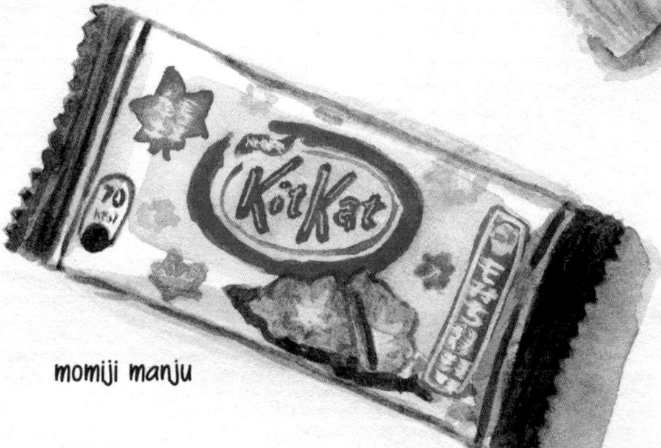
KitKat
70

momiji manju

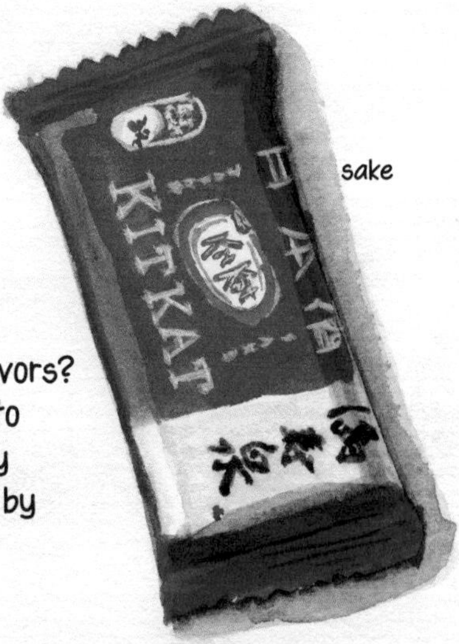
KITKAT

sake

Why does Japan have so many Kit Kat flavors? In Japanese, Kit Kat sounds similar to Kitto Katsu (きっと勝つ) meaning "You will surely win." They are used as good luck charms by students taking exams.

Armed with our Kit Kats, an omiyage for Connor's coworkers, and a Red King figurine from Ultraman for Connor's manager (which we thought was a weird Godzilla), we rushed to our gate.

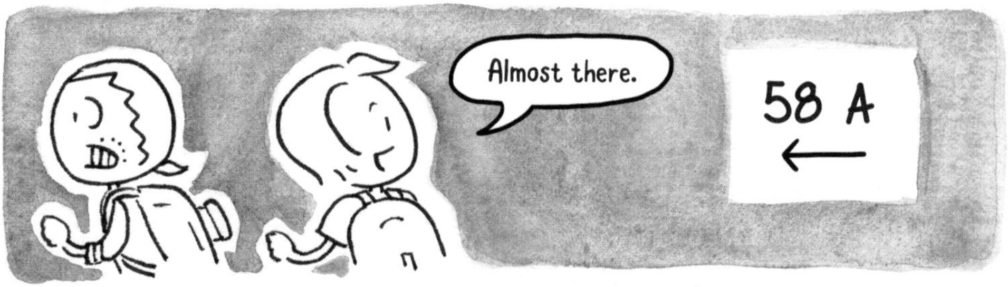
Almost there.
58 A

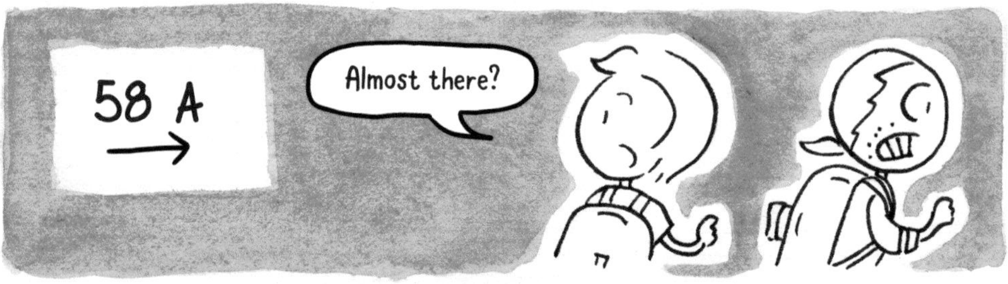
58 A
Almost there?

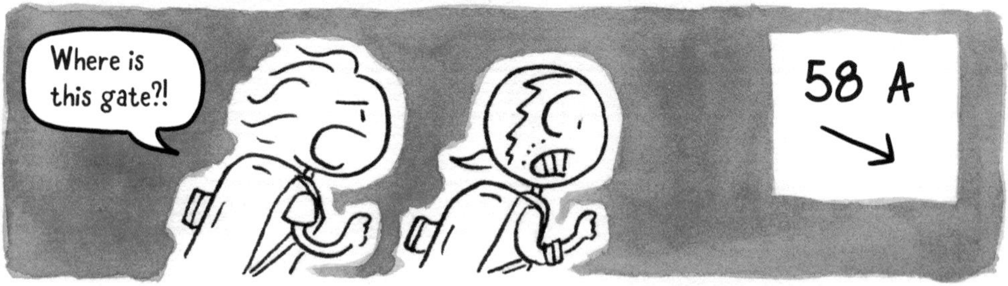
Where is this gate?!
58 A

Gate 58A must be in the furthest corner of Narita Airport. Sweaty and out of breath, we barely made it on time.

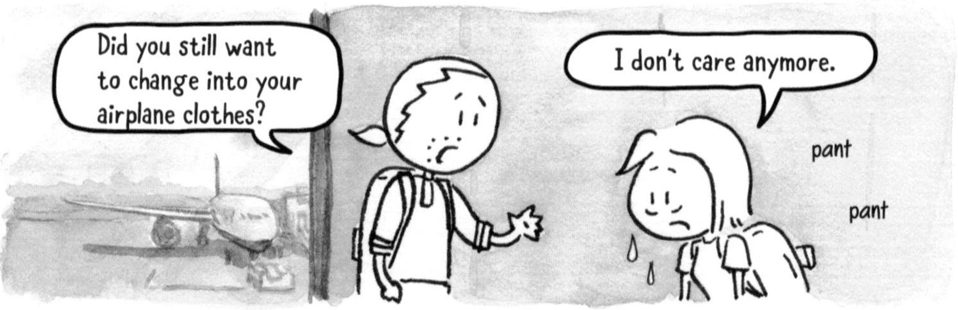
Did you still want to change into your airplane clothes?
I don't care anymore.
pant
pant

We took our seats and I looked forward to getting a cup of Kabosu. On the way to Japan I thought I'd find the drink everywhere, but that wasn't the case. Later I learned that Kabosu is a rare citrus fruit that is grown in a small area of Japan. The drink is more or less exclusive to ANA airlines.

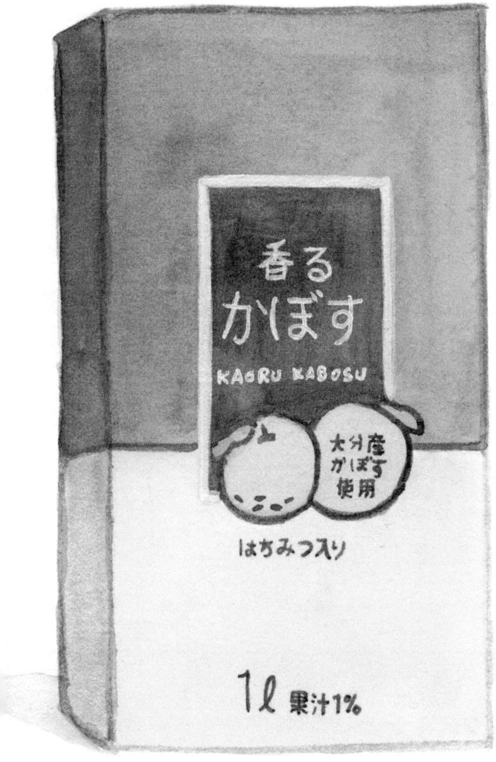
香る
かぼす
KAORU KABOSU
大分産
かぼす
使用
はちみつ入り
1ℓ 果汁1%

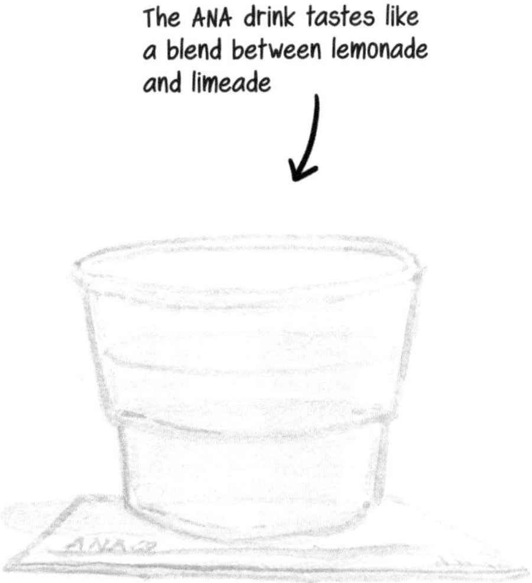
The ANA drink tastes like a blend between lemonade and limeade

As we settled in, I looked up. You'll never guess who we saw . . . my seatmates from the beginning of the trip!

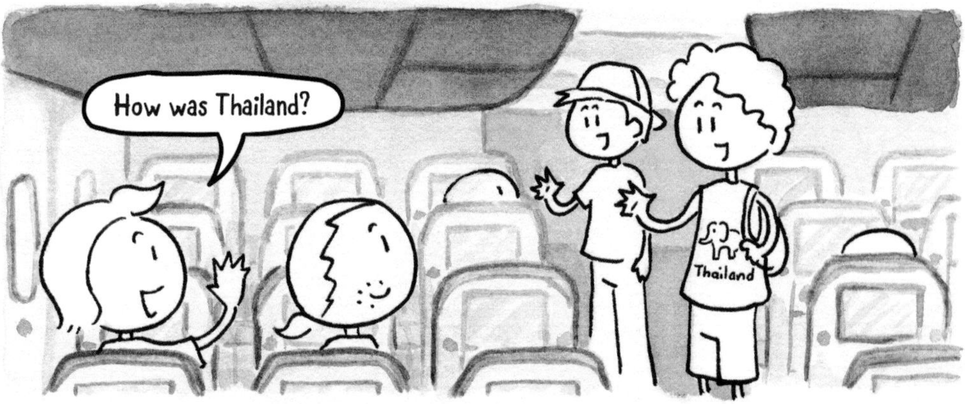
How was Thailand?
Thailand

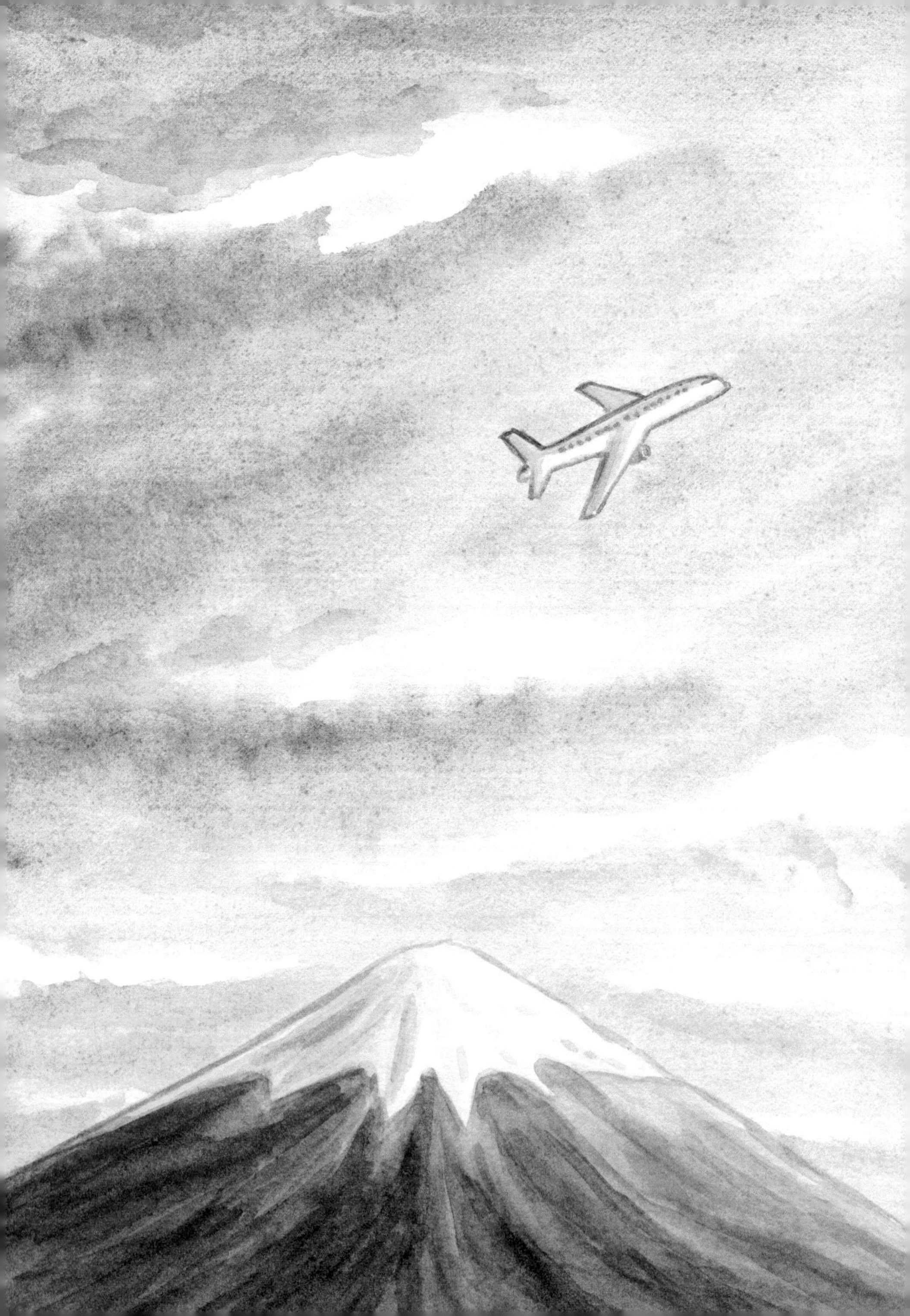

# How to Start Your Own
# Travel Journal

## Tools & Tips

# Travel Journal Tool Kit

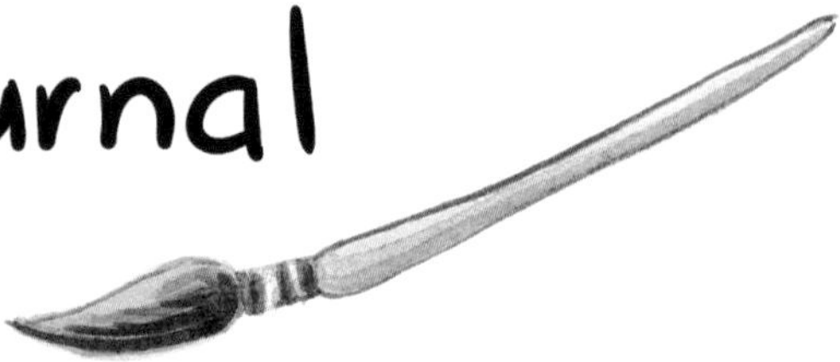

Whenever Connor and I travel, I like to take along a watercolor tool kit. While I continually adjust what I have in my kit, this is what I took with me to Japan.

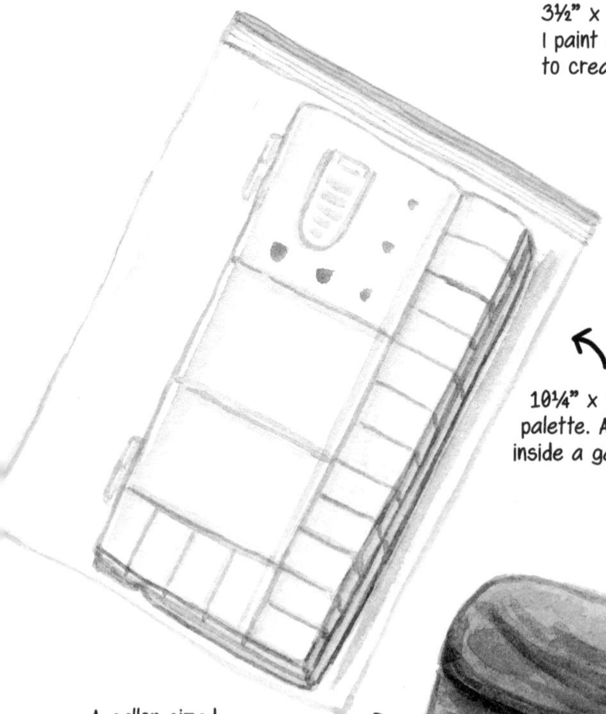

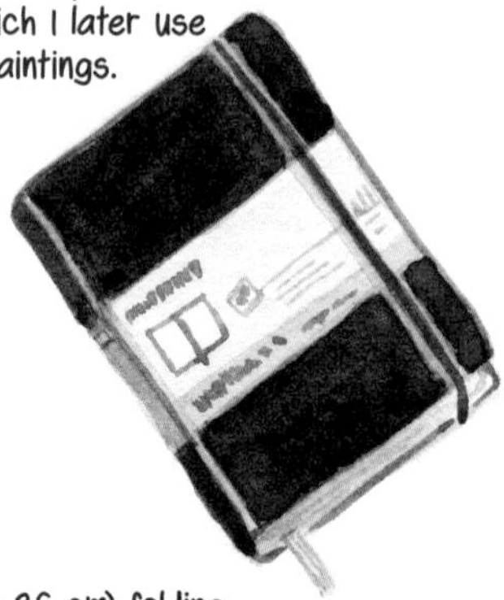

3½" x 5½" (9 x 14 cm) Moleskine Sketchbook. I paint studies, which I later use to create larger paintings.

10¼" x 10½" (25 x 26 cm) folding palette. Any bigger and it wouldn't fit inside a gallon-sized ziplock bag.

10" x 8" x 3½" (25 x 20 x 9 cm) ammo bag. This fits everything and more.

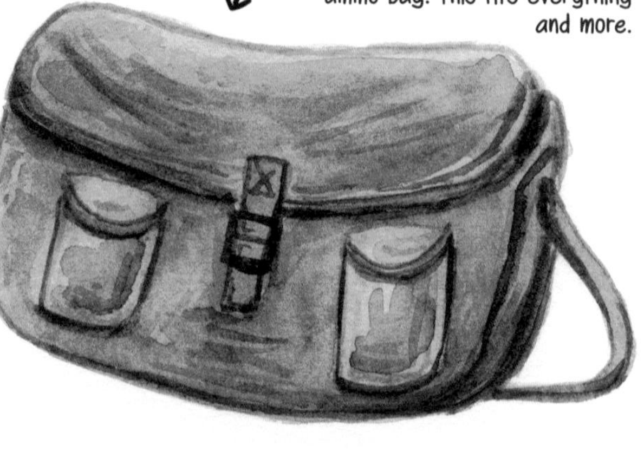

A gallon-sized ziplock bag to prevent the palette from leaking any wet paint.

2 oz (60 ml) Nalgene jars to hold water. I had three so I could switch between them when my water got too dirty.

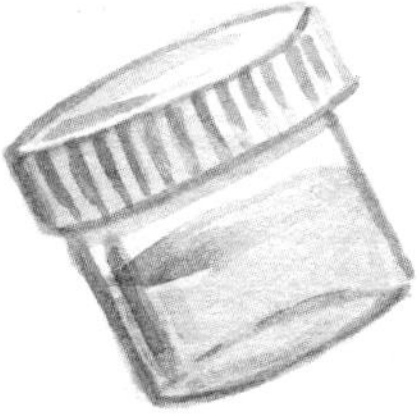

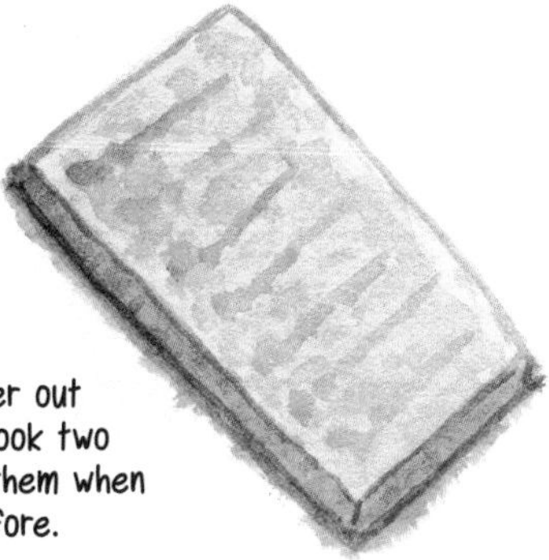

A sponge to wipe excess water out of the watercolor brushes. I took two so I could alternate between them when one was wet from the day before.

9"–14" (23–35 cm) telescoping plastic tube to hold the brushes.

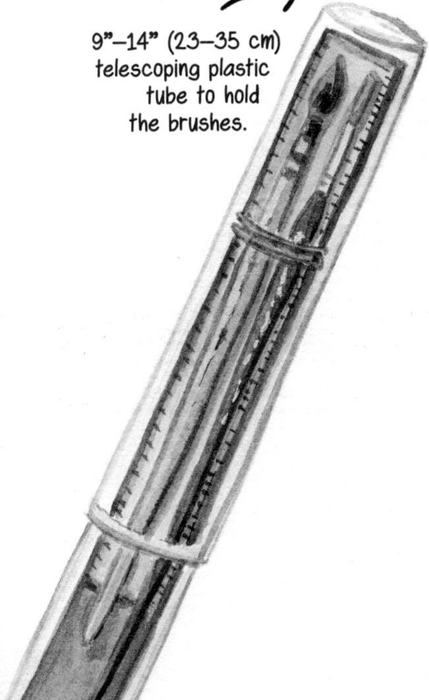

A plastic ruler and piece of cardboard rubber banded together inside the tube. To keep the brush heads in good shape, I rubber band them with the brush tips below the top of the ruler and cardboard.

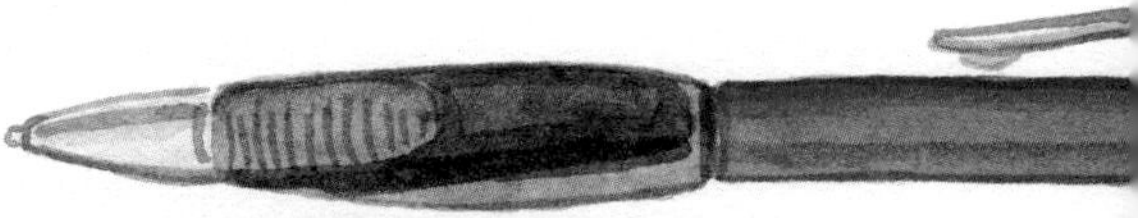

mechanical pencil

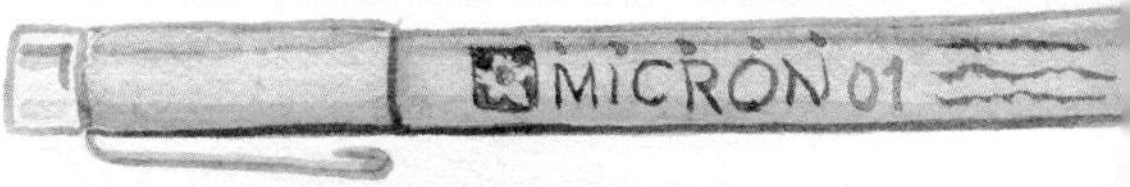
MICRON 01

0.01 black micron

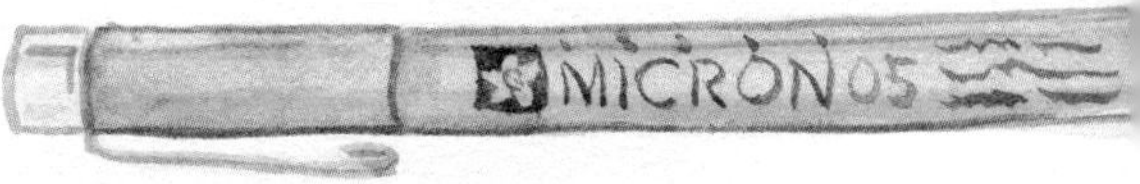
MICRON 05

0.5 black micron

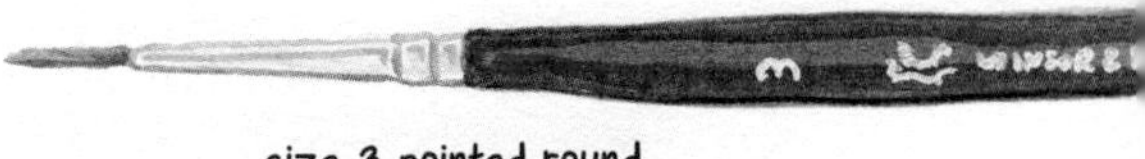

size 3 pointed round
Winsor & Newton
professional watercolor sable

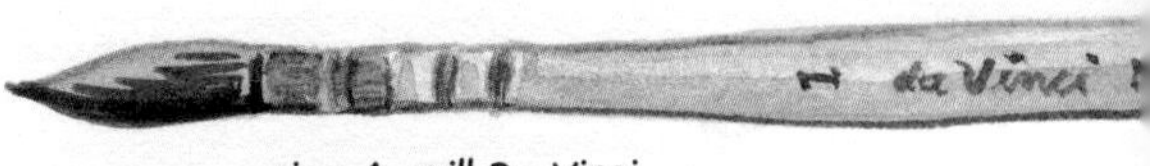
da Vinci

size 1 quill Da Vinci
Petit Gris Pur

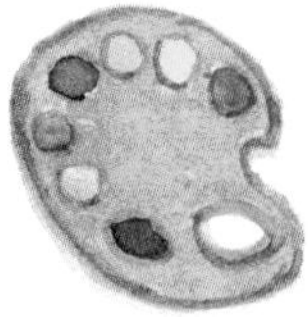

# Color Palette

While the colors found in my palette will sometimes change, my entire travel palette is made up of Daniel Smith brand watercolors. I like how well they dry in the palette and re-wet in the field. These are the colors I used while in Japan.

Quinacridone Rose (PV19)

Cerulean Blue Chromium (PB36)

Pyrrol Crimson (PR264)

Phthalo Blue (Green Shade) (PB15)

Pyrrol Red (PR254)

Ultramarine Blue (PB29)

Pyrrol Scarlet (PR255)

Buff Titanium (PW6:1)

Lemon Yellow (PY175)

Yellow Ochre (PY43)

Hansa Yellow Deep (PY65)

Burnt Umber (PBr7)

Phthalo Green (Blue Shade) (PG7)

Raw Umber (PBr7)

Cobalt Teal Blue (PG50)

Burnt Sienna (PBr7)

## My favorite color mixes:

Lemon Yellow

Pyrrol Scarlet

Hansa Yellow Deep

Phthalo Green (Blue Shade)

Phthalo Blue (Green Shade)

Quinacridone Rose

Phthalo Blue (Green Shade)

Ultramarine Blue

Burnt Umber

# Tips for Painting on Location

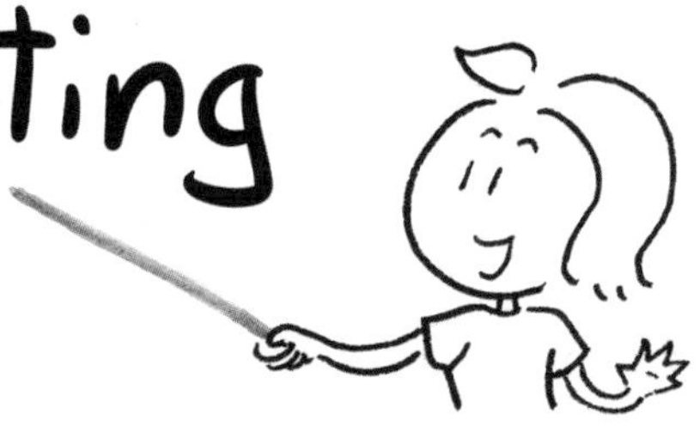

## Take a photo before you start painting

It's good to have a photo in case the scene changes or you aren't able to finish the painting in person. The photo I took at the floating gate on Miyajima came in handy when the tide went out faster than I expected. The photo taken at Fushimi Inari helped me put in the final details after mosquitoes chased us down the mountain.

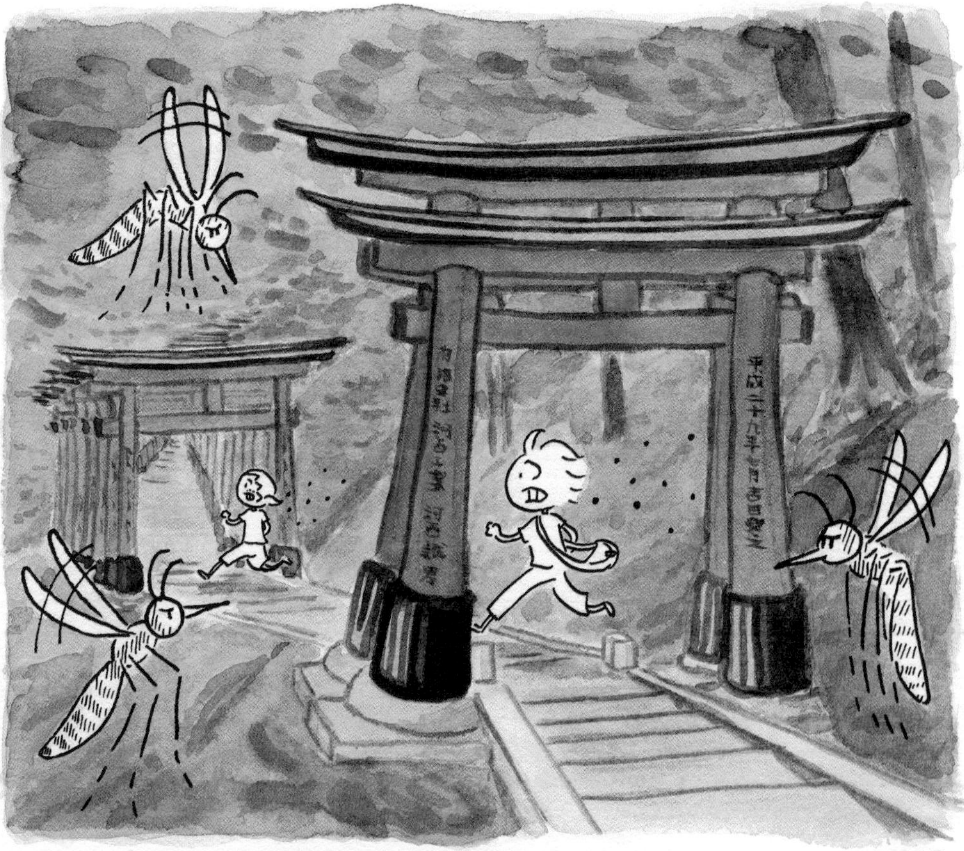

## Find a comfortable place to paint

Popular destinations will be full of people taking quick pictures so it's important to find a spot that keeps you from having to move out of the way. That doesn't mean not having a good painting angle. When I decided to paint the Cenotaph in Hiroshima, I watched to see where people were taking pictures first, then chose to stand in a place further back.

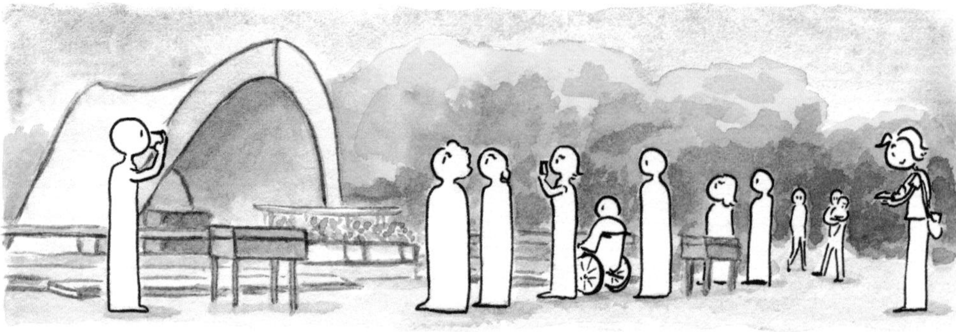

## How to graciously handle attention

Even if you're painting away from the crowds, people may get curious about what you're working on. Most of the time people only want to look. Those who feel brave enough to talk often wish they were painting too. Regardless of how you feel about the attention, it's good to be able to say thank you in the local language before continuing to paint. I made sure to practice my "arigato gozaimasu" (ah-ree-gah-toh goh-zah-ee-mas) before arriving in Japan.

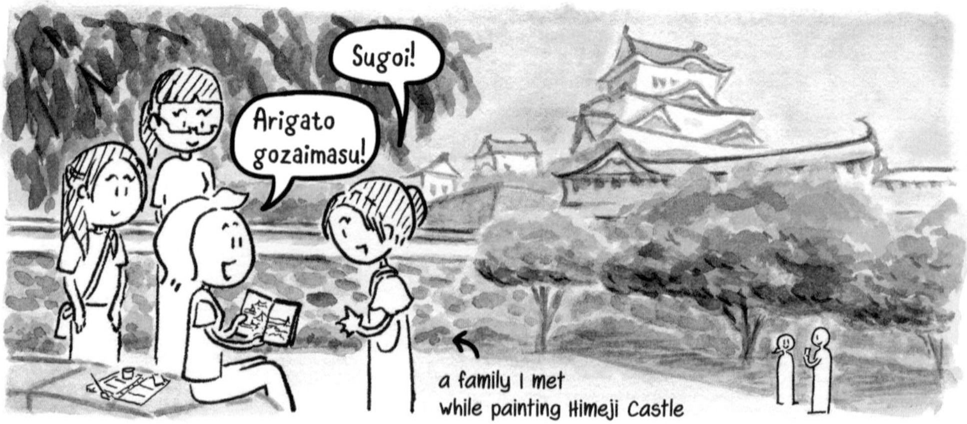
Sugoi!
Arigato gozaimasu!
a family I met while painting Himeji Castle

# Acknowledgments

First, I want to thank all my friends and family who have supported me over the years as I developed the skills that would one day allow me to make this book. I really couldn't have gotten to this point without you.

There are several people whose help directly impacted the quality of this book and I'd like to thank specifically.

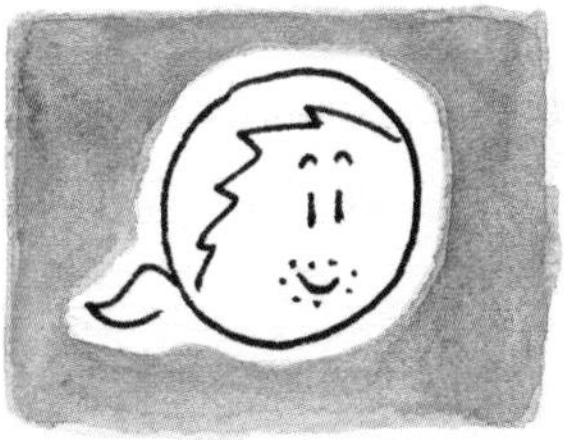

A big thank you to my husband, Connor. His loving support is the reason this book was both started and finished. He mopped me up off the floor on days I didn't think I could complete the manuscript, and he cheered loudly every time I finished a page.

Thanks to Takuya and Satoko who were kind hosts to us and helped us through our trip. Afterwards, both of them took the time to help me better understand Japanese culture. Takuya also kindly fielded my many, many, many translation questions.

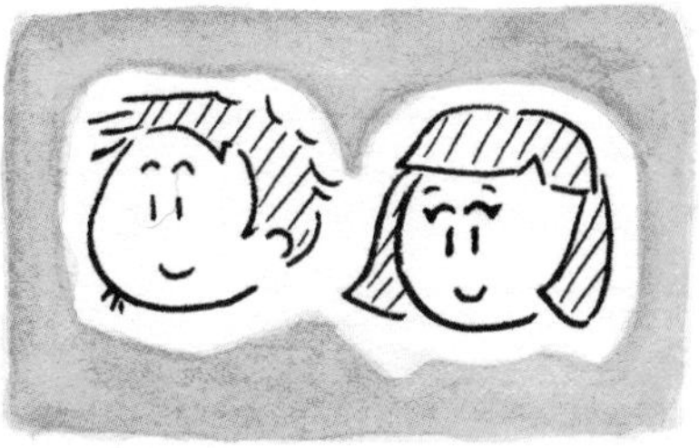

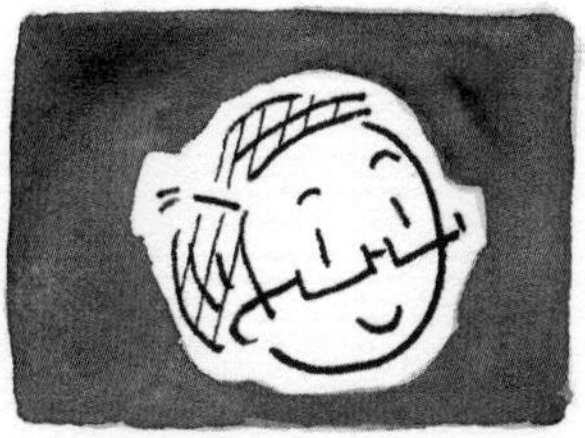

Thank you to Kiyohiro for not only sharing Japanese history with us, but also taking valuable time to answer my follow-up questions after the trip.

Additionally, I am grateful to you, the reader, for picking up this book. I hope it has given you a good taste of the rich culture that can be found in Japan.

## "Books to Span the East and West"

Tuttle Publishing was founded in 1832 in the small New England town of Rutland, Vermont [USA]. Our core values remain as strong today as they were then—to publish best-in-class books which bring people together one page at a time. In 1948, we established a publishing office in Japan—and Tuttle is now a leader in publishing English-language books about the arts, languages and cultures of Asia. The world has become a much smaller place today and Asia's economic and cultural influence has grown. Yet the need for meaningful dialogue and information about this diverse region has never been greater. Over the past seven decades, Tuttle has published thousands of books on subjects ranging from martial arts and paper crafts to language learning and literature—and our talented authors, illustrators, designers and photographers have won many prestigious awards. We welcome you to explore the wealth of information available on Asia at www.tuttlepublishing.com.

Published by Tuttle Publishing, an imprint of Periplus Editions (HK) Ltd.

www.tuttlepublishing.com

Copyright © 2022 Audry Nicklin

ISBN 978-4-8053-1643-6
Library of Congress in process

First edition
25 24 23 22     5 4 3 2 1

Printed in Malaysia     2204TO

Distributed by

**North America, Latin America & Europe**
Tuttle Publishing
364 Innovation Drive
North Clarendon, VT 05759-9436 U.S.A.
Tel: 1 (802) 773-8930
Fax: 1 (802) 773-6993
info@tuttlepublishing.com
www.tuttlepublishing.com

**Japan**
Tuttle Publishing
Yaekari Building, 3rd Floor, 5-4-12 Osaki
Shinagawa-ku, Tokyo 141 0032
Tel: (81) 3 5437-0171
Fax: (81) 3 5437-0755
sales@tuttle.co.jp
www.tuttle.co.jp

**Asia Pacific**
Berkeley Books Pte Ltd
3 Kallang Sector #04-01
Singapore 349278
Tel: (65) 6741 2178
Fax: (65) 6741 2179
inquiries@periplus.com.sg
www.tuttlepublishing.com

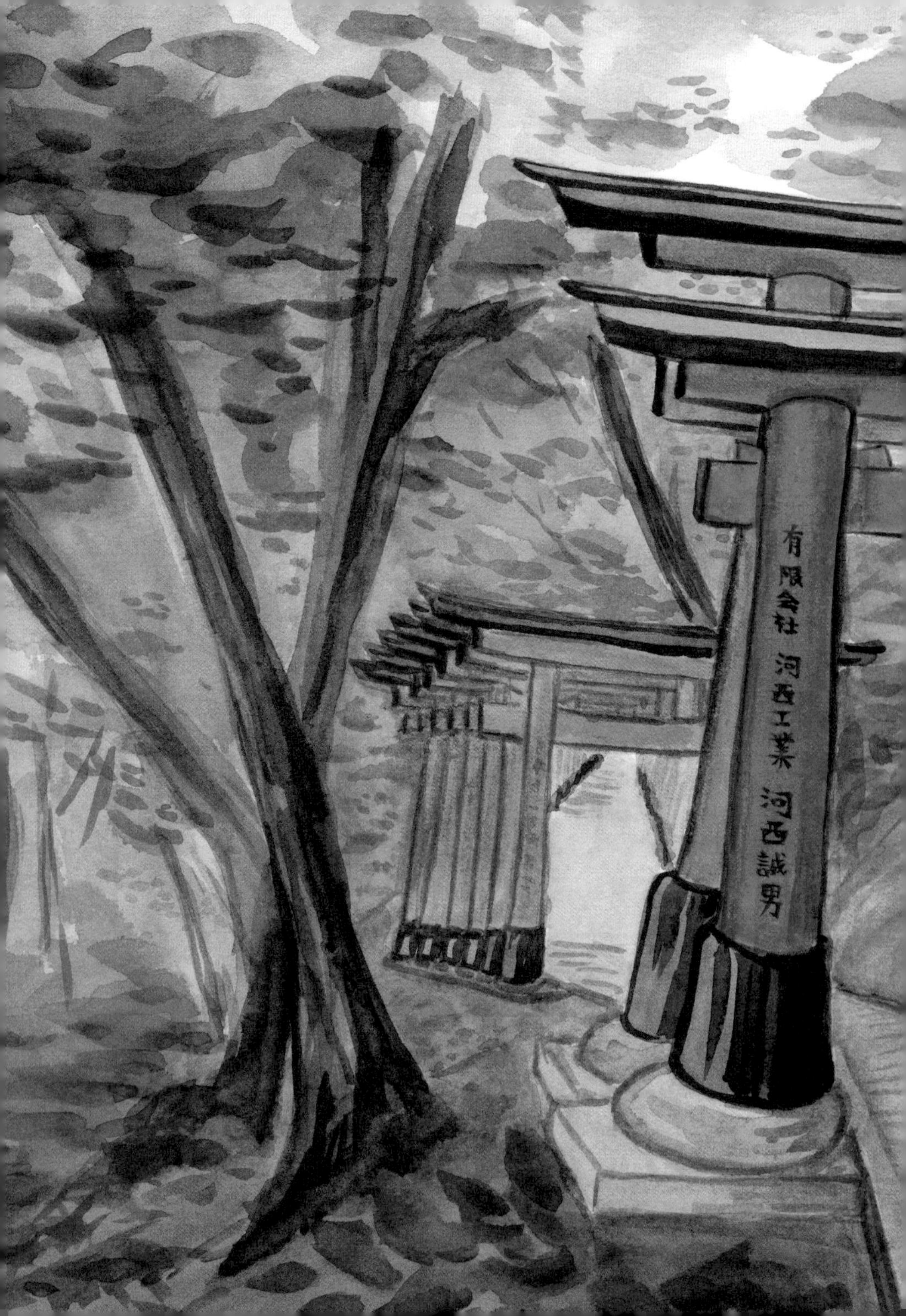
有限会社 河西工業 河西誠男